T0383192

Clausewitz Talks
Business

An Executive's Guide to
Thinking Like a Strategist

Clausewitz Talks
Business

An Executive's Guide to
Thinking Like a Strategist

Norton Paley

CRC Press
Taylor & Francis Group
Boca Raton   London   New York

CRC Press is an imprint of the
Taylor & Francis Group, an **informa** business

A PRODUCTIVITY PRESS BOOK

CRC Press
Taylor & Francis Group
6000 Broken Sound Parkway NW, Suite 300
Boca Raton, FL 33487-2742

© 2015 by Norton Paley
CRC Press is an imprint of Taylor & Francis Group, an Informa business

No claim to original U.S. Government works

Printed on acid-free paper
Version Date: 20140311

International Standard Book Number-13: 978-1-4822-2027-8 (Hardback)

This book contains information obtained from authentic and highly regarded sources. Reasonable efforts have been made to publish reliable data and information, but the author and publisher cannot assume responsibility for the validity of all materials or the consequences of their use. The authors and publishers have attempted to trace the copyright holders of all material reproduced in this publication and apologize to copyright holders if permission to publish in this form has not been obtained. If any copyright material has not been acknowledged please write and let us know so we may rectify in any future reprint.

Except as permitted under U.S. Copyright Law, no part of this book may be reprinted, reproduced, transmitted, or utilized in any form by any electronic, mechanical, or other means, now known or hereafter invented, including photocopying, microfilming, and recording, or in any information storage or retrieval system, without written permission from the publishers.

For permission to photocopy or use material electronically from this work, please access www.copyright. com (http://www.copyright.com/) or contact the Copyright Clearance Center, Inc. (CCC), 222 Rosewood Drive, Danvers, MA 01923, 978-750-8400. CCC is a not-for-profit organization that provides licenses and registration for a variety of users. For organizations that have been granted a photocopy license by the CCC, a separate system of payment has been arranged.

Trademark Notice: Product or corporate names may be trademarks or registered trademarks, and are used only for identification and explanation without intent to infringe.

Library of Congress Cataloging-in-Publication Data

Paley, Norton.
    Clausewitz talks business : an executive's guide to thinking like a strategist / Norton Paley.
        pages cm
    Includes bibliographical references and index.
    ISBN 978-1-4822-2027-8 (alk. paper)
    1. Strategic planning. 2. Clausewitz, Carl von, 1780-1831. I. Title.

HD30.28.P2848 2014
658.4'012--dc23   2014000458

Visit the Taylor & Francis Web site at
http://www.taylorandfrancis.com

and the CRC Press Web site at
http://www.crcpress.com

To my daughters,
Julia and Susan,
With love

Contents

Introduction

Carl von Clausewitz (1780–1831)* is regarded as one of the greatest Western military thinkers. His book, *On War,* published posthumously by his widow in 1832, is considered by many eminent scholars as the most distinguished Western work on war ever written.

On War has stimulated and influenced generations of soldiers, statesmen, historians, and intellectuals throughout the world—and is still being studied today at most military academies.

In recent years Clausewitz's insightful concepts have gained serious attention among business executives, as have other military classics, notably Sun Tzu's *The Art of War.* Such curiosity in the subject has spread from the C-suites to the lower echelons of organizations, as noted by the proliferation of books that interpret and apply the teachings of such giants of military history as Caesar, Napoleon, Alexander the Great, Frederick the Great, and others to business applications.

Why single out Clausewitz? Known as a soldier, philosopher, and author, many of his concepts have their origins in works reaching back to antiquity, which were known to him during his study and writing years. They reflect in some of Clausewitz's best known maxims, such as

- Even the ultimate outcome of a war is not to be regarded as final. The defeated state often considers the outcome merely as a transitory evil, for which a remedy may still be found at some later date.
- The natural goal of all campaign plans is the turning point at which the attack becomes defense. If one were to go beyond that point, it would not only be a useless effort, which could not add to success, it would in fact be a damaging one.
- War is not waged against an abstract enemy, but against a real one who must always be kept in mind.
- Another factor that can bring ... action to a standstill: imperfect knowledge of the situation. The only situation a commander can fully know is

---

* Highlights of Carl von Clausewitz's life are described at the end of this introduction.

his own; his opponent's he can only know from unreliable intelligence. His evaluation, therefore, may be mistaken and can lead him to suppose that the initiative lies with the enemy when in fact it remains with him.

- If you want to overcome your enemy you must match your effort against his power of resistance, which can be explained as the product of two inseparable factors, the total means at his disposal and the strength of his will.

- In short, absolute, so-called mathematical, factors never find a firm basis in calculations. From the very start, there is interplay of possibilities, probabilities, good luck and bad that weaves its way throughout the length and breadth of the tapestry. In the whole range of human activities, war most closely resembles a game of cards.

- What matters is to detect the culminating point of actions with discriminative judgment.

- We maintain unequivocally that the form of confrontation that we call defense offers greater probability of victory than attack.

If you would transpose some of the preceding terms, such as war for conflict, enemy for competitor, and commander for executive, those guidelines contain timeless qualities that are as vital in today's competitive business conflict as they were to war during the time Clausewitz wrote his book.

The intent of this book, then, is to interpret and transpose Clausewitz's core ideas and show their applications to today's competitive problems. It is meant to assist you as a leader with the managerial responsibilities for developing competitive strategies, making decisions with greater precision, and improving your chances of achieving your organization's objectives.

Expressed another way: The object of this book is to enhance your ability to *think like a strategist.*

What are the origins of the term strategy? It is derived from the Greek words *strategia,* which was used in ancient times to mean the art or skills of the general, and *strategos* to identify the general who practices strategy. One anonymous definition survives from antiquity, which reads:

> Strategy is the means by which a commander may defend his own lands and defeat his enemies. The general is the one who practices strategy. Strategy teaches us how to defend what is our own and to threaten what belongs to the enemy. The defensive is the means by which one acts to guard one's own people and their property; the offensive is the means by which one retaliates against one's opponents.

Then, there is Clausewitz's definition of strategy:

> Strategy is the use of the engagement for the purpose of war. The strategist must therefore define an aim for the entire operational side of the war that will be in accordance with its purpose. In other words, he will draft the plan of the war, and the aim will determine the series of actions intended to achieve it.

Clausewitz goes on to say: "We could more accurately compare war and strategy to commerce, which is also a conflict of human interests and activities, and it is still closer to politics, which may be considered as a kind of commerce on a larger scale."

THE CLAUSEWITZ MILITARY/BUSINESS CONNECTION

Clausewitz's latter comment, then, introduces the relationship of war to commerce. As cited previously, this connection is shown by the abundance of business books, seminars, and speeches that reference military concepts. In varying degrees they attempt to transpose military verbiage to business terms as the everyday language of business.

It is not uncommon to read and listen to war-like vocabulary with such phrases as attacking a competitor, developing a strong position, defending a market, strengthening logistics, deploying personnel, launching a campaign, developing a strategy, utilizing tactics, coping with price wars, doing battle with ... and other familiar comments.

Then, there are the more indirect references that connect military to business, such as holding reserves to exploit a market advantage, developing an intelligence network to track a competitor's actions, avoiding direct confrontation with the market leader, bypassing a market because of high entry barriers, reorganizing marketing and sales to strengthen a market position, or employing a new technology to create a competitive advantage over a weaker rival.

Taking the military/business connection another step forward, consider the business situations where strategy planning, with its military underpinnings, deals with confrontations and campaigns. These can be subdivided into the following categories, each requiring customized business strategies to confront an opposing competitor:

1. Campaigns to reclaim a former market position, which was given up after a failed competitive confrontation
2. Defensive campaigns to retain a share of market in a key region
3. Preemptive campaigns against a hard-hitting competitor to blunt his actions before he begins, thereby preventing drawn-out and costly market warfare
4. Conflicts of opportunity: discovering a competitor's weakness that is worth exploiting, such as poor product and service performance, lapses in technology, problems with the supply chain, or inept leadership
5. Campaigns tied to obligatory commitments entered into through joint-venture agreements
6. Campaigns that expand into additional market niches where there are dominant competitors
7. Campaigns to solidify an existing market position and make it more defensible

8. Campaigns into new markets or new businesses that support long-term strategic objectives
9. Campaigns initiated by senior management for reasons of ambition and personal gain or those driven by upward pressures from junior-level managers
10. Campaigns against the aggressive moves of a competitor attempting to weaken the defender's resistance
11. Limited-term campaigns versus mobilizing resources for longer term decisive campaigns
12. Campaigns intended to make the confrontation more costly for the rival to continue operations, thereby neutralizing the competitor and rendering him harmless

Where are these campaigns played out in the real world of competitive warfare? Think of the following classic and current examples of business competitors among organizations that have been and—in many cases still are—in no-holds-barred conflicts:

Coke versus Pepsi, Nike versus Reebok, Microsoft versus Apple, CVS versus Walgreens, UPS versus FEDEX, Google versus Facebook, BMW versus Mercedes-Benz, Visa versus MasterCard, Airbus versus Boeing, P&G versus Unilever, Bayer versus Tylenol—and the list remains in motion.[*]

This list of rivalries serves as an ongoing reality check of competitive conflicts in a volatile environment, where winning may be measured by gaining a single point of market share that could be worth millions in revenues. Or it can viewed as growth in a no-growth market where sales increases rely on taking sales from rivals—who, in turn, are intent on doing the same to you.

Within that framework, the further intent of this book is to maintain a pragmatic viewpoint by keeping in mind the kinds of competitive problems that you may face. For instance, consider the actual quotes from executives representing a variety of businesses. Some of their problems, in one form or another, may be happening to you at the present time[†]:

• How do we sustain growth in a sluggish market with increasing competition?
• With large organizations tending to dominate our industry, what strategies are possible?
• How do we deal with offshore competitors selling into our market with prices 30% to 40% below ours?
• What defensive strategies are effective to protect our market share?
• How can we maneuver into a market already occupied by the industry leader?
• How do we position our products effectively against the market leader?

---

[*] You may wish to add your own rivals to the list.
[†] The list of actual problems comes from a confidential survey of executives representing a variety of industries, which was conducted by a highly regarded management publication.

- What strategies can outdistance competitors when entering a new market?
- What strategies can we use to regain lost market share?

As indicated earlier, the origins of the term strategy come from the ancient Greeks. Commanders over the centuries have relied on military strategy to conquer territory and gain power. They faced formidable challenges as they crafted plans to outmaneuver competing forces, gain territory and power, and expand their influence. Faced with resistance, those leaders were forced to maximize the effectiveness of their resources to achieve their goals.

While the terminology varies, these challenges are not much different from many of the *preceding* business problems. Generally, confrontations involve a defense protecting the ground and an offense trying to overtake that ground—or, in business terminology, securing a market, as well as influencing a group's behavior.

Although the destructive aspects of war are not present in business, there is a reasonable parallel when considering the fall of organizations, including once mighty global leaders; the vast layoffs of thousands of personnel; and the closing of physical plants, with its devastating economic impact. And there are the societal disruptions that create demoralizing misery among large groups of individuals. In many instances those powerful shocks result in decimated regions, such as the 2013 bankruptcy of Detroit, Michigan.

Many C-suite executives and line managers readily accept the military/business connection and find practical wisdom in studying the chronicles of military conflicts. By examining the strategic and human elements of clashes, they gain valuable insights that provide an additional dimension to business study.

This book, then, taps the universal lessons of strategy and uncovers potential solutions for today's stubborn competitive problems—similar to the ones cited previously. It also overrides the narrower pathway of relying only on current business events or job experience, where those viewpoints tend to limit the range of opportunities and reduce judgment to a relatively short-term, constricted outlook.

Finally, Clausewitz provides foundation principles that can sharpen your skills to think like a strategist. In particular, his lessons can be indispensable in the pragmatic, everyday managing of people and resources, especially when applied to competitive issues. It is through the long lens of time and space that this additional perspective can fortify your judgment in such areas as leadership and employee behavior.

Thus, by focusing on his concepts of human behavior, leadership, and organizational culture, you can benefit from a broader viewpoint that leads to a better understanding of how you face up to competitive struggles. In turn, you will enhance your expertise for applying appropriate strategies to outmaneuver competitive obstacles.

ORGANIZATION OF THE BOOK

First, this book focuses entirely on Clausewitz's renowned classic *On War*. In interpreting and editing this massive work for business applications, I highlighted those portions of his text that in my judgment apply to the problems listed earlier, and I emphasized those concepts that are relevant to the broader strategic dimensions of operating a business in today's aggressive competitive environment.

Second, to enhance your understanding of Clausewitz's primary concepts, an "executive summary" of his key points is provided at the beginning of each chapter.

Third, where some of Clausewitz's writings seemed obscure and needed clarification, I added commentary to bridge the military–business gap. These commentaries, however, do not preclude you from adding your own interpretations and applications to fit your particular situations.

Fourth, where there is text that simply does not apply to today's business conditions, as in the case of Clausewitz discussing the tactical details of a particular battle, I have deleted those sections.

Fifth, my major input consists of interpreting and editing his work for business applications, yet retaining the essence and integrity of his original writings. In the process, I have substituted Clausewitz's military terminology for business verbiage—such as war with competitive conflict or confrontation, battle with campaign, fighting force with resources, destroying the enemy with neutralizing the opponent, soldiers with personnel, and the like.

What follows, then, is Clausewitz's classic *On War*. Altogether, you will find his writings especially valuable as you (1) take a broader look at your operating environment, (2) attempt to calculate and decode the intentions of your competitors, and (3) examine the behavior of your markets. In the process, you will gain a more acute awareness of the internal operating condition of your organization, as well as insights about the mind-sets and sensibilities of the people who will have to implement your company's plans.

As important, you will gain an insightful perspective about what is required of you as a leader when devising competitive strategies. All these areas are contained in your ability to think like a strategist. It is in this framework, then, that his rules, concepts, and strategies are presented in the following chapters.

Finally, an appendix is included that consists of two management tools to heighten your ability to think like a strategist:

1. Strategy diagnostic system. This tool helps you to evaluate your firm's internal capabilities and competitive strategies critically against those of your competitor. It functions as a reliable performance measure to candidly determine your organization's or group's competencies.
2. Appraising internal and external conditions. This 100-question checklist assists in analyzing key factors about your organization's capabilities. It also assists in determining the competitive readiness of your group or firm, as well as ability to implement your business plans successfully.

ABOUT CARL VON CLAUSEWITZ

Clausewitz, a Prussian soldier and writer, was born in 1780. He first encountered war in 1793 as a 13-year-old infantry ensign. During the Jena campaign, he was captured and while in service with the Russians he played a prominent part in the Moscow campaigns of 1812–1813.

On rejoining the Prussian service he became chief of staff and later director of the military academy in Berlin. There, he attracted the attention of the distinguished General Scharnhorst, whom he later helped to reform the Prussian army.

More than a soldier, Clausewitz was a philosopher. It is in this framework that he recognized war as a political phenomenon. Consequently, if conflict was meant to achieve a political purpose, everything that entered into war—social and economic preparation, strategic planning, the conduct of operations, and the use of force on all levels—should be determined by this purpose.

Clausewitz's lasting fame rests with *On War,* which he began work on in 1816. The book was published 1 year after his death in 1832. As an able philosopher and soldier, he understood the continual interaction between theory and practice, as his open mind grasped the lessons derived from his study of the wars of antiquity through his personal experiences during the Revolutionary and Napoleonic wars. His book is still used in the major military academies worldwide.

About the Author

Norton Paley has brought his world-class experience and unique approach to business strategy to some of the global community's most respected organizations.

Having launched his career with publishers McGraw–Hill and John Wiley & Sons, Paley founded Alexander-Norton Inc., bringing successful business techniques to clients around the globe, including the international training organization Strategic Management Group, where he served as senior consultant.

Throughout his career Paley has trained business managers and their staffs in the areas of planning and strategy development, raising the bar for achievement, and forging new approaches to problem solving and competitive edge.

His clients include

- American Express
- IBM
- Detroit Edison
- Chrysler (Parts Division)
- McDonnell-Douglas
- Dow Chemical (Worldwide)
- W. R. Grace
- Cargill (Worldwide)
- Chevron Chemical
- Ralston-Purina
- Johnson & Johnson
- USG
- Celanese
- Hoechst
- Mississippi Power
- Numerous midsized and small firms

Paley has lectured in the Republic of China and Mexico and he has presented training seminars throughout the Pacific Rim and Europe for Dow Chemical and Cargill.

As a seminar leader at the American Management Association, he conducted competitive strategy, marketing management, and strategic planning programs for over 20 years.

Published books include:

- *The Marketing Strategy Desktop Guide*
- *How to Develop a Strategic Marketing Plan*
- *The Manager's Guide to Competitive Marketing Strategies*
- *Marketing for the Nonmarketing Executive: An Integrated Management Resource Guide for the 21st Century*
- *Successful Business Planning: Energizing Your Company's Potential*
- *Manage to Win*
- *Mastering the Rules of Competitive Strategy: A Resource Guide for Managers*
- *Big Ideas for Small Businesses*
- *How to Outthink, Outmaneuver, and Outperform Your Competitors: Lessons from the Masters of Strategy*

On the cusp of the interactive movement, Paley developed three computer-based, interactive training systems: *the Marketing Learning Systems, Segmentation, Targeting & Positioning,* and *the Marketing Planning System.*

Paley's books have been translated into Chinese, Russian, Portuguese, and Turkish.

His byline columns have appeared in *The Management Review* and *Sales & Marketing Management* magazines.

Chapter 1

What Is Conflict?

Clausewitz makes these key points about conflict:

- To secure an objective, we must render the rival powerless; that is the true aim of conflict.
- To introduce moderation into conflict would always lead to logical absurdity.
- If you want to overcome your opponent, you must match your effort against his power of resistance.
- In conflict even the ultimate outcome is never to be regarded as final. The outcome is merely a transitory evil, for which a remedy may still be found in a variety of possible conditions at some later date.
- I am convinced that the superiority of the defense is very great, far greater than appears at first sight.
- A factor that can bring action to a standstill is imperfect knowledge of the situation.
- Only the element of chance is needed to make conflict a gamble, and that element is never absent.
- Conflict is an act of policy based on its strategic direction . . . and should never be an isolated incident.
- Conflict never breaks out wholly unexpectedly; nor can it be spread instantaneously. Each side can therefore gauge the other to a large extent by what he is and does.
- The strategic objective—the original motive for the conflict—will determine both the objective to be reached and the amount of effort it requires.

Clausewitz talks more extensively about conflict:

CONFLICT AS AN ACT OF FORCE

In conflict, more than in any other subject, we must begin by looking at the nature of the whole. Conflict is nothing but a duel on a larger scale with countless duels making up conflict. A picture of it as a whole can be formed by imagining a pair of wrestlers. Each tries through physical force to compel the other to do his will. His immediate aim is to throw his opponent in order to make him incapable of further resistance.

Conflict is thus an act of force to compel our rival to do our will. Force to counter opposing force is equipped with the inventions of art and science. Attached to force are certain self-imposed, imperceptible limitations, known as laws, regulations, and customs, but for the most part they scarcely weaken it. To impose our will on the rival is its object. To secure that objective, we must render the rival powerless and that, in theory, is the true aim of conflict.

COMMENTARY

Clausewitz's metaphors of conflicts with duels and wrestling are plausible images. You can reasonably experience such forms of confrontations in the everyday marketplace. Consider a company that puts up a strong resistance to retain an existing market position or the organization that attempts to expand into a market already occupied by strong competitors. Yet those defenders have no notion of relinquishing their dominant position without a fight.

Such was the case when Wal-Mart attacked Best Buy Stores' leadership position in consumer electronics through a major expansion into that category or the classic case of Canon and Ricoh moving aggressively into North America and taking on the then market titan Xerox.

In more recent times Google moved into China. However, once established, it was hindered by the Chinese government's requirement to self-censor its Web content. That ruling turned into an unaccustomed obstacle for Google, whereby its management pulled out and thereby ceded the market to Chinese competitor Baidu. That rival, eyeing a brilliant opportunity, moved rapidly to dominate China's search-ad market.

Yet Google decided not to abandon the market entirely to Baidu. Using an effective strategy, it drove back into China by waging war on its own terms: It targeted a then vacant niche of ads aimed at the growing mobile phone market, establishing a firm foothold that it was prepared to defend against any counterattacks from Baidu.

Clausewitz continues:

THE MAXIMUM USE OF FORCE

Some people might think there is some ingenious way to weaken or overwhelm a rival without too much harm. And they might imagine this is the true goal of the art of conflict. Pleasant as it sounds, it is a fallacy that must be exposed. Confrontation is such a risky business that the mistakes that come from a casual approach are the very worst.

The maximum use of force is in no way incompatible with the simultaneous use of the intellect. If one side uses force and harsh practices without compunction, undeterred by the damage it involves, while the other side refrains, the first will gain the upper hand. That side will force the other to follow suit. Each will drive its opponent toward extremes, and the only limiting factors are the counterbalances inherent in conflict.

To introduce the principle of moderation into the theory of conflict would always lead to logical absurdity.

Two different motives make individuals battle one another: hostile feelings and hostile intentions. Our definition is based on hostile intentions, since it is the universal element. Even the most antagonistic, instinctive passion cannot be conceived as existing without hostile intent.

If conflict is an act of force, the emotions cannot fail to be involved. Conflict may not spring from them, but they will still affect it to some degree. And the extent to which they do so will depend on how important the conflicting interests are and on how long the conflict lasts.

Each side, therefore, compels its opponent to follow suit; a reciprocal action is started, which must lead, in theory, to extremes. This is the first case of interaction and the first "extreme" we meet.

COMMENTARY

Clausewitz's reference to the use of maximum force is in deep contrast to the complacent attitudes of some executives with the mind-set that they were protected by a distinguished market history and a strong public image. Yet many of those once proud enterprises were left in shambles or were forced to exit their primary markets and go in entirely new directions, as in the case of the reorganized, downsized, and redirected Eastman Kodak Co. The company saw the digital photography market coming. It is even credited with inventing the digital camera in 1975. In the end, however, Kodak management remained focused on protecting its old technology and stoically watched as its market presence declined. The result: an industry identified with Kodak was relinquished to aggressive and forward-looking rivals.

Other organizations sought government intervention through tax relief or attempted to win through rulings in trade disputes, as in the case of Whirlpool's bottom-mount refrigerators against those made in South Korea and Mexico.* Still others, through neglect or self-assured attitudes, fell too far behind in technology, marketing, manufacturing, or supply-chain logistics and disappeared from the market altogether.

Further, Clausewitz's comment about "confrontation is such a risky business" has an intensified truth with potentially tragic outcomes. His viewpoint translates to remaining totally aware of the consequences behind the "hostile intentions" of your competitor. In the Introduction, you will find 10 categories that indicate intentions for conflict that, in turn, find application for Clausewitz's cautionary advice, "To introduce . . . moderation into . . . conflict would always lead to logical absurdity."

---

* Whirlpool lost the case at the US International Commission.

THE AIM IS TO WEAKEN THE RIVAL

The aim of conflict is to weaken the rival. You must put him in a situation that is even more unpleasant than the sacrifice you call on him to make.

The hardships of that situation must not be merely temporary—at least not in appearance. Otherwise, the opponent would not give in, but would wait for things to improve. Any change that might be brought about by continuing combative actions must then be of a kind to bring the rival still greater disadvantages.

The worst of all conditions in which an opponent can find himself is utter defenselessness. Consequently, if you are to force the rival, by creating confrontations against him, to do your bidding, you must either make him literally defenseless or at least put him in a position that makes this danger probable.

It follows, then, that to overcome the adversary, or weaken him, must always be the aim of a confrontation.

So long as I have not overthrown my opponent, I am bound to fear he may overthrow me. Thus, I am not in control: He dictates to me as much as I dictate to him. This is the second case of interaction and it leads to the second "extreme."

If you want to overcome your rival, you must match your effort against his power of resistance, which can be expressed as the product of two inseparable factors: first, the total means at his disposal and, second, the strength of his will. The extent of the means at his disposal is a matter—though not exclusively—of figures and should be measurable.

But the strength of his will is much less easy to determine and can only be gauged approximately by the strength of the motive stimulating it. Assuming you arrive in this way at a reasonably accurate estimate of the opponent's power of resistance, you can adjust your own efforts accordingly. You can either increase them until they surpass the rival's or, if this is beyond your means, you can make your efforts as great as possible.

But expect the rival to do the same. Confrontation will again result and it must again force you both to extremes. This is the third case of interaction and the third "extreme."

COMMENTARY

Clausewitz talks about "the strength of his will." That is an issue with two faces: the will of your own people, which is matched against the strength of will of your opponent's. From a leader's viewpoint, that issue refers to the morale of personnel who are directly involved in the conflict.

Morale is the dominant issue that affects day-to-day employee performance and contributes ultimately to how well a business plan is implemented and, more precisely, in the context of Clausewitz's meaning, how it is used to weaken the competitor's resolve and power of resistance.

Morale, then, is shaped by common values, such as loyalty to fellow workers and a belief that the organization will care for them. Where morale is at a high level, it results in a cohesive team effort with a sheer determination to win at a competitive confrontation. Successful leaders also know that when the inevitable problems and reversals occur, morale holds a group together and keeps it going in the face of adversity.

THE HUMAN WILL: NOT A WHOLLY UNKNOWN FACTOR

Even assuming an extreme effort can be quantified and easily calculated, you must admit that the human mind is unlikely to consent to being ruled by such logic. It would often result in strength being wasted. An effort of will out of all proportion to the objective would be needed, but would not in fact be realized. Such efforts at forming logical conclusions do not motivate the human will.

Would this ever be the case in practice? Yes, it would if (a) conflict were a wholly isolated act, occurring suddenly and not produced by previous events in the world; (b) it consisted of a single decisive act or a set of simultaneous ones; (c) the decision achieved was complete and perfect in itself, uninfluenced by any previous estimate of the strategic situation.

As to the first of these conditions, conflict is never an isolated act. It must be remembered that neither opponent is an abstract person to the other—not even to the extent of the power of resistance, which is expressed as the will to resist, although dependent on external factors.

Yet the will is not a wholly unknown factor. We can base a forecast of its state tomorrow on what it is today. Conflict never breaks out wholly unexpectedly; nor can it be spread instantaneously. Each side can therefore gauge the other to a large extent by what he is and does, instead of judging him by what he ought to be or do.

Individuals and their affairs, however, are always something short of perfect and will never quite achieve the absolute best. Such shortcomings affect both sides alike and therefore constitute a moderating force.

COMMENTARY

Clausewitz's comment, "the will to resist … is not a wholly unknown factor," justifies leaning heavily on competitor intelligence to uncover and monitor a rival's behavior. By monitoring those patterns under a variety of market conditions you can shape a more accurate strategy. Simply observing if a rival is normally active, passive, or impulsive under a variety of competitive conditions can provide useable clues to future behavior.

CONFLICT CONSISTS OF SEVERAL SUCCESSIVE ACTS

As for the second condition: Conflict does not consist of a single short campaign. If conflict consisted of one decisive campaign, or of a set of simultaneous decisions, the sole criterion for preparations would be the strategies used by the competitor—so far as they are known. The rest would once more be reduced to forecasts, estimates, and, ultimately, judgment.

But if the decision in conflict consists of several successive acts, then each of them will provide a gauge for those that follow. Here again, the rough calculations and conclusions are replaced by the real ones and the trends to the extreme are thereby moderated.

Yet, if all the means available were, or could be, simultaneously employed, all conflicts would automatically be confined to a single decisive campaign or a set of simultaneous ones. Any subsequent actions would merely be an extension of the initial single act.

Moreover, even if the first confrontation is not the only one, the influence it has on subsequent actions will be on a scale proportionate to its original effort. In reality, however, it is contrary to human nature to make an extreme effort, and the tendency therefore is always to plead that a decision may be possible later on.

Lastly, in conflict even the ultimate outcome is never to be regarded as final. The defeated unit, or administration, often considers the outcome merely as a transitory evil, for which a remedy may still be found in a variety of possible conditions at some later date. It is obvious how this, too, can slacken tension and reduce the vigor of the effort.

COMMENTARY

Clausewitz's comment about "the ultimate outcome is never to be regarded as final" is one of his more famous statements. Internalizing that point has tremendous ramifications for any leader. For instance, the human tendency is to lean back on success and absorb the rewarding rays of the moment. In failure, the inclination is to drop into a state of despondency, which would have severe repercussions on employee morale, as it deteriorates and spreads uncontrolled throughout the organization or business group.

Each extreme should be considered a temporary moment in time and dealt with accordingly. This is where leadership takes control. That means influencing employees by providing purpose, direction, and motivation, so that you do not place the entire burden of responsibility on them.

Further, leadership demands calmness and patience, which are exhibited in how you react in a variety of competitive situations. It is also reflected by attitudes toward the marketplace and, specifically, with customers. Such ways of thinking characterize Cisco Systems with its near-religious convergence on the customer, a total belief in employees as intellectual capital, and an energetic willingness to team up with outsiders to develop active partnerships. This passion for molding such an outside-in focus is credited to the leadership of CEO John T. Chambers, who clearly saw those attributes as a value system to drive subsequent actions.

In turn, other levels of employees recognized such values and used them to shape strategies that conformed to the culture of the organization, thereby increasing the chances of successfully implementing business plans. As a result, line managers were able to reliably predict the success or failure of their respective strategies.

STRATEGIC AIM IS A CALCULATION OF PROBABILITIES

Once the opponents have ceased to be mere figments of any theory and become targeted adversaries, and when conflict becomes a series of actions obeying its own peculiar laws, reality supplies the data from which we can deduce the unknown that lies ahead.

From the opponent's character, from his organization's culture, and from the state of his general situation, each side, using the laws of probability, forms an estimate of the opponent's likely course and acts accordingly.

Strategic aim becomes a calculation of probabilities based on individuals and conditions. The smaller the price you demand from your rival, the less you can expect him to deny it to you. Therefore, the smaller the effort he makes, the less you need make yourself.

Moreover, the more modest your own strategic aim, the less importance you attach to it and the less reluctantly you will abandon it, if you must. This is another reason why your effort will be modified.

The strategic objective—the original motive for the conflict—will thus determine both the objective to be reached and the amount of effort it requires. The strategic objective cannot, however, in itself provide the standard of measurement. Since we are dealing with realities, not with abstractions, it can do so only in the overall context of two organizations in conflict.

Yet the same strategic objective can elicit differing reactions from different peoples and even from the same people at different times. Between two leaders and two organizations there can be such tensions that even the slightest quarrel can produce a wholly disproportionate effect—a real confrontation.

Thus, it follows that, without any inconsistency, conflicts can have all degrees of importance and intensity, ranging from a total confrontation down to simple wait-and-see observation.

COMMENTARY

Clausewitz's point that the "strategic objective can elicit differing reactions" is an essential point about the types of long-term goals you set for your company or business unit. In turn, his statement can impact your operational business plan and provide guidance to help you determine the amount of effort and types of strategies you can employ. Consequently, developing serious, well thought out strategic objectives is essential to good leadership, as well as for sharpening your ability to think like a strategist.

Thus, the strategic direction you have set for your group or company becomes your compass for directing the conflict and determining the level of resistance you can expect from your competitor. It determines the level of resources you have to commit in such areas as marketing, technologies, personnel, and capital.

The strategic direction also becomes the foundation for the year-to-year objectives you list in your plan. Some of the questions you would address in refining your strategic objective are the following*:

1. What are our organization's distinctive strengths or areas of expertise?
2. What business should our organization be in over the next 3 to 5 years?
3. What segments or categories of customers will our company or business unit serve?

---

* These eight questions take on a pragmatic reality when applied to the previously cited Kodak case.

4. What additional functions will be required to fulfill customers' needs as we see the market evolve and competition intensify?
5. What new technologies will our firm require to satisfy future customer needs and stay ahead of competitors?
6. What changes are taking place in markets, consumer behavior, competition, environment, and the economy that are likely to impact our company?
7. Is our corporate culture compatible with the company's or group's strategic goals?
8. Is the organization's leadership able to maintain a high enough level of employee morale to sustain the long-term efforts—especially during those periods of inevitable conflicts?

ACTIONS CANNOT BE INTERRUPTED

However modest the executive demands may be, however small the resources employed, and however limited the objective, once an effort is under way, actions cannot be interrupted even for a moment. Every action needs a certain time to be completed. That period is called its duration, and its length will depend on the speed at which individuals work.

Without concern for individual differences here, every person performs a task in his own way. A slow person does not do a task more slowly because he wants to spend more time over it, but because his nature causes him to need more time. If he made more haste, he would do the job less well.

COMMENTARY

Whereas Clausewitz recognized the differences in individuals and their innate capabilities in completing a task, the realities of today's competitive world dictate some remedies—for instance, pairing individuals together to complement each other's capabilities, assigning the appropriate task to an individual that matches the skill set needed to do the job, and providing the proper work environment.

Then, there is the issue of leadership and discipline. Preparing your staff to bear up under intense competitive conditions involves a good deal of leadership skill. This is particularly essential when individuals are naturally predisposed to back away from the realities of an uncertain and erratic competitive threat.

Therefore, your aim is to motivate individuals to make audacious efforts to reverse a situation and turn potential defeat into victory. Clausewitz's sage advice once again holds true: "In conflict even the ultimate outcome is never to be regarded as final."

Accordingly, your intention is to be totally aware of what psychological effects competitive conditions have on your employees. Your central task, therefore, is to inspire individuals by reinforcing the idea that there are always actions that can change dire conditions into successful outcomes.

The central point: If handled skillfully, you can reignite your staff's creativity and energy to find solutions to a supposed untenable situation. Doing so also goes a long way in strengthening how you are viewed by your subordinates.

DEFENSE AS A STRONGER FORM OF FIGHTING

If two rivals have prepared for conflict, some aggressive motive must have brought them to that point. Moreover, so long as they remain ready to confront each other that motive of opposition must still be active. Only one consideration can restrain it: a desire to wait for a better moment before acting, and it never can be present on more than one side.

One could, however, conceive of a state of balance in which the side with the stronger grounds for action was the one that had the weaker forces. The balance would then result from the combined effects of aim and strength. Were that the case, one would have to say that unless some shift in the balance were in prospect, the two sides should make peace.

As we shall show, defense is a stronger form of fighting than attack. I am convinced that the superiority of the defensive is very great, far greater than appears at first sight. Thus, the weaker the motives for action are, the more frequently will action be suspended.

COMMENTARY

Defense should be further defined as an active defense versus a passive defense. That is, for the defender to achieve a successful outcome, it has to absorb the competitor's attack by blunting his efforts, followed by strategies to actively regain the advantage. Clausewitz elaborates on the advantages of defense in the later chapters.

FACTORS THAT CAN SUSPEND ACTION

Another factor that can bring action to a standstill is imperfect knowledge of the situation. The only situation a leader can know fully is his own; he can know his opponent's only from unreliable intelligence. His evaluation, therefore, may be mistaken and can lead him to suppose that the initiative lies with the rival when in fact it remains with him.

Of course such faulty appreciation is as likely to lead to ill-timed action as to ill-timed inaction, and it is no more conducive to slowing down operations than it is to speeding them up. Nevertheless, it must rank among the natural causes that, without entailing inconsistency, can bring activity to a halt.

Individuals are always more inclined to pitch their estimate of the opponent's strength too high than too low; such is human nature. Bearing this in mind, one must admit that partial ignorance of the situation is, generally speaking, a major factor in delaying the progress of action.

The possibility of inaction has a further moderating effect on the progress of the conflict by diluting it, thereby increasing the means of restoring a balance between the two sides. The greater the tensions that have led to conflict are and the greater the consequent aggressive effort is, the shorter these periods of inaction will be.

Conversely, the weaker the motive for conflict is, the longer is the interval between actions. The stronger motive increases willpower and willpower, as we know, is always both an element in and the product of strength.

COMMENTARY

Even acknowledging Clausewitz's assertion about the "imperfect knowledge of the situation," there are still recurring patterns of behavior that you can monitor and interpret. And notwithstanding that flaws in competitor intelligence do exist, it does not preclude your gathering the most reliable information available. Remaining completely blind in any competitive situation can jeopardize virtually any plan.

Consequently, paying close attention to incoming intelligence becomes an imperative. Once you have assembled what you believe to be reliable data and you have carefully deliberated on all that is meaningful, use your best judgment to develop and implement your strategy with speed. It would be a far greater error to wait for a situation to clear up entirely. The reality of working in a dynamic confrontational marketplace is that decisions are required—even in the fog of uncertainty.

Therefore, work with the attitude that the competitor intelligence you have assembled and screened and the assessments you have made can improve your chances of producing the results you expect. And even in the penetrating light of reality, should you discover that some intelligence is contradictory, false, or contains "imperfect knowledge," then you have little recourse but to lean heavily on your years of experience and your knowledge of the industry. That includes showing confidence in those key individuals with whom you work, recognizing the value of your training, and relying on the richness of your intuition.

CHANCE MAKES CONFLICT A GAMBLE

The slower the progress, the more frequent the interruptions of aggressive activity, the easier it is to retrieve a mistake, the bolder will be the leader's assessments. And the more likely he will be to avoid extremes and to base his plans on data, probability, and inference. Any given situation requires that probabilities be calculated in the light of circumstances, and the amount of time available for such assessments will depend on the pace at which operations are taking place.

Only one more element is needed to make conflict a gamble and that element is never absent: chance.* It is the very last thing that conflict lacks. No other human activity is so continuously or universally bound up with chance. And through the element of chance, guesswork and luck come to play a great part in conflict.

Now consider the subjective nature of conflict. That is, the means by which aggressive activity has to be fought will look more than ever like a gamble. The element in which conflict exists is menacing.

The highest of all moral qualities in time of danger is certainly courage. Now courage is perfectly compatible with prudent calculations, but the two differ nonetheless and pertain to different psychological forces. On the other hand, daring, boldness, rashness, and trusting in luck are only variants of courage. And all these traits of character seek their proper element: chance.

In short, absolute, so-called mathematical factors never find a firm basis in all calculations. From the very start, there is interplay of possibilities, probabilities, good luck and bad that weaves its way throughout the length and breadth of the tapestry.

COMMENTARY

Even taking into account all the sophisticated methodologies and absolute claims associated with the providers of analytics, there is still the unpredictability of human behavior spiraling in a maelstrom of internal and external forces. Or as Clausewitz states, "There is interplay of possibilities, probabilities, good luck and bad." These dynamics at play, in turn, form the foundations of chance, which continually vibrate in every conflict.

As for Clausewitz's comment about courage: History teaches that an enterprise, accented with determination and purpose, leads more often than not to successful performance. Other factors being somewhat equal, when boldness meets caution, boldness wins. It is this quality that emerges as the first prerequisite of the great leader.

---

* Clausewitz uses *chance* as it relates to conflict, courage, and the unpredictability of reliable intelligence as a recurring theme in the following chapters.

Audacity in plans and action, therefore, has a powerful emotional impact on the mind and the leader's subsequent behavior, whereas excessive caution is handicapped by a loss of stability, initiative, and momentum. Thus, when in doubt, some action is better than no action.

The following case provides a tangible perspective to this personality trait.

Apple Inc. had a long history of being a niche player in the personal computer market. At one point, when overall market sales plateaued, Apple's share hovered in the paltry 3 percent range, which it held for several years.

When presented with the uncertain consequences, yet driven by the need to grow or go downhill, the late Steven Jobs saw opportunities. He made the bold leap out of his comfort zone and moved aggressively into the mainstream of the consumer-electronics market.

Jobs launched iPod. Original industry estimates pegged sales at 12 million units, with sales growth predicted at a rate of 74 percent annually for several years. By moving rapidly, Apple gained a solid market position and avoided fighting costly battles against slower moving competitors attempting to latch on to the soaring product category.

What initially gave the iPod a boost was its ability to work with most PCs. As a further advantage, the product was then at the introduction stage of the product life cycle.

Even for individuals who do not have the innate personality and temperament to act with boldness, some measure of audacity still remains a practical and even prudent course of action—that is, as long as the display of courage is supported by a sound business plan, ongoing competitive intelligence, clearly stated objectives, and skillfully crafted strategies. Then boldness is justified with the strong likelihood of ending up with profitable outcomes.

CHANCE BEST SUITS HUMAN NATURE

Although our intellect always longs for clarity and certainty, our nature often finds uncertainty fascinating. It prefers to daydream in the realms of chance and luck, rather than accompany the intellect on its narrow and tortuous path of philosophical enquiry and logical deduction.

Unconfined by narrow necessity, chance can revel in a wealth of possibilities, which inspire courage to take wing and dive into the element of daring and danger like a fearless swimmer into the current. It must also take the human factor into account and find room for courage, boldness, even foolhardiness.

The art of conflict deals with living and with moral forces. Consequently, it cannot attain the absolute, or certainty. It must always leave a margin for uncertainty, in the greatest things as much as in the smallest. With uncertainty in one scale, courage and self-confidence must be thrown into the other to correct the balance. Thus, courage and self-confidence are essential in conducting business operations.

CONFLICT IS BASED ON STRATEGIC DIRECTION— NEVER AS AN ISOLATED INCIDENT

Such is conflict, such is the leader who directs it, and such is the theory that governs it. Conflict is no pastime. It is no mere joy in daring and winning and no place for enthusiasts who lack the training and experience.

It is a serious means to a serious end. And all its colorful resemblance to a game of chance, all the vicissitudes of courage, imagination, and enthusiasm it includes are merely its special characteristics.

When groups engage in conflict, the reason always lies in the organization's long-term strategic situation. Conflict, therefore, is an act of policy based on its strategic direction. At times, the conflict will expand sufficiently to overcome the resistance of inertia or friction. At other times, the activities are too weak to have any effect.

The central issue is that conflict should never be an isolated incident. Rather, it should always be tested against the strategic direction set out in the operational plan.

Consequently, we keep in mind that conflict springs from some strategic purpose. It is natural, then, that the prime causes remain the supreme consideration in conducting it.

Conflict must adapt itself to its chosen means, a process that can radically change it. Yet the political aim remains the first consideration. Strategic aim, then, will permeate all operations. And, insofar as their aggressive nature will admit, it will have a continuous influence on them.

CONFLICT IS THE CONTINUATION OF POLICY BY OTHER MEANS

Engaging in conflict is not a mere act of policy, but rather a true statement of strategic direction. That is, it is a continuation of the long-term policies and strategic objectives by other means. And the trend and designs of policy shall not be inconsistent with the means.

The strategic aim is the goal; conflict is the means of reaching it. And means can never be considered in isolation from their overall purpose.

The more powerful and diverse the nature of motives for conflict is, the greater are the tensions that precede the confrontation and the more aggressive and less appeasing will the conflict appear to be.

On the other hand, the less intense the motives are, the less will be the tendency toward being more confrontational. As a result, actions will be driven further from their natural course; appeasement and peaceful coexistence will characterize the conflict.

At times, however, emotions might be so aroused that, looking at the strategic implications, one would be hard put to maintain overriding control. Yet if the motivations are so powerful, there must be a policy of proportionate magnitude. And in situations where policy is directed only toward minor objectives, the emotions of personnel will be little stirred and they will have to be stimulated rather than held back.

Clausewitz concludes by reviewing one of his major points about conflict:

ALL CONFLICTS CAN BE CONSIDERED ACTS OF STRATEGIC DIRECTION

Therefore, it is clear that conflict should never be thought of as something autonomous, but always as an instrument of strategic direction and policy.

Conflicts must vary with the nature of their motives and of the situations that give rise to them. The first, the supreme, the most far-reaching act of judgment that the highest level of leaders has to make is to establish by that test the kind of conflict on which they are embarking—neither mistaking it for nor trying to turn it into something that is alien to its nature.

The passions that are to be kindled in conflict must already be inherent in the people. That is, the scope that the play of courage and talent will enjoy in the realm of probability and chance depends on the particular character of the leader and his personnel. However, policy and strategic aims remain the business of the senior leader alone.

Chapter 2

Purpose and Means in Competitive Conflict

Clausewitz makes these key points about conflict:

- The opponent's capabilities must be neutralized: that is, they must be put in such a condition that they can no longer carry on the conflict. All plans are ultimately based on this.
- To make the adversary fear for the final outcome can be considered as a shortcut to a successful outcome.
- Make the conflict more costly for the opponent by wasting his human, material, and financial resources.
- Resistance is a form of action, aimed at reducing enough of the rival's power to force him to abandon his intentions.
- If a mere presence is enough to cause the opponent to abandon his position, the objective has been achieved.
- Preserving our own forces has a negative purpose: It amounts to pure resistance, whose ultimate aim can only be to prolong the conflict until the rival is exhausted.
- When we speak of reducing the opponent's forces, we must emphasize that nothing obliges us to limit this idea to physical forces. The morale element must also be considered.
- Choose objectives that will bring about the opponent relinquishing the area to you.
- If we wish to gain total victory, then the weakening of the opponent's capabilities is the most appropriate action; to seize a dominant position is only a consequence.
- In conflict many roads lead to success. They range from wasting the rival's resources and rendering him harmless, his loss of a favorable field

position, to passively awaiting the rival's attacks. Any one of these may be used to overcome the opponent's will.

- How far waiting may be maintained means a policy whereby waiting must never become passive endurance.

Clausewitz talks in more detail about the purpose and means of competitive conflict:

The preceding chapter showed that the nature of conflict is complex and changeable. I now propose to inquire how its nature influences its purpose and its means.

For a start, the objective of a particular conflict must guide actions if the strategic long-term objectives are to be achieved. It is the object of any conflict that can vary, just as much as its purpose and actual circumstances.[*]

If for the moment we consider the pure concept of conflict, we should have to say that the strategic aim of conflict has no connection with conflict itself. That is, if conflict is an act of aggressive movements meant to force the rival to do our will, its aim would always be to overcome the opponent and reduce his effectiveness. Since many conflicts do actually come very close to fulfilling that purpose, let us examine this kind of conflict first. Later, when we are dealing with strategic plans, we shall investigate in greater detail what is meant by lessening the capabilities of a rival.

REDUCING THE OPPONENT'S EFFECTIVENESS

The opponent's capabilities must be neutralized. That is, it must be put in such a condition that its personnel can no longer carry on the conflict. But the aim of reducing the rival's effectiveness is not always encountered in reality, and needs not be fully achieved as a condition of achieving one's objectives. Not every conflict needs to be fought until one side collapses—or exits.

When the motives and tensions of confrontations are slight, we can imagine that the very faintest prospect of defeat might be enough to cause one side to yield. If from the very start the other side feels that this is probable, it will obviously concentrate on bringing about this probability rather than take the long way round and totally ruin the opponent.

Of greater influence on the decision to make peace is the consciousness of all the effort that has already been made and of the efforts yet to come. We see then that if one side cannot completely weaken the other, the desire for a live-and-let-live approach on either side will rise and fall with the probability of further successes on both sides; then the two would resolve their disputes by meeting halfway. If the incentive grows on one side, it should diminish on the other.

The question now arises how success can be made more likely. One way, of course, is to choose objectives that will incidentally bring about the rival's

---

[*] A listing of types of conflicts is shown in the Introduction.

relinquishing the field to you. When we assault the opponent, it is one thing if we mean our first effort to be followed by others until all resistance has been broken. It is quite another if our aim is only to obtain a single victory, in order to make the opponent insecure, to impress our greater strength upon him, and to give him doubts about his future.

If that is the extent of our aim, we will employ no more strength than is absolutely necessary. In the same way, taking control is a different matter, if the rival's collapse is not the object.

If we wish to gain total victory, then the weakening of the opponent's capabilities is the most appropriate action and to seize a dominant position only a consequence. Consequently, to occupy a field before the rival's capabilities are defeated should be considered at best a necessary evil. If, on the other hand, we do not aim at totally weakening the opposition, and if we are convinced that the opponent does not see a final decision, but rather fears it, then the seizure of a lightly defended territory is an advantage in itself.

Should this advantage be enough to make the rival fear for the final outcome, it can be considered as a shortcut on the road to a successful outcome. But there is another way: It is possible to increase the likelihood of success without defeating the opponent's physical capabilities.

I refer to operations that have direct policy and strategic repercussions. If such operations are possible, it is obvious that they can greatly improve our prospects and can form a much shorter route to the goal than making the rival's efforts totally ineffectual.

COMMENTARY

Clausewitz's concept about "reducing the opponent's effectiveness" has its business applications through the following maneuvers:

First, look for ways to apply your strengths against a competitor's weaknesses. The essence of the move is that you position your resources so that your rival cannot, will not, or simply lacks the capability and spirit to challenge your efforts.

Second, focus greater attention toward serving customers' needs and resolving their problems in a manner that visibly outperforms those of your competitors.

Third, search for a psychological advantage by creating an unbalancing effect in the rival manager's mind, whereby he or she hesitates in indecision. The aim is to disorient and unbalance the competing manager into wasting time and making irreversible mistakes.

Fourth, attempt to hold a long-term position in a target market, as gauged by attaining a market share objective, securing a position on the supply train, reaching a profitability goal, or similar metrics.

One relatively new company illustrates some of these points when it maneuvered to gain an advantage over an established organization in a specialized market. Such is the case with a mobile payments company, Square, which enables small businesses from local hardware stores to restaurants to accept credit card payments via a small plastic reader that attaches to a smartphone.

In 1 year, the St. Louis, Missouri, firm processed $15 billion in transactions, up from $5 billion during a previous 12-month period. Not unexpectedly, Square was being watched by a strong, deep-pocketed competitor, Intuit. The rival serves a substantial customer base of five million small businesses with its popular QuickBooks. It, too, sells a Square-like credit reader called GoPayment.

Square founder Jack Dorsey claims that his approach to "reducing the opponent's effectiveness" sits in a line of attack that his rival can't claim: an ability to get people to come together behind him, to believe in his vision, and to buy into the cool image that Square has managed to accumulate.

The central issues: Will such an advantage be powerful enough to increase Square's market share? Is the advantage sustainable to spearhead an ongoing offensive and secure a sizeable market penetration? To date, progress has been exceptional. The sustainable part, however, will be determined at some later time depending, first, on when and how Intuit decides to react and, second, on the durability of Dorsey's strategy to "get people to come together."

MAKE THE CONFLICT MORE COSTLY FOR THE OPPONENT

The next question is how to influence the opponent's expenditure of effort. In other words, how can we make the conflict more costly to him? The objective in such a case would show as, first, the rival's wasting his human, material, and financial resources, which would render him virtually harmless, and, second, in his loss of territory—all of which gives us victory.

Closer study will make it obvious that these two factors can vary in their significance with the deviation in objectives. As a rule the differences will be slight, but that should not mislead us. In practice, when strong motives are not present, the slightest nuances often divide between the different uses of force.

For the moment all that matters is to show that, given certain conditions, different ways of reaching the objective are possible and that they are not inconstant, absurd, or even mistaken.

There is yet a third method, and thus far the most important, judging from the frequency of its use, directly aimed at increasing the rival's expenditure of effort: It is to wear down the challenger.

That expression is more than a label. It describes the process precisely and is not as figurative as it may seem at first. Wearing down the opponent in a confrontation means that we use the duration of the conflict gradually to exhaust his physical and morale resistance.

If we intend to hold out longer than our opponent, we must be content with the smallest possible objectives, for obviously a major objective requires more effort than a minor one. The minimum objective is pure self-defense—that is, fighting without a positive goal. With such a policy our relative strength will be at its height, and thus the prospects for a favorable outcome will be greatest.

But how far can this negativity be pushed? Obviously not to the point of absolute passivity, for sheer endurance would not be fighting at all. But resistance is a form of action, aimed at reducing enough of the rival's power to force him to abandon his intentions.

Every single act of our resistance is directed to that act alone, and that is what makes our policy negative. Undoubtedly, a single action, assuming it succeeds, would do less for a negative aim than it would for a positive one. But that is just the difference: The former is more likely to succeed and to give you more security.

What it lacks in immediate effectiveness it must make up for in its use of time—that is, by prolonging the conflict. Thus, the negative aim, which lies at the heart of pure resistance, is also the natural formula for outlasting the opponent and wearing him down.

COMMENTARY

Clausewitz's points about "prolonging the conflict" and "wearing him [the competitor] down" raise this additional meaning: Maintaining a maximum effort for a prolonged period can be counterproductive if it consumes excessive amounts of your resources and ends-up weakening your position.

WEARING DOWN THE OPPONENT

Here lies the origin of the distinction that dominates the whole of conflict: the difference between attack and defense. We shall pursue the matter in depth later, but let us just say this: From the negative purpose derive all the advantages of confrontation, which is expressed by the dynamic relationship between the magnitude and the likelihood of success.

If a negative aim—that is, the use of every means available for pure resistance—gives an advantage in conflict, the advantage need only be enough to balance any superiority the opponent may possess. In the end his strategic objective will not seem worth the effort it costs. He must then give up his policy.

It is evident that this method of wearing down the rival applies to the great number of cases where the weak endeavor to resist the strong. We can now see that in conflict many roads lead to success, and that they do not all involve the opponent's outright defeat.

They range from wasting his resources and rendering him harmless, his loss of a favorable field position, to passively awaiting the rival's attacks. Any one of these may be used to overcome the opponent's will. The choice depends on circumstances.

COMMENTARY

Clausewitz's point about "many roads lead to success" deserves further explanation. He advises destroying—or for our purposes neutralizing—the opponent's forces, which opens-up a wide range of interpretations for business application.

For instance, consider the following direct and indirect approaches that could have a positive effect on weakening a competitor:

- Pursue revenue-expansion opportunities, as well as cost-reduction opportunities. By latching on to new systems and advanced technologies, it is possible to create a meaningful competitive advantage and possibly neutralize the opponent's capabilities.
- Position yourself in the market through rapid maneuvers, so that the competitor cannot anticipate your moves in sufficient time to counter them with a meaningful defense.
- Focus your resources on an emerging, neglected, or poorly served market. Your aim is to avoid a direct, head-on confrontation with a stronger rival. An alternative aim is to cause the competitor to spread his resources by attempting to anticipate your moves, thereby weakening his primary efforts.
- Create a differentiated product, or value-added service, that is not easily cloned.
- Develop a system that provides accurate market intelligence so that you can take fast action against market opportunities and, as important, that allows you to react quickly to any areas of a competitor's vulnerabilities.
- Initiate constructive relationships with customers that lock out competitors for an extended sales cycle.

Electrolux, the Swedish appliance maker, exhibits several of these approaches in its efforts to keep up with and even surpass its chief rivals, Whirlpool and China's Haier, where the company was experiencing brutal price competition.

Electrolux's primary strategy was to create a differentiated product. To begin, the company sent its market researchers to homes in Australia, France, and Russia where they spent hours observing and questioning people on their uses of the vacuum cleaner. They were especially anxious to find out about complaints with the product and any troublesome problems the people were encountering.

The resulting market intelligence led Electrolux to develop a bagless vacuum cleaner. The inventive product design uses a unique technology that compresses dust into a spongy pellet, thereby eliminating for the user any irritating and harmful dust from circulating in the air.

The company refers to the product design as a result of "consumer-focused innovation," which initiated an "innovation triangle," bringing together the design, research and development, and marketing departments to jointly come up with a marketable new product that could solve customers' complaints. The aim was also to lock out competitors for an extended sales cycle.

THE HUMAN DIMENSION: PERSONALITY AND PERSONAL RELATIONSHIPS

Is there a field of human affairs where personal relationships do not count, where the sparks they strike do not leap across all practical considerations? The personalities of leaders and staff are such important factors that, in conflict, it is vital not to underrate them. It can be said that this question of personality and personal relationships raises the number of possible ways of achieving the goal of policy to infinity.

To think of them as rare exceptions or to minimize the differences in the conduct of a conflict would be to underrate them. To avoid that error we need only bear in mind how wide a range of strategic interests can lead to conflict. Or think for a moment of the gulf that separates a struggle for survival from a conflict that does not reflect the organization's true interests.

Between these extremes lie numerous gradations. If we reject a single one of them on theoretical grounds, we may as well reject them all and lose contact with the real world. There is only one: confrontation. However many forms confrontation takes, it is inherent in the very concept of conflict that everything that occurs must originally derive from a confrontation.

It is easy to show that this is always so, no matter how many forms reality takes. Everything that occurs in conflict results from the existence of forces. But whenever forces are used, the idea of confrontation must be present.

COMMENTARY

Clausewitz's reference to human relationships and the personalities of leaders and staff raises several issues:

First, from a managerial viewpoint, the aim is to strengthen employee relationships by binding their hearts and minds to positive actions when facing the inevitable conflicts that lie ahead. Your purpose is to expand their views of what is going on beyond their limited access to information and to get them tuned in to their surroundings, especially to the immediate competitive world.

By taking such positive action, you harness your human capital to its full potential. You also acknowledge that your people are a major influence in market performance to the extent that they function as a key competitive differentiator.

Second, as for leadership, the following is a summary of the generally accepted attributes of a leader. If acquired, strengthened, or perfected, they can enhance your ability to manage people and resources, and implement effective strategies under the various circumstances of how Clausewitz defines conflict.

The primary qualities include: insightfulness, straightforwardness, compassion, boldness, and strictness.

Insightful. A leader recognizes early on the impact of conflict as it applies to a rival attacking you in your market space.

Straightforward. Employees have no doubt how and when rewards or reprimands would be handed out.

Compassionate. The leader respects the staff, appreciates their hard work, and empathizes with them during stressful times.

Bold. The leader finds innovative ways to market the company or product by seizing opportunities, neutralizing the effectiveness of the competition, and avoiding getting bogged down in indecision.

Strict. The leader is dedicated to the strategic objectives of the company. In turn, the staff respects the leader's discipline and optimistic outlook.

In contrast, a serious situation exists where signs indicate that the personalities and relationships between leader and staff are failing.

Some of the primary signals include:

1. Lack of trust by the leader in his employees' discipline, capabilities, or skills
2. Lack of confidence by employees in their leader's ability to make correct decisions
3. Inadequate support from senior management
4. Disagreement and open arguments with others about objectives, priorities, and strategies
5. A highly conservative and plodding company culture prevents projects moving forward
6. Lack of urgency in developing new products to deal with short product life cycles

7. No simplified system of control exists, so cumbersome committees prolong deliberation and result in unwarranted delays
8. Threats from aggressive competitors strike fear among employees,
   which damages morale and results in lost momentum

Clausewitz continues:

EMPLOYING FORCES

Confrontation comprises everything related to employing forces. And it
includes everything to do with their creation, maintenance, and their use.

If the idea of a confrontation underlies every use of forces, then their
employment means simply the planning and organizing of a series of campaigns. The whole activity must therefore relate directly or indirectly to the
engagement.

If all threads of activity lead to the campaign, then if we control the
engagement, we understand them all. Their results are produced by our orders
and by the execution of these orders, never directly by other conditions.

Since in the engagement everything is concentrated on weakening the
opponent, or rather his capabilities, it follows that the elimination of the rival's
forces is always the means by which the purpose of the campaign is achieved.

The purpose in question may be the weakening of the opponent's forces,
but not necessarily so. It may be quite different, when there are other objectives for which the conflict is waged. It follows that other objectives can also
become the purpose of particular operations and thus also the purpose of
campaigns.*

Even when subordinate engagements are directly intended to weaken the
rival, that action need not be the immediate concern. Bearing in mind the
elaborate structure of an organization and the numerous factors that determine its employment, one can see that the activity of such a force is also
subject to complex functions and combinations.

Separate units of the organization often are assigned tasks that are not in
themselves concerned with the weakening of the rival's capabilities, which
may increase their losses, but do so only indirectly. If the true purpose is normally to occupy a territory, reducing the rival's capabilities is only a means to
an end, a secondary matter.

If a mere presence is enough to cause the opponent to abandon his position, the objective has been achieved. If this is the case in a small geographic
region, it will be even more so in the entire area, where it is not merely two
groups that are facing each other, but two total organizations.

---

* Once again, refer to the Introduction and the listing of types of campaigns.

Thus, there are many reasons why the purpose of an engagement may not be the elimination of the opponent's presence. Elimination may be merely a means to some other end. In such a case, the campaign is nothing but a trial of strength. In itself it is of no value; its significance lies in the outcome.

When one force is a great deal stronger than the other, an estimate may be enough. There will be no fighting; the weaker side will yield at once.

The fact that engagements do not always aim at blunting the rival's efforts, their objectives can often be attained without any confrontation at all, but merely by an evaluation of the situation. That explains why entire campaigns can be conducted with great energy, even though actual confrontation plays an unimportant part in them.

COMMENTARY

Clausewitz's point that "objectives can often be attained without any confrontation" is supported by other writers on strategy.

The renowned twentieth century British historian B. H. Liddell Hart takes a very firm viewpoint that a direct confrontation should be avoided at all costs. Most often it results in exhausting budgets, demoralizing employees, and using hard to replace resources without achieving the objectives.*

In business terms, "direct" translates to (1) going up against a competitor's strongest position without any areas of differentiation or (2) spreading resources by not concentrating on a decisive point of a competitor's weakness.

Liddell Hart goes on to say that if the direct attack requires the aggressor to expend an enormous quantity of resources, it thereby deprives itself of the strength for further market penetration. In that case, an alternative approach must do the opposite. Such an approach means placing the competitor at a disadvantage by concentrating on its weaknesses.

Liddell Hart views the indirect attack as the most fruitful approach. It has the greatest chance of success while conserving the greatest amount of strength. Typically, when an indirect attack is applied as a business strategy, the aggressor concentrates on a weakness in those market segments that are emerging, neglected, or poorly served by competitors. Such a segment is usually the initial point of entry.

Other commentators have added their comments about acting without direct confrontation. Two individuals from different times and different disciplines wrote:

"The object of business is to create a customer."—Peter Drucker, twentieth century management scholar

"To win one hundred victories in one hundred battles is not the acme of skill. To subdue the enemy without fighting is the acme of skill."—Sun Tzu, ancient Chinese strategist, ca. 544 BCE–ca. 496 BCE

* See B. H. Liddell Hart, *Strategy.* New York: Praeger, 1954.

REDUCING THE OPPONENT'S CAPABILITIES

We have shown that the neutralization of a rival's activities is one of the many objects that can be pursued in a conflict, and we have left aside the question of its importance relative to other purposes. In any given case the answer will depend on circumstances; its importance to a conflict in general remains to be clarified.

We shall now go into this question, and we shall see what value must necessarily be attributed to this object of total collapse. Actual confrontation is the only effective force in a conflict. Its aim is to eliminate or reduce the opponent's capabilities as a means to a further end.

That holds true even if no actual confrontation occurs, because the outcome rests on the assumption that if it came to fighting, the rival would be neutralized. It follows that the reduction of the rival's force underlies all actions. All plans are ultimately based on it. Consequently, all action is undertaken in the belief that if the ultimate test of a confrontation should actually occur, the outcome would be favorable.

The decision through conflict is for all major and minor operations. Regardless of how complex the relationship between the two parties is and how rarely settlements actually occur, they can never be entirely absent.

If a decision by confrontation is the basis of all plans and operations, it follows that the rival can frustrate everything through a successful campaign. This occurs not only when the encounter affects an essential factor in our plans, but also when any victory that is won is of sufficient scope.

For every important victory, it is evident that blunting and thereby eliminating the opponent's threat is always the superior, more effective means with which others cannot compete. But of course, we can only say elimination is more effective if we can assume that all other conditions are equal.

It would be a great mistake to deduce from this argument that a headlong rush must always triumph over skillful caution. Blind aggressiveness would destroy the campaign itself, not the defense, and this is not what we are talking about. Greater effectiveness relates not to the means but to the end. We are simply comparing the effect of different outcomes.

THE INTERACTION OF PHYSICAL AND MORALE FACTORS

When we speak of reducing the rival's forces we must emphasize that nothing obliges us to limit this idea to physical forces. The morale element must also be considered. The two interact throughout. They are inseparable.

We have just mentioned the effect that a major victory inevitably exerts on all other actions. And it is exactly at such times that the morale factor is the most fluid element of all and therefore spreads most easily to affect everything else.

The advantage that reducing the rival's threat possesses over all other means is balanced by its cost and danger. And it is only in order to avoid these risks that other policies are employed.

That the method of reduction cannot fail to be expensive is understandable. Other things being equal, the more intent we are on canceling the effectiveness of the rival's forces, the greater our own efforts must be.

The danger of this method is that the greater the success we seek, the greater will be the damage if we fail. Other methods, therefore, are less costly if they succeed and less damaging if they fail, though this holds true only if both sides act identically.

If the opponent pursues the same course as we do—if he were to seek the decision through a major confrontation, his choice would force us against our will to do likewise. Then the outcome of the confrontation would be decisive. But it is clear—other things again being equal—that we would be at an overall disadvantage, since our plans and resources had been in part intended to achieve other goals, whereas the rival's were not.

Two objectives, neither of which is part of the other, are mutually exclusive: One force cannot simultaneously be used for both. If, therefore, one of the two leaders is resolved to seek a decision through major confrontations, he will have an excellent chance of success if he is certain that his opponent is pursuing a different policy.

Conversely, the leader who wishes to adopt different means can reasonably do so only if he assumes his opponent to be equally unwilling to resort to major confrontations. What has been said about plans and forces being directed to other uses refers only to the positive purposes, other than the reduction in the opponent's capabilities. It pertains in no way to pure resistance, which seeks to wear down the opponent's strength.

Pure resistance has no positive intention. We can use our forces only to frustrate the opponent's intentions, and not divert them to other objectives. Here we must consider the negative side of neutralizing the opponent's capabilities—that is, the preservation of our own.

These two efforts always go together; they interact. They are integral parts of a single purpose, and we only need to consider the result if one or the other dominates.

The effort to reduce or eliminate the rival's capabilities has a positive purpose and leads to positive results, whose final aim is the opponent being neutralized. Preserving our own forces has a negative purpose; it frustrates the enemy's intentions. That is, it amounts to pure resistance, whose ultimate aim can only be to prolong the conflict until the rival is exhausted.

How far such a waiting attitude may or should be maintained means a policy whereby waiting must never become passive endurance. It would be a fundamental error to imagine that a negative aim implies a preference for a passive decision over neutralizing the rival.

This usually means that action is postponed in time and space to the extent that space is relevant and circumstances permit. If the time arrives when further waiting would bring excessive disadvantages, then the benefit of the negative policy has been exhausted.

COMMENTARY

Four examples describe various marketplace conditions where conflict exists, yet "waiting would bring excessive disadvantages":

Google, the Internet company, built a new computer operating system and attacked Microsoft in virtually all of its businesses.

In response, Microsoft fought back rapidly by offering a free, Web-based version of its Office software.

Panasonic attempted to reach out and acquire a larger share in emerging markets. Yet the Japanese company became quickly aware that its $1,200 large-screen plasma-display TV sets and $3,000 nanotechnology refrigerators were beyond the reach of low-wage families. Moving forward with its new line of offerings, the company included TVs for $50, air conditioners for $100, and washing machines in the $200 range.

Meanwhile, local manufacturers relying on years of experience squeezing costs and working on paper-thin margins responded aggressively with similar products at bargain prices.

TiVo popularized a technology that makes it routine for viewers to save TV shows on a hard drive so that they can watch them later and fast-forward through the commercials. The company threatened to disrupt the industry and competitors by trying to remake itself as the Google of television.

Responding to the threat, cable companies counterattacked by rolling out their own digital video recorders and began taking subscribers away from TiVo.

AT&T looked to turn mobile access into a big business. It began by assembling a team to operate like a start-up. Its mission: Come up with innovative ways for people to use its wireless network. The strategy: Go beyond cell phones and hook up all manner of electronics to the Internet—from digital cameras and navigation devices to parking meters.

Verizon and other rivals immediately responded by entering the conflict pursuing similar avenues of growth by selling inexpensive netbooks and signing up customers to their networks.

Clausewitz sums up his major points on conflict:

Our discussion has shown that while many different roads can lead to the attainment of the strategic objective, confrontation is the only possible means. Everything is governed by a supreme law, the decision by force.

If the opponent does seek a confrontation, this recourse can never be denied him. A leader who prefers another strategy must first be sure that his opponent either will not appeal to force or that he will lose the verdict if he does.

To sum up: Of all the possible aims in conflict, the reduction of the rival's capabilities always appears as the highest. At a later stage and by degrees we shall see what other kinds of strategies can be achieved in conflict.

All we need to do for the moment is to admit the general possibility of their existence, the possibility of deviating from the basic concept of conflict under the pressure of special circumstances. The leader may exploit any weaknesses in the opponent's capabilities and strategy and finally reach a peaceful settlement. If his assumptions are sound and promise success, we are not entitled to criticize him.

But he must never forget that he is moving on devious paths where conflict may catch him unaware. He must keep his eye on the opponent in order to be prepared adequately should he suddenly be confronted with massive force.

Chapter 3

On Genius

Clausewitz makes these key points about genius:

- Intelligence alone is not courage; we often see that the most intelligent people are indecisive.
- Determination, which dispels doubt, is a quality that can be aroused only by the intellect.
- Determination proceeds from a special type of mind, from a strong rather than a brilliant one.
- Of all the passions that inspire man in conflict, none is so powerful and so constant as the longing for honor and renown.
- Strength of mind or of character ... is the ability to keep one's head at times of exceptional stress and violent emotion.
- The individual responsible for evaluating the whole must bring to his task the quality of intuition that perceives the truth at every point.
- If we ask what sort of mind is likeliest to display the qualities of genius, it is the inquiring, rather than the creative mind, the comprehensive rather than the specialized approach, the calm rather than the excitable head to which we entrust the fate of our personnel, and the safety and honor of our organization.
- The role of determination is to limit the agonies of doubt and the perils of hesitation when the motives for action are inadequate.
- Four elements make up the climate of competitive encounters: danger, exertion, uncertainty, chance.

Clausewitz continues to talk about intellect, courage, temperament, intuition, and determination as attributes associated with achievement—and genius:
Any complex activity, if it is to be carried on with any degree of brilliance, calls for appropriate gifts of intellect and temperament. If they are outstanding

and reveal themselves in exceptional achievements, their possessor is called a "genius."

Let us discuss this faculty, this distinction of mind for a moment, setting out its claims in greater detail, so as to gain a better understanding of the concept. Genius consists in a harmonious combination of elements, in which one or the other may predominate, but none may be in conflict with the rest.

We can already guess how great a role intellectual powers play in the higher forms of genius. Let us now examine the matter more closely. Confrontation is in the realm of danger; therefore, courage is the individual's first requirement.

Courage is of two kinds: first, courage in the face of personal danger and, second, courage to accept responsibility, either before the tribunal of some outside power or before the court of one's own conscience. Only the first kind will be discussed here.

Courage in the face of personal danger is also of two kinds. It may be indifference to danger, which could be due to the individual's constitution, or to his holding life cheap, or to habit. In any case, it must be regarded as a permanent condition. Alternatively, courage may result from such positive motives as ambition, patriotism, or enthusiasm of any kind. In that case courage is a feeling—an emotion—not a permanent state.

These two kinds of courage act in different ways. The first is the more dependable; having become second nature, it will never fail. The other will often achieve more. There is more reliability in the first kind, more boldness in the second. The first leaves the mind calmer; the second tends to stimulate, but it can also blind. The highest kind of courage is a compound of both.

Conflict is the realm of physical and mental exertions. These will seriously impact us unless we can make ourselves indifferent to them, and for this, birth or training must provide us with certain strength of body and soul. If we do possess those qualities, then even if we have nothing but common sense to guide them, we shall be well equipped for conflict.

If we pursue the demands that confrontation makes on those who practice it, we come to the region dominated by the powers of intellect. Conflict is the realm of uncertainty; three-quarters of the factors on which action is based are wrapped in a fog of greater or lesser uncertainty. A sensitive and discriminating judgment is called for—a skilled intelligence to scent out the truth. Average intelligence may recognize the truth occasionally, and exceptional courage may now and then retrieve a blunder, but usually intellectual inadequacy will be shown up by indifferent achievement.

INFORMATION IS THE REALM OF UNCERTAINTY

Since all information and assumptions are open to doubt, and with chance at work everywhere, the leader continually finds that things are not as he expected. These are bound to influence his plans, or at least the assumptions underlying them. If such influences are sufficiently powerful to cause a change in his plans, he must usually work out new ones, but for these the necessary information may not be immediately available.

During a campaign, decisions have usually to be made at once. There may be no time to review the situation or even to think it through. Usually, new information and reevaluation are not enough to make us give up our intentions; they only call them in question.

We now know more, but this makes us more, not less, uncertain. The latest reports do not arrive all at once; they merely trickle in. They continually impinge on our decisions, and our mind must be permanently armed to deal with them.

If the mind is to emerge unscathed from this relentless struggle with the unforeseen, two qualities are indispensable:

First, an intellect that, even in the darkest hour, retains some glimmerings
   of the inner light which leads to truth
Second, the courage to follow this faint light wherever it may lead

The first of these qualities is described by the French term, *coup d'oeil.** The second is determination. *Coup d'oeil* refers not alone to the physical but also, more commonly, to the inward eye. The expression, like the quality itself, has certainly always been more applicable to tactics, but it must also have its place in strategy, since here, as well, quick decisions are often needed.

Stripped of metaphor and of the restrictions imposed on it by the phrase, the concept merely refers to the quick recognition of a truth that the mind would ordinarily miss or would perceive only after long study and reflection.

Determination in a single instance is an expression of courage; if it becomes characteristic, a mental habit. Here we are referring not to physical courage but to the courage to accept responsibility, courage in the face of a moral danger. This has often been called *courage d'esprit,* because it is created by the intellect. That, however, does not make it an act of the intellect; rather, it is an act of temperament.

COMMENTARY

As discussed in Chapter 2, chance and luck play a part in every venture when there is no reliable way to know, or calculate, the outcome. You thereby open yourself to a level of risk. Expressed another way, chance is the absence of predictability. You cannot say for certain what the

---

* Clausewitz's meaning of the term is the commander's ability to see things simply, to identify the whole business of war (conflict) completely with himself, which is the essence of good generalship. Only if the mind works in this comprehensive fashion can it achieve the freedom it needs to dominate events and not be dominated by them. A more popular definition is the leader's ability to size up a situation at a glance.

result of a particular action will be. Without risk it is almost axiomatic to state that there is little opportunity for a favorable outcome.

The central issue: How far are you willing to extend yourself and your resources in an unknown situation? Part of the answer depends on the level of investigation, thought, and planning that precedes your decision.

Consider the following guidelines:

First, evaluate the action you are considering. How would you rank the level of risk? Also list the things you imagine could go wrong as a result of taking that chance.

Second, develop a plan that will allow for contingencies. That is, determine alternate objectives if the primary ones are unattainable. And, if possible, determine a fallback position to reduce any damaging effects of plans going awry.

Third, adopt the flexible attitude that in failure there are always possibilities for success. Or, as Clausewitz phrases it, "In war the result is never final ... merely a transitory evil."

Fourth, whenever you take a chance and events turn in your favor, take the opportunity to exploit the situation by involving members of your staff. Use the moment to boost their morale and sincerely thank them for their efforts. The underlying issue is to maintain momentum, for success, too, is never final.

These points introduce Clausewitz's next issue: intelligence versus courage.

INTELLIGENCE ALONE IS NOT COURAGE

We often see that the most intelligent people are indecisive. Since in the rush of events a man is governed by feelings rather than by thought, the intellect needs to arouse the quality of courage, which then supports and sustains it in action. Looked at in this way, the role of determination is to limit the agonies of doubt and the perils of hesitation when the motives for action are inadequate.

Determination also applies to a propensity for daring, pugnacity, boldness, or audacity. But when a man has adequate grounds for action—whether subjective or objective, valid or false—he cannot properly be called "determined." This would amount to putting oneself in his position and weighting the scale with a doubt that he never felt. In such a case it is only a question of strength or weakness.

Determination, which dispels doubt, is a quality that can be aroused only by the intellect, and by a specific cast of mind at that. More is required to create determination than a mere conjunction of superior insight with the appropriate emotions.

Some may bring the keenest brains to the most formidable problems and may possess the courage to accept serious responsibilities. But when faced with a difficult situation, they still find themselves unable to reach a decision.

Their courage and their intellect work in separate compartments, not together. Determination, therefore, does not result. It is engendered only by a mental act. The mind tells man that boldness is required, and thus gives direction to his will. This particular cast of mind, which employs the fear of wavering and hesitating to suppress all other fears, is the force that makes strong men determined.

Men of low intelligence, therefore, cannot possess determination in the sense in which we use the word. They may act without hesitation in a crisis, but if they do, they act without reflection. And a man who acts without reflection cannot be torn by doubt. From time to time, action of this type may even be appropriate.

As I have said before, it is the average result that indicates the existence of genius. This statement may surprise the reader who knows some determined leaders who are little given to deep thought. But he must remember that we are talking about a special kind of intelligence, not about great powers of meditation.

In short, we believe that determination proceeds from a special type of mind, from a strong rather than a brilliant one. We can give further proof of this interpretation by pointing to the many examples of men who show great determination at the junior levels, but lose it as they rise in rank. Conscious of the need to be decisive, they also recognize the risks entailed by a wrong decision.

Since they are unfamiliar with the problems now facing them, their minds lose their former incisiveness. The more they had been used to instant action, the more their timidity increases as they realize the dangers of the vacillation that ensnares them.

COMMENTARY

Clausewitz's emphasis on determination deserves further support, as noted by the following quotes from a cross section of famous personalities:

"A dream doesn't become reality through magic; it takes sweat, determination and hard work."—Colin Powell

"I never could have done what I have done without the habits of punctuality, order, and diligence, without the determination to concentrate myself on one subject at a time."—Charles Dickens

"Not only our future economic soundness but the very soundness of our democratic institutions depends on the determination of our government to give employment to idle men."—Franklin D. Roosevelt

"The truest wisdom is a resolute determination."—Napoleon Bonaparte

"Let us not be content to wait and see what will happen, but give us
the determination to make the right things happen."—Horace Mann
"If your determination is fixed, I do not counsel you to despair. Few
things are impossible to diligence and skill. Great works are performed not by strength, but perseverance."—Samuel Johnson

PRESENCE OF MIND: THE CAPACITY
TO DEAL WITH THE UNEXPECTED

Having discussed *coup d'oeil* and determination, it is natural to pass to a
related subject: presence of mind. This must play a great role in conflict, the
domain of the unexpected, since it is nothing but an increased capacity of
dealing with the unexpected.

We admire presence of mind in an apt repartee, as we admire quick thinking in the face of danger. Neither needs to be exceptional, so long as it meets
the situation. A reaction following long and deep reflection may seem quite
commonplace; as an immediate response, it may give keen pleasure.

The expression "presence of mind" precisely conveys the speed and
immediacy of the help provided by the intellect. Whether this splendid quality is due to a special cast of mind or to steady nerves depends on the nature of
the incident, but neither can ever be entirely lacking. A quick retort shows wit;
resourcefulness in sudden danger calls, above all, for steady nerve.

Four elements make up the climate of competitive encounters: danger,
exertion, uncertainty, and chance.

If we consider them together, it becomes evident how much fortitude of
mind and character is needed to make progress in these impeding elements
with safety and success. According to circumstance, reporters and historians use such terms as energy, firmness, staunchness, emotional balance, and
strength of character.

These products of a heroic nature could almost be treated as one and the
same force—strength of will—which adjusts itself to circumstances. Though
closely linked, they are not identical.

A closer study of the interplay of mental forces at work here may be
worthwhile. To begin with, clear thought demands that we keep one point
in mind: the weight, the burden, the resistance that challenge the mental and
emotional strengths of the individual. Only a small part of these is the direct
result of the rival's activity, his resistance, or his operations.

The deep anxiety that he must experience works on his strength of will
and puts it to the test. Yet we believe that this is not by any means the heaviest
burden he must bear, for he is answerable to himself alone. All other effects of
action, however, are felt by the people under his command and, through them,
react on him.

So long as a unit advances cheerfully, with spirit and élan, great strength of will is rarely needed. But once conditions become difficult, as they must when much is at stake, things no longer run like a well-oiled machine. The machine itself begins to resist, and the leader needs tremendous willpower to overcome this resistance.

The machine's resistance need not consist of disobedience and argument, though this occurs often enough in individuals. It is the impact of the ebbing of morale and physical strength that the leader has to withstand: first in himself, and then in all those who, directly or indirectly, have entrusted him with their thoughts and feelings, hopes and fears.

As each man's strength gives out, as it no longer responds to his will, the inertia of the whole gradually comes to rest on the leader's will alone. The ardor of his spirit must rekindle the flame of purpose in all others.

His inward fire must revive their hope. Only to the extent that he can do this will he retain his hold on his men and keep control. Once that hold is lost, once his own courage can no longer revive the courage of his men, the mass will drag him down to the world where danger is shirked and shame is unknown.

Such are the burdens that the leader's courage and strength of will must overcome, if he hopes to achieve outstanding success. The burdens increase with the number of men in his command, and therefore the higher his position is, the greater the strength of character he needs to bear the mounting load.

COMMENTARY

Clausewitz covers many points in his views on intelligence, courage, presence of mind, and morale—much of which reflects on "the burdens that the leader's courage and strength of will must overcome." The following generally accepted guidelines can provide a measure of relief from some of those burdens:

- Hold fast to the definitive object of all businesses, which according to the late management scholar, Peter Drucker, is to "create a customer."
- Remove obstacles that deprive your people from gaining pride in providing quality of service and in delivering innovative products.
- Break down inhibiting barriers within your company or business unit by establishing cross-functional teams of workers.
- Introduce a work environment where the emphasis is on junior managers leading, not merely supervising.
- Commit to long-term goals, such as developing leading-edge products or maintaining superior service and product quality.
- Eliminate the use of fear as a motivator.
- Encourage employees to express ideas; listen to them and respond.

- Promote self-improvement as an ongoing obligation.
- Institute continuing employee training and education to advance their skills, personal growth, and chances for career advancement.

A recent example of a leader's courage and determination was exhibited by CEO Marissa Mayer of Yahoo. Within 1 year of taking over the top corporate spot, she took rapid and sweeping actions. Several key executives were replaced, a string of 22 acquisitions was made, and the company's culture was overhauled, including substantial changes in human resource rules.

The central aims behind those changes, which committed major amounts of financial and material resources, were to reverse declining revenues, rebuild market presence, revitalize Yahoo, and generally get personnel ready to confront equally committed competitors who were not expected to sit quietly on the sidelines. In effect, the stages were set for a competitive conflict when Mayer began introducing those audacious moves.

THE LONGING FOR HONOR AND RENOWN

Energy in action varies in proportion to the strength of its motive, whether the motive is the result of intellectual conviction or of emotion. Great strength is not easily produced where there is no emotion. Of all the passions that inspire man in conflict, none, we have to admit, is so powerful and so constant as the longing for honor and renown.

Other emotions may be more common and more venerated—loyalty, idealism, enthusiasm of every kind—but they are no substitute for a thirst for fame and honor. They may, indeed, rouse the mass to action and inspire it, but they cannot give the leader the ambition to strive higher than the rest, as he must if he is to distinguish himself. They cannot give him, as can ambition, a personal, almost proprietary interest in every aspect of a campaign so that he turns each opportunity to best advantage, plowing with vigor and sowing with care, in the hope of reaping with abundance.

It is primarily this spirit of endeavor on the part of leaders at all levels—this inventiveness, energy, and competitive enthusiasm—that vitalizes a group and makes it victorious. And so far as the leader is concerned, we may well ask whether history has ever known a great leader who was not ambitious—whether, indeed, such a figure is conceivable.

COMMENTARY

Clausewitz talks about two issues: "the longing for honor and renown" and a leader's personal quality of ambition.

First, as for honors, the seemingly insatiable demand for awards continues in the form of medals, decorations, prizes, titles, and other tributes. There seems to be no limit to inventing new awards with recognition given to the manager of the month, of the year, by industry, by age, as in the outstanding leader under 40, and so on.

Psychologists have shown that people often value status above and beyond the monetary rewards. It reaches the point where such individuals are even willing to incur their own costs to "buy" high status. The object of these cravings is to satisfy the deep-seated human needs for social status, identity, recognition, self-esteem, reputation, and fame. The endgame is to inspire motivation, productivity, morale, and job satisfaction.

Psychologists further point out that individuals have an innate desire to distinguish themselves from other individuals to the extent of harboring a strong urge to be better than others. Thus, the quest for social distinction is taken as a hardwired trait of human nature—a characteristic Clausewitz emphasizes in his comment that "of all the passions that inspire man ... none is so powerful and so constant as the longing for honor and renown."

Second, as for ambition: Clausewitz raises the question "whether history has ever known a great leader who was not ambitious ... whether such a figure is conceivable."

It is generally accepted that ambition can be considered one of the essential qualities of a leader. However, for pragmatic application, ambition must be worthy of the organization's mission and not a pathway to personal power.

Yet, from another viewpoint, ambition is difficult to separate from courage. In thinking about outstanding leaders, it is difficult to decide which of their actions in the face of severe problems bore the mark of boldness or that of ambition. Both are characteristics of the truly outstanding leader.

Constructive ambition and the intense desire to excel are the combination that stimulates ambition in others—meaning that the magic of winning always arouses determination, which gives momentum to the organization. Thus, nurturing positive ambition is an essential duty of the leader.

That said, the unwelcome reality also exists that unrestrained personal ambition does live on, with all its excesses and potentially harmful outcomes. It is uncontrolled raw ambition that can destroy employees' careers and the economic livelihood of the community in which the organization operates. Such excesses and scandalous executive behavior within the financial community decimated even the loftiest organizations during the height of the 2008–2009 recession.

Consequently, if you seek competence in leadership, understand how the power of ambition interfaces with the goals and culture of the organization.

STRENGTH OF MIND

We now turn to strength of mind, or of character, and must first ask what we mean by these terms. Is it not the vehement display of feeling or passionate temperament? That would strain the meaning of the phrase. We mean the ability to keep one's head at times of exceptional stress and violent emotion.

Could strength of intellect alone account for such a faculty? We doubt it. Of course the opposite does not deny the fact that some men of outstanding intellect do lose their self-control. It could be argued that a powerful rather than a large mind is what is needed.

It might be closer to the truth to assume that the faculty known as self-control—the gift of keeping calm even under the greatest stress—is rooted in temperament. It is itself an emotion that serves to balance the passionate feelings in strong characters without destroying them.

And it is this balance alone that assures the dominance of the intellect. The counterweight we mean is simply the sense of human dignity, the noblest pride and deepest need of all: the urge to act rationally at all times.

Therefore, we would argue that a strong character is one that will not be unbalanced by the most powerful emotions—that is, if we consider how men differ in their emotional reactions. For instance:

First, we find a group with small capacity for being roused, usually known as unemotional or calm.

Second, there are men who are extremely active, but whose feelings never rise above a certain level, men whom we know to be sensitive but calm.

Third, there are men whose passions are easily inflamed, in whom excitement flares up suddenly but soon burns out.

Fourth, we come to those who do not react to minor matters, who will be moved only very gradually, not suddenly, but whose emotions attain great strength and durability.

These are the men whose passions are strong, deep, and concealed. These variants are probably related to the physical forces operating in the human being. They are part of that dual organism we call the nervous system, one side of which is physical and the other emotional. It is important to note the ways in which these various combinations can affect activity, and to find out how far one can look for great strength of character among them.

In the first group, impassive men are hard to throw off balance, but total lack of vigor cannot really be interpreted as strength of character. It cannot be denied, however, that the imperturbability of such men gives them a certain narrow usefulness in conflict. They are seldom strongly motivated, lack initiative, and consequently are not particularly active. On the other hand, they seldom make a serious mistake.

The salient point about the second group is that trifles can suddenly stir them to act, whereas great issues are likely to overwhelm them. This kind of man will gladly help an individual in need, but the misfortune of an entire people will only sadden him and will not stimulate him to action.

In conflict, men in the third group show no lack of energy or balance but they are unlikely to achieve anything significant unless they possess a very powerful intellect to provide the needed stimulus. But it is rare to find this type of temperament combined with a strong and independent mind.

Their volatile emotions make it doubly hard for such men to preserve their balance. They often lose their heads, and nothing is worse on active service. All the same, it must be untrue to say that highly excitable minds could never be strong—that is, could never keep their balance even under the greatest strain.

Lastly, we come to men who are difficult to move, but have strong feelings—men who are to the previous type like heat to a shower of sparks. These are the men who are best able to summon the titanic strength it takes to clear away the enormous burdens that obstruct activity in conflict.

Their emotions move as great masses do—slowly but irresistibly. These men are not swept away by their emotions as often as is the previous group. Experience shows that they too can lose their balance and be overcome by blind passion. This can happen whenever they lack the noble pride of self-control, or whenever it is inadequate.

We say a man has strength of character, or simply has character, if he sticks to his convictions, whether these derive from his own opinions or someone else's, and whether they represent principles, attitudes, sudden insights, or any other mental force. Such firmness cannot show itself, of course, if a man keeps changing his mind.

This need not be the consequence of external influence. The cause may be the workings of his own intelligence, but this would suggest a peculiarly insecure mind.

Obviously a man whose opinions are constantly changing, even though this is in response to his own reflections, would not be called a man of character. The term is applied only to men whose views are stable and constant.

This may be because they are well thought-out, clear, and scarcely open to revision. Or, in the case of lethargic men, because such people are not in the habit of mental effort and therefore have no reason for altering their views.

And, finally, because a firm decision, based on fundamental principles, is relatively immune to changes of opinion, there is no activity to rob men of confidence in themselves and in others, and to divert them from their original course of action.

COMMENTARY

Clausewitz refers to the man "whose opinions are constantly changing" and relates it to character. Such behavior often shows up in a manager's indecisiveness, lack of vision, unwillingness to attack a problem, or reluctance to pursue an opportunity with vigor and boldness. These displays of negative behavior in leadership are often too visible to hide from employees.

Consequently, a display of volatile behavior that is inconsistent with a market situation could become a serious leadership issue. Employees can understand the need for a flexible managerial style or even a certain amount of unconventional behavior, if it is understood and accepted as part of a manager's inherent personality. However, they are unable to tolerate inconsistency and sudden erratic mannerisms, particularly if there is no apparent reason for what could be perceived as chaotic behavior.

Like an epidemic, such damaging traits can spread to all those who are exposed to them. If the lack of self-confidence cannot be converted to a positive attitude, then the manager might consider stepping down before any further harm is done.

STRENGTH OF CHARACTER

Action can never be based on anything firmer than instinct, a sensing of the truth. Nowhere, in consequence, are differences of opinion so acute as in conflict, and fresh opinions never cease to batter at one's convictions. No degree of calm can provide enough protection. New impressions are too powerful, too vivid, and always assault the emotions as well as the intellect.

Only those general principles and attitudes that result from clear and deep understanding can provide a comprehensive guide to action. It is to these that opinions on specific problems should be anchored. The difficulty is to hold fast to these results of contemplation in the torrent of events and new opinions.

Often there is a gap between principles and actual events that cannot always be bridged by a succession of logical deductions. Then a measure of self-confidence is needed, and a degree of skepticism is also beneficial. Frequently, nothing short of an authoritative principle will suffice, which is not part of the immediate thought process but does dominate it.

That principle is in all doubtful cases to stick to one's first opinion and to refuse to change unless forced to do so by a clear conviction. A strong faith in the overriding truth of tested principles is needed.

The vividness of transient impressions must not make us forget that such truth as they contain is of a lesser stamp. By giving preference, in case of doubt, to our earlier convictions, by holding to them stubbornly, our actions acquire that quality of steadiness and consistency termed strength of character.

It is evident how greatly strength of character depends on balanced temperament. Most men of emotional strength and stability are therefore men of powerful character as well. Strength of character can degenerate into obstinacy. The line between them is often hard to draw in a specific case; but surely it is easy to distinguish them in theory.

Obstinacy is not an intellectual defect. It comes from reluctance to admit that one is wrong. To attribute this to the mind would be illogical, for the mind is the seat of judgment. Obstinacy is a fault of temperament.

Stubbornness and intolerance of contradiction result from a special kind of egotism, which elevates above everything else the pleasure of its autonomous intellect, to which others must bow. It might also be called vanity, if it were not something superior. We would therefore argue that strength of character turns to obstinacy as soon as a man resists another point of view—not from superior insight or attachment to some higher principle, but rather because he objects instinctively.

Admittedly, this definition may not be of much practical use. But it will nevertheless help us avoid the interpretation that obstinacy is simply a more intense form of strong character. There is a basic difference between the two. They are closely related, but one is so far from being a higher degree of the other that we can even find extremely obstinate men who are too dense to have much strength of character.

COMMENTARY

Clausewitz's comment that "strength of character depends on balanced temperament" is another way of saying to remain calm and firm and avoid being easily unbalanced by negative events. Often this balancing effect can be achieved by looking at the big picture—or, more pragmatically, focusing on the long-term strategic direction of your operation as a way of gaining an unclouded perspective.

In such a state of physical and mental composure, you are in a better state of mind to reduce any emotions of anger, fear, worry, or resentment. If left unattended, those feelings can cause you to lose your grip on the situation and possibly end up losing your advantage to a rival.

CONFLICT AND THE PHYSICAL NATURE OF THE FIELD

So far our survey of the attributes that a great leader needs in conflict has been concerned with qualities in which mind and temperament work together. Now we must address ourselves to a special feature of competitive confrontation—possibly the most striking even though it is not the most important—which is not related to temperament and involves merely the intellect. I mean the relationship between conflict and the physical nature of the field.

First, this relationship is a permanent factor—so much so that one cannot conceive of a campaign operating except in a definite physical space.

Second, its importance is decisive in the highest degree, for it affects the operations of all forces and, at times, entirely alters them.

Third, its influence may be felt in the very smallest feature of the field, but it can also dominate enormous areas.

In these ways the relationship between the conflict and the field determines the peculiar character of action. If we consider activities connected with the soil—gardening, farming, building, hydraulic engineering, mining, or forestry—none extends to more than a very limited area, and a working knowledge of that area is soon acquired.

But a leader must submit his work to a partner, space, which he can never completely scrutinize, and that, because of the constant movement and change to which he is subject, he can never really come to know. To be sure, the rival is generally no better off. But the handicap, though shared, is still a handicap, and the man with enough talent and experience to overcome it will have a real advantage.

Moreover, it is only in a general sense that the difficulty is the same for both sides. In any particular case the defender usually knows the area far better than his opponent. This problem is unique. To master it a special gift is needed, which is given the too restricted name of a sense of locality.

It is the faculty of quickly and accurately grasping the topography of any area, which enables a man to find his way about at any time. If imagination is entirely lacking, however, it would be difficult to combine details into a clear, coherent image.

That practice and a trained mind have much to do with it is undeniable. A leader, on the other hand, must aim at acquiring an overall knowledge of the configuration of an entire area, without ever losing a sense of his immediate surroundings. Of course, he can draw general information from reports of all kinds, from maps, books, and local studies. Other details will be furnished by his staff.

Nevertheless, it is true that with a quick, unerring sense of locality his dispositions will be more rapid and assured. He will run less risk of certain awkwardness in his concepts and be less dependent on others. We attribute this ability to the imagination.

COMMENTARY

Clausewitz talks about "the relationship between conflict and the physical nature of the field." Further, he says that "the relationship between the confrontation and the field determines the peculiar character of action."

For our purposes, there are useful ways to look at the physical nature of the competitive market. For instance, there are markets that can be categorized as natural, leading edge, key, linked, central, challenging, difficult, and encircled.

NATURAL MARKETS

In this type of space, you are likely to operate in the familiar setting of established markets. The implication is that within such customary surroundings, personnel tend to be at ease and may not be motivated to venture out of their comfort zone.

Yet, to expand, you have to motivate them to move beyond the confines of existing markets. That means that you should get back to the issue of your organization's culture. That is, does your organization's culture permit venturing out of familiar territory?

For the most part, in a natural market, you and your rivals have learned to adopt a live-and-let-live policy. That condition exists as long as each company sticks to its own dedicated segment. Generally, outright aggressive confrontations are seldom used.

The primary reason for this uncharacteristic display of togetherness in a highly competitive world is that you and your rivals share a common interest in furthering the long-term growth and prosperity of the market.

On the other hand, if any one competitor chooses to move forward and gain a meaningful benefit, a likely strategy might include securing a more advantageous position on the supply chain by adjusting its position. Or it can be done by adding or deleting a link in the distribution network. Or it may choose to gain additional market share by recasting itself as a low-cost producer.

LEADING EDGE MARKETS

Leading edge means exploring markets by making minor penetrations into a competitor's territory. The intent is to investigate the possibility of opening another revenue stream.

Such a movement out of a natural market requires that you obtain market intelligence to determine the following accurately:

- The feasibility for generating a revenue stream over the long term and the possibility for expanding into additional niches
- The investment needed to enter and gain a foothold in the market
- A time frame for payback and eventual profitability
- An assessment of competitors: their market position, strengths/ weaknesses, and nature of the opposition you will likely face

A classic example of a leading edge market is the initial penetration by a few Japanese companies into North America with their small copier machines. Xerox, the market leader in those early years, concentrated its marketing efforts at large corporations with a line of large copiers.

Xerox managers initially avoided the small copier market. That oversight proved to be a critical error. Armed with a low-cost, no-frills desk-top copier, enterprising Japanese copier makers moved in virtually unopposed and exploited a wide-open opportunity in the vast market of small- and midsize firms. Once established, they moved upscale in a segment-by-segment assault and took over a significant amount of Xerox's primary market share.

KEY MARKETS

Key means that you and many of your competitors seem evenly matched within key market segments. The general behavior is that you would not openly create a conflict with an equally strong rival.

However, you may find that some competitor is attempting to dislodge you from a long-held position with the clear aim of taking away customers or disrupting your supply chain relationships. Then you may be forced to launch a counter effort by concentrating as many resources as possible to blunt the effort. Such actions are appropriate, however, if they fit your overall strategic objectives.

Therefore, keep the big picture in mind: If you expend excessive resources in hawkish-style actions such as price wars, then you may be left with a restricted budget to defend your overall market position.

LINKED MARKETS

In this category, you and your competitors are linked with easy access to markets. Your best strategy is to pay strict attention to constructing defensive barriers around those niches that you value most, and from which you can best defend your position. (Remember, too, that according to Clausewitz, when in a defense mode, time is on your side.)

Barriers include:

- Above-average quality
- Feature-loaded products
- First-class customer service
- Superior technical support
- Competitive pricing
- Generous warranties
- Patent protection of advanced technologies

Not only do you build barriers against competitors' incursions, you also benefit by solidifying customer relationships. In particular, customer loyalty gives you a long-lasting, profit-generating advantage that is difficult for a competitor to overcome. It is the one area that makes a meaningful addition to your growth. As one management analyst put it, "If you currently retain 70 percent of your customers and you start a program to improve that to 80 percent, you'll add an additional 10 percent to your growth rate."

CENTRAL MARKETS

Central means that you may face powerful forces that threaten your market position. These forces are as diverse as watching competitors eat away at your position through aggressive pricing or by offering dazzling feature-laden products, or by technology-rich firms generating new applications overlaid with value-added services.

To counter such threats, look for joint ventures so that the cumulative effects yield greater market advantages and offer more strategy options than you can achieve independently. For many companies the merger and acquisition (M&A) route and other forms of joint ventures have proven the strategy of choice.

CHALLENGING MARKETS

In this category, if you enter a market dominated by a strong and aggressive competitor, be watchful. You could place your company at excessively high risk.

If, however, your long-term strategic objectives strongly support maintaining a presence in a challenging market, and if the expenditures of financial, material, and human resources are consistent with your overall strategy, then find a secure position, for example, on the supply chain.

Dell Computer is a prime example of excellent supply chain management. In its original climb toward prominence, the company activated its manufacturing process and supply chain only when an order was received from a customer. That strategy eliminated the cost of storing excessive inventory. Dell benefited by shipping just the right amount of components to its factories, thereby avoiding investing in expensive warehousing.[*]

DIFFICULT MARKETS

This type of market segment is characterized as one where progress is erratic and highly competitive. For instance, in attempting a meaningful market penetration, securing key accounts, or maintaining reasonable levels of logistical support, you are likely to be blocked by asset-draining barriers.

And should a competitor take you totally off-guard, and you subsequently lose your market position, it is difficult to return to your former

---

[*] That strategy has worked remarkably well in past decades. However, as of 2013, with the decline in laptop computer sales, Dell changed direction and moved into corporate services and related products.

position. In effect, you are entrapped in an untenable situation and your entire business plan could be in jeopardy. Your best course of action is to go forward only as long as the effort is consistent with your mission and long-term strategic objectives.

ENCIRCLED MARKETS

Encircled segments foretell a potentially risky situation. This market condition exists where you control limited resources, and any aggressive action by a stronger, well-positioned competitor can force you to consider pulling out of a market.

In such a situation, it is in your best interest to maintain ongoing competitive intelligence so that you can accurately assess the vulnerability of your position against that of your opponent.

Armed with the intelligence, you are able to develop a contingency plan that highlights your strengths and exposes your competitor's weaknesses. If in your judgment you still lack maneuverability and a capability to mount a meaningful competitive response, then exiting the market is prudent, as long as it minimizes disruption to your main line of business.

If, on the other hand, your competitor foresees an encircled position, it is wise to give the rival a way out of the market and not force him into a fight-to-the-end mind-set. Your aim is to encourage him to take the more tempting approach and exit the market.

INTELLECTUAL STANDARDS

We have reached the end of our review of the intellectual and moral powers that human nature needs to draw upon in conflict. The vital contribution of intelligence is clear throughout. No wonder then, that conflict, though it may appear to be uncomplicated, cannot be waged with distinction except by men of outstanding intellect.

Once this view is adopted, there is no longer any need to think that it takes a great intellectual effort to outflank an opponent's position, or to carry out a multitude of similar operations. It is true that we normally regard the plain, efficient individual as the very opposite of the contemplative scholar, or of the inventive intellectual with his dazzling range of knowledge.

This opposite is not entirely unrealistic. It does not prove that courage alone will make an efficient member of the staff or that having brains and using them is not a necessary part of being a good individual. Once again we must insist: No case is more common than that of the leader whose energy declines as he rises in rank and fills positions that are beyond his abilities.

But we must also remind the reader that outstanding effort, the kind that gives men a distinguished name, is what we have in mind. Every level of command has its own intellectual standards, its own prerequisites for fame and honor. A major gulf exists between a senior-level leader and those immediately subordinate to him.

The reason is simple: The second level is subjected to much closer control and supervision, and thus gives far less scope for independent thought. People, therefore, often think that outstanding intellectual ability is called for only at the top and that for all other duties common intelligence will suffice.

A leader of lesser responsibility, one grown gray in the service, his mind well blinkered by long years of routine, may often be considered to have developed a certain stodginess. His gallantry is respected, but his simplemindedness makes us smile.

Since in our view junior positions require outstanding intellectual qualities for outstanding achievement, and since the standard rises with every step, it follows that we recognize the abilities that are needed if the second positions in a group are to be filled with distinction. Such individuals may appear to be rather simple compared to the sage scholar, the far-ranging leader, and the statesman; but we should not dismiss the value of their practical intelligence.

It sometimes happens of course that someone who made his reputation in one rank carries it with him when he is promoted, without really deserving to. If not much is demanded of him and he can avoid exposing his incompetence, it is difficult to decide what reputation he really deserves. Such cases often cause one to hold in low estimate individuals who in less responsible positions might do excellent work.

Appropriate talent is needed at all levels if distinguished service is to be performed. But history and posterity reserve the name of "'genius" for those who have excelled in the highest positions, since here the demands for intellectual and moral powers are vastly greater. To bring a conflict or one of its campaigns to a successful close requires a thorough grasp of the organization's policy. On that level strategy and policy coalesce.

The great range of business that a leader must swiftly absorb and accurately evaluate has been indicated earlier. We argue that a senior-level person must also be a statesman, but he must not cease to be a leader. On the one hand, he is aware of the entire strategic situation. On the other, he knows exactly how much he can achieve with the means at his disposal.

Circumstances vary so enormously in competitive conflict and are so indefinable that a vast array of factors has to be appreciated—mostly in the light of probabilities alone. The individual responsible for evaluating the whole must bring to his task the quality of intuition that perceives the truth at every point. Otherwise, a chaos of opinions and considerations would arise and fatally entangle judgment.

COMMENTARY

Clausewitz singles out the quality of "intuition that perceives the truth at every point." What exactly is intuition and how does it relate to competitive conflict and pursuing a market opportunity?

Think of intuition as an inner voice that presents you with possible courses of action. It unlocks the mind and guides you by means of flashes of insights, ideas, images, metaphors, or symbols. "The intuitive mind tells the rational thinking mind where to look next," declared the renowned Dr. Jonas Salk.

While intuition is often thought of as something elusive, spontaneous, and outside your control, nevertheless, it is possible to make intuition more accessible and more reliable. It begins by paying attention to your feelings. That means starting with a quiet mind and turning off the constant monologue that clutters the mind.

You then adopt a mind-set where simply knowing transcends reason. Just perceiving possibilities is also an intuitive function. Of course, you can never be certain what the outcome of a decision is going to be. But you can have a strong intuitive sense of the direction you want to pursue.

Yet such a leap of understanding is not in opposition to or a substitute for reason. And it certainly is not in conflict with the input of reliable market intelligence. Intuition is inner power that you use in addition to reason and factual information. In effect, there is an integration of intuition with the logical and linear thinking mind.

You may have to personalize how you reach the receptive state where your intuition can flourish. It may be through meditation, solitude, being out in nature alone and quiet, or using slow breathing techniques.

Other approaches include using mental imagery, which is more associated with thinking and tends to be the type of intuition used by business executives, especially entrepreneurs, who tend to be highly intuitive.

The benefits come when you can perceive possibilities in the future. In its most practical business application, intuition applies to developing a strategic business plan where the first planning step is to develop a mission (or vision) statement for your company or business unit, or to define a long-term strategic direction for a product line.

Anything that breaks new ground, provides a future-directed vision, or pushes you beyond the boundaries of what you already know, is intuitive. If any mystery exists about intuition, it is that people seem to get information and they do not know how they got it.

"No problem is solved by the same consciousness that created it," observed the celebrated Albert Einstein, who was known for his reliance on intuition.

What is required is a shift in consciousness; through this shift you tap the subconscious mind to show you the way to solve a problem, which is revealed as intuition. What follows is for you to use logic, reason, and market research to follow up on the intuition for proof and validation. However, if time does not permit that luxury and you must react to a severe competitive situation, then you have sound reason to trust in your intuition.

Clausewitz summarizes:

Truth in itself is rarely sufficient to make men act. Hence the step is always long from awareness to decision, from knowledge to ability. The most powerful springs of action in man lie in his emotions. He derives his most vigorous support from that blend of brains and temperament that we have learned to recognize in the qualities of determination, firmness, staunchness, and strength of character.

Naturally enough, if a leader's superior intellect and strength of character did not express themselves in the final success of his work and were only taken on trust, they would rarely achieve historical importance. What the layman gets to know of the course of events is usually nondescript. One action resembles another, and from a mere recital of events it would be impossible to guess what obstacles were faced and overcome.

Only now and then, in the memoirs of leaders or as the result of close historical study, are some of the countless threads of the tapestry revealed. Most of the arguments and clashes of opinion that precede a major campaign are deliberately concealed because they touch political interests. Or they are simply forgotten, being considered as scaffolding to be demolished when the building is complete.

Finally, and without wishing to risk a closer definition of the higher reaches of the spirit, let us assert that the human mind is far from uniform. If we then ask what sort of mind is likeliest to display the qualities of business genius, experience and observation will both tell us that it is:

> The inquiring, rather than the creative mind, the comprehensive rather than the specialized approach, the calm rather than the excitable head, to which in conflict we would choose to entrust the fate of our personnel and the safety and honor of our organization.

Chapter 4

Strategy (Part 1)*

Clausewitz makes these key points about strategy:

- Everything in conflict is very simple, but the simplest thing is difficult.
- Friction is the only concept that distinguishes real conflict from conflict on paper. It is the force that makes the apparently easy so difficult.
- Action in conflict is like movement in a resistant element. Just as the simplest movement, walking, cannot easily be performed in water, in conflict it is difficult for normal efforts to achieve even moderate results.
- Danger, physical exertion, intelligence, and friction coalesce to form the atmosphere of conflict.
- Campaigns are never directed against material forces alone; they are always aimed simultaneously at the moral forces, which give them life.
- Conflict is an expression of hostile feelings.
- Action in conflict is never completely free from risk.
- Emotions easily associated with conflict include: ambition, love of power, and enthusiasms of all kinds.
- Courage is not a conscious act; like fear, it is an emotion.
- For lack of objective knowledge, one has to trust to talent or to luck.
- The senses make a more vivid impression on the mind than systematic thought.

Clausewitz talks more extensively about the various forces that interact with strategy:

---

* This chapter combines several chapters from *On War,* as each of the original ones varies from one to three pages in length.

PHYSICAL EFFORT: ONE OF THE GREAT SOURCES OF FRICTION

Among the many factors in a conflict with a determined rival that cannot be measured, physical effort is the most important. Unless it is wasted, its exact limit cannot be determined. But it is significant that it takes a powerful mind to drive his group to the limit.

The inexperienced observer now comes to recognize one of the elements that seem to chain the spirit and secretly wear away men's energies. Although we are dealing only with the efforts that a leader can require of his personnel, we are concerned with the courage it takes to make the demands and the skills to keep up the response. And we must not forget the physical exertion required of the leader himself.

Our reason for dealing with physical effort here is that, like danger, it is one of the great sources of friction in conflict. Because its limits are uncertain, it resembles one of those substances whose elasticity makes the degree of its friction exceedingly hard to gauge.

COMMENTARY

Physical energy expended by personnel under prolonged and stressful conditions should be a major concern to any manager. The consequences of fatigue, which is certain to impact morale, can affect the abilities for both manager and subordinates to make lucid decisions. And it is likely to make the critical difference between success and failure in reaching planned objectives.

It is noteworthy, too, that Clausewitz looks at physical energy as a form of friction, which he says is difficult to measure. Notwithstanding, and to the extent that credible insights can be processed, the physical dimensions affecting performance should be carefully watched at all personnel levels.

As Sun Tzu points out: "Pay heed to nourishing the troops; do not unnecessarily fatigue them. Unite them in spirit; conserve their strength. Make unfathomable plans."

Organizations respond in various ways to the issues of how their staffs relate to expending physical energy and the resulting impact of fatigue and friction on job performance. Their approaches take into account such variables as attitudes, morale, physical and mental well-being. They also include creature comforts, pathways to professional growth, and confident feelings about job security. For example, a survey of privately owned and midsize organizations revealed the following approaches:

An advertising agency rewards employees with 5-week, paid sabbaticals on their fifth anniversary with the company, a mining company gives profit-sharing bonuses every quarter, a consulting firm helps colleagues plan personal and professional goals from buying homes to building careers, a software maker takes a 2-week break to form new teams and develop ideas, and a consumer research firm conducts innovation Fridays to improve workplace practices. Then, there is a case of a municipal government that eliminates bureaucratic red tape by allowing staff to make many decisions that were previously reserved for senior-level executives.

These examples recognize and focus on the indispensable asset of an organization: its people. Thus, protecting them, nurturing them, and enhancing their intrinsic capabilities into top-performing and skilled individuals legitimately rank among management's top priorities. They are the ones who become essential at successfully activating offensive or defensive strategies. There is more on friction ahead.

INTELLIGENCE: A SERIOUS SOURCE OF FRICTION IN CONFLICT

By intelligence we mean every sort of information about the rival, which is the basis, in short, of our own plans and operations. If we consider the actual basis of this information, how unreliable and transient it is, we soon realize that conflict is a flimsy structure that can easily collapse and bury us in its ruins.

The textbooks agree, of course, that we should only believe reliable intelligence, and should never cease to be suspicious. But what is the use of such feeble maxims? Many intelligence reports in conflict are contradictory; even more are false, and most are uncertain.

What one can reasonably ask of a leader is that he should possess a standard of judgment, which he can gain only from knowledge of men and affairs and from common sense. He should be guided by the laws of probability.

These are difficult enough to apply when plans are drafted in an office, far from the sphere of action. The task becomes infinitely harder in the thick of a campaign itself, with reports streaming in. At such times one is lucky if their contradictions cancel each other out and leave a kind of balance to be critically assessed.

It is much worse for the novice if chance does not help him. As in the situation where one contrary report tallies with another, he has to make a quick decision that is soon recognized to be mistaken as the reports turn out to be lies, exaggerations, and errors.

In short, most intelligence is false, and the effect of fear is to multiply lies and inaccuracies. As a rule most men would rather believe bad news than good, and rather tend to exaggerate the bad news. The dangers that are reported may soon, like waves, subside; but like waves they keep recurring, without apparent reason.

The leader must trust his judgment and stand like a rock on which the waves break in vain. It is not an easy thing to do. If he does not have a buoyant disposition and if experience has not trained him and matured his judgment, he had better make it a rule to suppress his personal convictions and give his hopes, rather than his fears, the benefit of the doubt. Only thusly can he preserve a proper balance.

This difficulty of accurate recognition constitutes one of the most serious sources of friction in conflict, by making things appear entirely different from what one had expected. The senses make a more vivid impression on the mind than systematic thought—so much so that I doubt if a leader ever launched a campaign of any magnitude without being forced to repress new misgivings from the start.

Ordinary men, who normally follow the initiative of others, tend to lose self-confidence when they reach the scene of action. Things are not what they expected, the more so as they let others influence them. But even the man who planned the operation and now sees it being carried out may well lose confidence in his earlier judgment, whereas self-reliance is his best defense against the pressures of the moment.

Confrontations have a way of masking the stage with scenery crudely daubed with fearsome visions. Once this is cleared away, and the horizon becomes unobstructed, developments will confirm his earlier convictions. This is one of the great chasms between planning and execution.

COMMENTARY

Notwithstanding Clausewitz's mistrust of intelligence, such an activity absolutely forms the underpinnings of strategy development. If you are to determine weaknesses and strengths of a competitor, then intelligence gathering is required. If you are to develop a maneuver to skirt areas of strength and attack weaknesses, intelligence is needed to deploy your resources at a decisive point. If you are to identify a market position in which to concentrate, intelligence is essential to the selection.

One credible area where Clausewitz focuses attention is on the frailties of the individual who receives the intelligence. Such factors as judgment, confidence, and self-reliance—or lack of them—are causes of friction. These, in turn, impact how a manager interprets the information, what attitude and mind-set are present, and the extent to which he gives "his hopes and not his fears the benefit of the doubt," at the time of decision making.

There is one hopeful conclusion to take away about the intelligence issue: Reliable market and competitor intelligence are essential for the reasons mentioned previously. However, it is equally essential that vigorous efforts are made to validate, confirm, and reconfirm incoming intelligence. Then, level-headed judgment, intuition, experience, and a positive mind-set are required to apply the intelligence in developing strategies. The human factor, therefore, still remains one of the all-important variables in decision making.

FRICTION DISTINGUISHES REAL CONFLICT FROM CONFLICT ON PAPER

If one has never personally experienced a serious confrontation, one cannot understand what the constant difficulties really consist of or why a leader should need any brilliance and exceptional ability. Everything looks simple; the knowledge required does not look remarkable. The strategic options are so obvious that by comparison the simplest problem of higher mathematics has an impressive scientific dignity.

Once conflict has actually been seen, the difficulties become clear. Yet it is still extremely hard to describe the unseen, all-pervading element that brings about this change of perspective.

Everything in conflict is very simple, but the simplest thing is difficult. The difficulties accumulate and end by producing a kind of friction that is inconceivable unless one has experienced conflict.

Countless minor incidents, the kinds you can never really foresee, combine to lower the general level of performance, so that one always falls far short of the intended goal. Iron willpower can overcome this friction. It pulverizes every obstacle, but of course it wears down the machine as well. We shall often return to this point.

Friction is the only concept that more or less corresponds to the factors that distinguish real conflict from conflict on paper. The organization and everything related to it are basically very simple and therefore seem easy to manage. But we should bear in mind that none of the components is of one piece. Each part is composed of individuals, every one of whom retains his potential of friction.

In theory it sounds reasonable enough: A leader's duty is to carry out his orders. Discipline welds the group together. Its leader must be a man of tested capacity, so that the great beam turns on its iron swivel with a minimum of friction.

A group is made up of individuals, the least important of whom may, by chance, delay things or somehow make them go wrong. The obstacles and the physical exertions can aggravate the problem to such an extent that they must be ranked among its principal causes.

This tremendous friction, which cannot, as in mechanics, be reduced to a few points, is everywhere in contact with chance. It brings about effects that cannot be measured, just because they are largely due to chance. It would take volumes to cover all difficulties. We could exhaust the reader with illustrations alone if we really tried to deal with the whole range of minor troubles that must be faced in conflict.

COMMENTARY

According to Clausewitz, friction in its innumerable forms remains chronic and ever present in a conflict. For personnel enduring such an unsettling environment, any effort on your part to mitigate their harmful effects should be actively pursued. One remedial approach is through ongoing, substantive training.

Although not a total panacea, in marginal situations, properly trained personnel can be the determining factor in the success of a campaign by eliminating some areas of friction. For instance, market maneuvers often require audacious and circuitous moves to throw competitors off-track. Such maneuvers can only take place by individuals who exhibit the skills and discipline honed through ongoing training.

The unfaltering lesson endures: Only the skilled will survive. And the quality of your individuals is far superior to quantity. Ultimately, it could become a key differentiator in a conflict. Consequently, do not sacrifice quality. If you do, there is reason to expect failure—unless the competition is far inferior to you.

Sun Tzu adds this perspective: "A skilled commander selects his men and they exploit the situation. Now the valiant can fight, the cautious defend, and the wise counsel. Thus, there is none whose talent is wasted."

Field Marshal Archibald Wavell takes this viewpoint: "The final deciding factor of all engagements…is the morale of the opposing forces. Better weapons, better food, and superiority in numbers will influence morale, but it is a sheer determination to win, by whomever or whatever inspired, that counts in the end. Study men and their morale always."

While no situation offers certain results, as Clausewitz points out with the uncertainty of friction and chance, it is axiomatic that the skilled and watchful eyes of highly trained and motivated individuals can turn disadvantage to advantage and prevent an advantage from turning into a rout.

One adherent to highly trained and motivated individuals is the global consumer-goods company, Unilever. They build an ambiance into their training, which incorporates the values of integrity, empowerment, and trust. Where fundamental skills such as accounting, finance, and operations are vital, the company views them as generally available skills that can be learned online and at numerous other venues.

Instead, Unilever's training emphasizes traits related to being inspirational and having a global sensibility. At the company's training centers in London and Singapore, attention is given to helping employees connect to developing their personal values and giving purpose to their work. In the end, however, training focuses on a highly pragmatic goal of creating energy and commitment as a means to compete and win.

ACTION IN CONFLICT IS LIKE MOVEMENT IN A RESISTANT ELEMENT

Just as the simplest and most natural of movements, walking, cannot easily be performed in water, in conflict it is difficult for normal efforts to achieve even moderate results.

A genuine theorist is like a swimming teacher who makes his pupils practice motions on land that are meant to be performed in water. To those who are not thinking of swimming, the motions will appear grotesque and exaggerated. By the same token, theorists who have never swum, or who have not learned to generalize from experience, are impractical and even ridiculous. They teach only what is already common knowledge: how to walk.

Moreover, every conflict is rich in unique episodes. Each is an uncharted sea, full of reefs. The leader may suspect the reefs' existence without ever having seen them. Now he has to steer past them in the dark. If a contrary wind springs up or if some major mischance appears, he will need the greatest skill and personal exertion, and the utmost presence of mind—even though, from a distance, everything may seem to be proceeding automatically.

An understanding of friction is a large part of that much admired sense of conflict, which a good leader is supposed to possess. To be sure, the best leader is not the one who is most familiar with the idea of friction and takes it most to heart. The good leader must know friction in order to overcome it whenever possible and in order not to expect a standard of achievement in his operations, which friction makes impossible.

Friction is the force that makes the apparently easy so difficult. We shall frequently revert to this subject, and it will become evident that an eminent leader needs more than experience and a strong will. He must have other exceptional abilities as well.

Clausewitz summarizes the preceding sections:
We have identified danger—physical exertion, intelligence, and friction—as the elements that combine to form the atmosphere of conflict and turn it into a medium that impedes activity. In their restrictive effects they can be grouped into a single concept of general friction. Is there any lubricant that will reduce this abrasion? Only one. And a leader will not always have it readily available: real-world experience.

Habit hardens the body for great exertions, strengthens the heart in peril, and fortifies judgment against first impressions. Habit breeds that priceless quality, calm, which, passing from individual to individual up to the senior leader himself, will lighten the leader's task.

In conflict, the experienced individual reacts rather in the same way as the human eye does in the dark. The pupil expands to admit what little light there is, discerning objects by degrees, and finally seeing them distinctly. By contrast, the novice is plunged into the deepest night. No leader can accustom his personnel to serious competitive confrontation.

To plan campaigns so that some of the elements of friction are involved, which will train managers' judgment, common sense, and resolution, is far more worthwhile than inexperienced people might think. It is immensely important that no individual, whatever his position, should wait for conflict to expose him to those aspects of active service that amaze and confuse him when he first comes across them.

If he has met them even once before, they will begin to be familiar to him. This is true even of physical effort. Exertions must be practiced, and the mind must be made even more familiar with them than the body.

When exceptional efforts are required of him in conflict, the novice is apt to think that they result from mistakes, miscalculations, and confusion at the top. In consequence, his morale is doubly depressed.

If campaigns prepare him for exertions, this will not occur. Another very useful, though more limited, way of gaining familiarity with conflict is to attract individuals who have seen active service.

However, few highly experienced individuals may be in proportion to an organization. Yet their influence can be very real. Their experience, their insights, and the maturity of their characters will affect their subordinates and peers. Even when they cannot be given authority, they should be considered as guides who can be consulted in specific eventualities.

COMMENTARY

Clausewitz makes it quite clear about the value of "real-world experience," as well as the benefits of training—preferably through simulations that duplicate actual problems—that can "expose [them] to those aspects of active service that amaze and confuse."

As for Clausewitz's comment about "highly experienced individuals ... and their influence can be very real," the following example shows how individuals with experience, insight, and maturity "should be considered as guides who can be consulted in specific eventualities."

John Deere, producers of farm equipment, tapped the experience of its workforce to implement the company's customer loyalty strategies. To execute Deere's strategy, teams of assembly-line workers crisscrossed North America and talked to dealers and farmers about Deere equipment.

They traveled singly or in small groups and pitched their product stories to farmers at regional trade exhibits. Workers in various job functions routinely made unscheduled visits to local farmers to discuss their problems and needs.

In most places the "new" reps were accepted as friendly, nonthreatening individuals who had no ulterior motives other than to present an honest, grassroots account of what goes into making a quality Deere product. At the time of initiating the strategy, enlisting the workforce for marketing-related duties was triggered by the weakening of demand for farm equipment during a recession, as well as by the aggressive actions of competition—in particular from Deere's chief rival, Caterpillar Inc.

Underlying the workforce strategy was Deere's view of customer loyalty: All employees are valuable resources to serve the needs of customers. Further, many of the workers supporting the effort had over 15 years' experience with the company.

They were trained in advanced manufacturing methods, total quality programs, and teamwork. According to Deere's management, har-
nessing that expertise demonstrated to customers that, as makers of the
products, the Deere employees were the best company spokespeople.
Noteworthy benefits of Deere's strategy included:

- Identified customers' problems early on
- Detected potential threats from competitors
- Uncovered new benefits for customers
- Mobilized the workforce to support the customer-loyalty effort,
  which represented its underlying competencies, products, ser-
  vices, and cultural values
- Communicated a powerful image of management–labor harmony
- Strengthened customer relationships

Capitalizing on its employees' experience, insight, and maturity
contributed to a sharp increase in net income, along with sizable jumps
in sales and market share.

Clausewitz now talks about the moral factors in conflict:

MORAL VALUES CANNOT BE IGNORED IN CONFLICT

Campaigns are never directed against material forces alone. They are always
aimed simultaneously at the moral forces, which give it life. The two cannot be
separated. But moral values can only be perceived by the inner eye, which differs
in each person. And they are often different in the same person at different times.

Since danger is the common element in which everything moves in conflict, courage—the sense of one's own strength—is the principal factor that
influences judgment. It is the lens through which impressions pass to the brain.
And yet there can be no doubt that experience will by itself provide a degree
of objectivity to these impressions.

Everyone knows the moral effects of a trap or an attack in a vulnerable
area. Everyone rates the rival's bravery lower once his back is turned and
then takes much greater risks in pursuit than while being pursued. Everyone
gauges his opponent in the light of his reputed talents, age, and experience
and acts accordingly. Everyone tries to assess the spirit and temper of his own
personnel and those of the rival's.

All these and similar effects in the sphere of mind and spirit have been proved
by experience. They recur constantly and are therefore entitled to receive their
due as objective factors. Of course, these truths must be rooted in experience.
No theorist or leader should bother himself with clever but flawed arguments.

PRINCIPAL PROBLEMS IN FORMULATING A THEORY OF THE CONDUCT OF A CONFLICT

In order to get a clear idea of the difficulties involved in formulating a theory of the conduct of conflict and thus be able to deduce its character, we must look more closely at the major characteristics of campaigns.

First Characteristic: Moral Forces and Effect

Hostile Feelings

The first of these characteristics consists of moral forces and the effects they produce. Essentially, confrontation is an expression of hostile feelings. But in the larger scale of conflict, hostile feelings often have become merely hostile intentions. At any rate, there are usually no hostile feelings between individuals. Yet such emotions can never be completely absent from conflict.

Even where there is no overall resentment and no animosity to start with, the confrontation itself will stir up hostile feelings. That is only human, but it is a fact. Apart from emotions stimulated by the nature of conflict, there are others that are not so intimately linked with confrontation: ambition, love of power, enthusiasms of all kinds, and so forth.

The Effects of Danger—Courage

Confrontation gives rise to the element of risk in which all activity must move and be maintained like birds in air and fish in water. The effects of exposure, however, produce an emotional reaction, either as a matter of immediate instinct, or consciously. The former results in an effort to avoid the danger or, where that is not possible, fear and anxiety.

Where these effects do not arise, it is because instinct has been outweighed by courage. But courage is by no means a conscious act. Like fear, it is an emotion.

Fear is concerned with physical and courage with moral survival. Courage is the nobler instinct, and as such cannot be treated as an inanimate instrument that functions simply as prescribed. Thus, courage is not simply a counterweight to danger to be used for neutralizing its effects. It is a quality on its own.

COMMENTARY

Clausewitz refers to the emotional effects of courage. In turn, psychologists ascribe specific attributes to courage, such as boldness, tenacity, integrity, and enthusiasm. Clausewitz also talks about these four qualities in his various themes about conflict, which appear in numerous sections of previous chapters and in those that follow.

Extent of the Influence Exercised by Risk

In order to appreciate properly the influence that risk exerts in conflict, one should not limit its sphere to the physical hazards of the moment. Hazards dominate the leader not merely by intimidating him personally, but also by threatening all those entrusted to him: not only at the moment where it is actually present, but also through the imagination and at all other times when it is relevant—not just directly but also indirectly through the responsibilities that lay a tenfold burden on the leader's mind.

He could hardly recommend or decide on a major campaign without a certain feeling of strain and distress at the thought of the danger and responsibility such a decision implies. One can make the point that action in conflict is never completely free from risk.

Second Characteristic: Positive Reaction

The second characteristic connected with a confrontation: Expect positive reactions. Here we are not concerned with the problem of calculating moral forces. Rather, it is with the very nature of interaction, which is bound to make it unpredictable and must be left to judgment and talent. Thus, it is natural that a campaign, with plans based on general circumstances, is so frequently disrupted by unexpected events. And these should remain largely a matter of talent, so theoretical directives tend to be less useful.

Third Characteristic: Uncertainty of Information

Finally, the general unreliability of all information presents a special problem in conflict: All activity takes place in a kind of twilight, which, like fog or moonlight, often tends to make things seem grotesque and larger than they really are.

Whatever is hidden from full view in this feeble light has to be guessed at by talent or simply left to chance. So, once again for lack of objective knowledge, one has to trust to talent or to luck.

COMMENTARY

Clausewitz continues to talk about the unpredictable conditions that can exist in a confrontation with a rival. While he discounts the value of intelligence because of its unreliability, he relies heavily on talent and values luck.

Talent can have a quantitative and qualitative dimension to it. For instance, if you accept the broad definitions of talent as a special natural ability or aptitude, a capacity for achievement or success, or a talented individual with a special capability, then you can track individuals' innate capabilities. Your aim is to single out and nurture those special talents through specialized training and mentoring, and then deploy them for particular competitive situations.

A POSITIVE DOCTRINE IS UNATTAINABLE

Given the nature of the subject, we must remind ourselves that it is simply not possible to construct a model for the art of conflict that can serve as scaffolding on which the leader can rely for support at any time. Whenever he has to fall back on his innate talent, he will find himself outside the model and in conflict with it. No matter how versatile the code, the situation will always lead to the consequences we have already alluded to: Talent and genius operate outside the rules and clash with practice.

ALTERNATIVES THAT MAKE A THEORY POSSIBLE: THE DIFFICULTIES VARY IN MAGNITUDE

There are two ways out of the difficulties. In the first place, our comments on the nature of a campaign in general should not be taken as applying equally to activities at all levels. What is most needed in the lower ranks is courage and dedication, but there are far fewer problems to be solved by intelligence and judgment. The field of action is more limited; means and ends are fewer in number, and the data more concrete, usually limited to what is actually visible.

But the higher the rank is, the more the problems multiply, reaching their highest point in the most senior individual. At this level, almost all solutions must be left to imaginative intellect. Even if we break down conflict into its various activities, we will find that the difficulties are not uniform throughout.

The more physical the activity is, the less the difficulties will be. The more the activity becomes intellectual and turns into motives, which exercise a determining influence on the leader's will, the more the difficulties will increase.

Thus, it is easier to use theory to organize, plan, and conduct an engagement than it is to use it in determining the engagement's purpose. Confrontation is conducted physically, and although the intellect does play a part, material factors will dominate. But when one comes to the effect of the engagement, where material successes turn into motives for further action, the intellect alone is decisive. In brief, tactics will present far fewer difficulties to the theorist than will strategy.

COMMENTARY

Clausewitz's preceding comments call for a more precise agreement on strategy and tactics. The differences between strategy and tactics consist of level, time, and space. Whereas there are numerous definitions lodged with academics, consultants, and line executives, the following business classifications are used here:

First, corporate strategy. At this level, strategies are developed at the highest echelons of the organization. The aim here is to deploy company resources through a series of actions that would fulfill the senior executives' visions and objectives for the future of the organization.

Second, midlevel strategy. At this juncture, strategy operates at the business-unit, department, or product-line level. It is more precise than corporate strategy. Typically, it covers actions covering a 3- to 5-year period and focuses on fulfilling specific objectives.

Also at this level, strategy covers two zones of activity: first, actions to create and retain customers, and, second, actions geared to preventing competitors from dislodging the company from its market position by seizing market share and key customers.

Third, tactics. These are actions designed to achieve short-term objectives, while in support of longer term objectives and strategies. The time frame normally correlates with a company's or business unit's business plan and the yearly budgetary process.

Tactics are precise actions that cover such areas as pricing and discounts, advertising media and copy themes, the Internet, sales force deployment and selling aids, supply chain methods and relationships, training, product packaging, value-added services, and the selection of market segments for product launch.

Thus, they involve the generally accepted marketing mix, consisting of product, price, promotion, and distribution, which translates to the physical and material factors described by Clausewitz.

As an overall definition, strategy is the art of coordinating the means (money, human resources, and materials) to achieve the ends (profit, customer satisfaction, and company growth) as defined by company policy and objectives.

In an abbreviated form: Strategies are actions to achieve long-term objectives. Tactics are actions to achieve short-term objectives. Yet, they must all synchronize with the longer term strategic goals of the organization.

THEORY SHOULD BE STUDY, NOT DOCTRINE

The second way out of this difficulty is to argue that a theory need not be a positive doctrine, a sort of manual for action. Whenever an activity deals primarily with the same things again and again—with the same ends and the same means, even though there may be minor variations and an infinite diversity of combinations, these things are susceptible to rational study.

It is precisely this inquiry that is the most essential part of my theory and that may quite appropriately claim that title. It is an analytical investigation leading to a close acquaintance with the subject applied to experience—in our case, to history.

The closer it comes to that goal and the more it proceeds from the objective form of a science to the subjective form of a skill, the more effective it will prove in areas where nature admits no arbiter but talent. It will, in fact, become an active ingredient of talent.

Theory will have fulfilled its main task when it is used to analyze the constituent elements of conflict—that is, to explain in full the properties of the means employed and to show their probable effects, to define clearly the nature of the ends in view, and to illuminate all phases of conflict in a thorough critical inquiry.

Theory then becomes a guide to anyone who wants to learn about conflict from books. It will light his way, ease his progress, train his judgment, and help him to avoid pitfalls. A specialist who has spent half his life trying to master every aspect of some obscure subject is surely more likely to make headway than a man who is trying to master it in a short time.

Theory exists so that one need not start afresh each time, sorting out the material and plowing through it, but will find it ready in hand and in good order. It is meant to educate the mind of the future leader.

More accurately, it is to guide him in his self-education, not to accompany him to the confrontation—just as a wise teacher guides and stimulates a young man's intellectual development, but is careful not to lead him by the hand for the rest of his life.

If the theorist's studies automatically result in principles and rules, and if truth spontaneously crystallizes into these forms, theory will not resist this natural tendency of the mind. On the contrary, where the arch of truth culminates in such a keystone, this tendency will be underlined.

But this is simply in accordance with the scientific law of reason, to indicate the point at which all lines converge, but never to construct an algebraic formula for use on the field. Even these principles and rules are intended to provide a thinking man with a frame of reference for the movements he has been trained to carry out, rather than to serve as a guide that, at the moment of action, lays down precisely the path he must take.

THE NATURE OF ENDS AND MEANS, AND MEANS AND ENDS IN TACTICS

It is the task of theory, then, to study the nature of ends and means. In tactics the means are the forces trained for confrontation. The end is victory. A more precise definition of this concept will be offered later on, in the context of the engagement. Here, it is enough to say that the rival's withdrawal is the sign of victory.

Strategy thereby gains the end it had ascribed to the engagement, the end that constitutes its real significance. This significance admittedly will exert a certain influence on the kind of victory achieved. A victory aimed at weakening the rival's capabilities is different from one that is only meant to seize a certain position.

The significance of an engagement may therefore have a noticeable influence on its planning and conduct. And it is therefore to be studied in connection with tactics.

ENDS AND MEANS IN STRATEGY

The original means of strategy is victory—that is, tactical success. Its ends, in the final analysis, are those objects that will lead directly to peace. The application of these means for these ends will also be attended by factors that will influence it to a greater or lesser degree.

These factors are the geographical surroundings and nature of the terrain, the time of day and time of year, and the weather. These factors form new means.

Strategy, in connecting these factors with the outcome of an engagement, confers a special significance on that outcome. It assigns a particular aim to it. Yet insofar as that aim is not the one that will lead directly to peace, it remains subsidiary and is also to be thought of as a means. Successful engagements or victories in all stages of importance may therefore be considered as strategic means.

COMMENTARY

Clausewitz's references to geographical surroundings, terrain, time of day, and weather have a parallel in business campaigns. Consider, too, seasonal forces and the consequences of natural climate-related conditions. These influence how you manage your business within the variables of weather and logistics, such as recurring outcomes of winter's cold and summer's heat or the extremes and greater frequency of earthquakes and hurricanes.

For instance, what impact does weather have on such industries as home building and road construction, on transporting materials to meet critical delivery schedules, on installing communications systems, and on supplying energy, as well as all the ancillary products and services associated with those industries? Further, what is the weather or seasonal impact on food supplies, fashion, entertainment, and retailing?

Chapter 5

Strategy (Part 2)

Clausewitz makes these key points in part 2 of strategy:

- Rather than comparing conflict to art we could more accurately compare it to commerce, which is also a conflict of human interests and activities.
- Any method by which strategic plans are turned out ready-made, as if from some machine, must be totally rejected.
- Constant practice leads to brisk, precise, and reliable leadership, reducing natural friction and easing the working of the machine.
- Conflict consists of single, great decisive actions, each of which needs to be handled individually.
- So long as no intelligent analysis of the conduct of conflict exists, routine methods will tend to take over even at the highest levels.
- The highest level that routine may reach in action is determined not by rank, but by the nature of each situation.
- A leader can best demonstrate his genius by managing a campaign exactly to suit his objectives and his resources, doing neither too much nor too little.
- Strategy is the use of the engagement for the purpose of the conflict. The strategist must define an aim for the entire operational side of the conflict in accordance with its purpose.
- The strategist will draft the plan. He will shape the individual campaigns and decide on the individual engagements.
- Strategic theory must therefore study the engagement in terms of its possible results and of the moral forces that largely determine its course.

Clausewitz talks in greater detail about the preceding points of strategy and tactics:

We have divided the acts of conflict into the two fields of tactics and strategy. The theory of tactics, as we have already stated, will unquestionably encounter the greater problems since strategy is virtually limited to material factors. As for strategy, dealing as it does with ends, which bear directly on the restoration of peace, the range of possibilities is unlimited.

As these ends will have to be considered primarily by the leader, the problems mainly arise in those fields that lie within his competence. In the field of strategy, therefore, even more than in tactics, theory will be content with the simple consideration of material factors. It will be sufficient if it helps the leader acquire those insights that, once absorbed into his way of thinking, will smooth and protect his progress and will never force him to abandon his convictions.

COMMENTARY

Clausewitz's insightful comments about "dealing ... with ends, which bear directly on the restoration of peace [and] the range of possibilities is unlimited," raise these questions: What are the "ends," or objectives, of your strategic and operational plans? Are they clearly stated and based on the strategic vision for the organization or group over the long term, as defined by senior management?

As for the tactical short-term portion of the plan, are the objectives independent actions or, as they should be, subsets of the longer term strategic objectives? And are they stated in quantitative terms for precise monitoring of performance? As important, are appropriate metrics indicated to red-flag threats or deviations for remedial action?

In a growing number of companies shaping a strategic vision is being handled by individuals in what is known as collaborative, community-based, or social strategy planning. The process is taking hold in such organizations as 3M, Dutch insurer AEGON, global IT services provider HCL Technologies, Linux software provider Red Hat, and defense contractor Rite-Solutions.

Clausewitz also talks about the "restoration of peace." That idyllic end can readily translate to a marketplace where all companies are actively involved in the mutual benefits of nurturing a market for long-term profitable growth.

The late management scholar Peter Drucker succinctly stated the end: "The object of business is to create a customer." In part that means developing peaceful coexistence among all those organizations that serve the market with the intention of not actively looking for confrontation.

There are other planning goals, with more limited aims as shown in the 11 categories of conflict listed in the Introduction. Consequently, understand the ends. From there, you can devise the appropriate means, or strategies, to "shape the individual campaign" and achieve a successful outcome.

ART OF CONFLICT OR SCIENCE OF CONFLICT?

The object of science is knowledge; the object of art is creative ability. The use of these terms still seems to be unsettled. And simple though the matter may be, we apparently do not know on what basis we should choose between them. We have already argued that knowledge and ability are different things—so different that there should be no cause for confusion.

We have become used to summarizing the knowledge required for the practice of art (individual branches of which may be complete sciences in themselves) by the term "theory of art," or simply "art." It is therefore consistent to keep this basis of distinction and call everything "art" whose object is creative ability, as, for instance, architecture.

The term "science" should be kept for disciplines such as mathematics or astronomy, whose object is pure knowledge. That every theory of art may contain discrete sciences goes without saying and need not worry us. But it is also to be noted that no science can exist without some element of art.

In mathematics, for instance, the use of arithmetic and algebra is an art. But art may go still further. The reason is that, no matter how obvious and palpable the difference between knowledge and ability may be in the totality of human achievement, it is still extremely difficult to separate them entirely in the individual.

Of course, all thought is art. The point where the logician draws the line, where the premises resulting from perceptions end and where judgment starts, is the point where art begins. But further, perception by the mind is already a judgment and therefore an art. So, too, in the last analysis, is perception by the senses.

In brief, if it is impossible to imagine a human being capable of perception, but not of judgment, or vice versa. It is likewise impossible to separate art and knowledge altogether. To repeat, creation and production lie in the realm of art; science will dominate where the object is inquiry and knowledge.

CONFLICT IS AN ACT OF HUMAN INTERCOURSE

We therefore conclude that conflict does not belong in the realm of arts and sciences. Rather, it is part of man's social existence. Conflict is a clash between major interests, which is resolved by bloodshed—the only way in which it differs from other conflicts.

COMMENTARY

"Bloodshed" needs clarification—a context, a reasonable interpretation—to extract any meaning from Clausewitz's usage. For instance, one can interpret it to mean a type of confrontation that forces a rival to exit the market with substantial losses that stagger the organization.

> Another meaning, more extreme, would be a conflict with a finality so conclusive that it causes the competitor to go out of business through bankruptcy. In such a case the explosive event would create shock waves that reach out and cause failures among a variety of businesses within a supply chain, as well as among fringe businesses.
>
> Not much research is needed to compile a list of industries and individual companies in the Rust Belt that have been so affected. Other consequences follow with the resulting economic devastation to large geographic areas. Again, think of the 2013 bankruptcy of Detroit, Michigan. Or consider the bankruptcy of Kodak and its reorganization into a fraction of its original size. Within those ruins is the disruptive toll among working-class individuals, their families, and their communities that suffer psychological, financial, and social upheavals.

Clausewitz continues his discussion of conflict:

Rather than comparing conflict to art, we could more accurately compare it to commerce, which is also a conflict of human interests and activities. And it is still closer to politics, which in turn may be considered as a kind of commerce on a larger scale. Politics, moreover, is the womb in which conflict develops, where its outlines already exist in their hidden rudimentary form, like the characteristics of living creatures in their embryos.

Part of the object of this book is to examine whether a conflict of living forces—as it develops and is resolved in conflict—remains subject to general laws, and whether these can provide a useful guide to action. This much is clear: This subject, like any other that does not surpass man's intellectual capacity, can be clarified by an inquiring mind. And its internal structure can, to some degree, be revealed. That alone is enough to turn the concept of theory into reality.

METHOD AND ROUTINE

In order to explain succinctly the concepts of method and routine, which play such an important role in conflict, we must glance briefly at the logical hierarchy that governs the world of action. Law is the broadest concept applicable to both perception and action.

In its literal sense, law contains a subjective, arbitrary element. And yet it expresses the very thing on which man and his environment essentially depend. Law, then, is the relationship between things and their effects.

Method is a constantly recurring procedure that has been selected from several possibilities. It becomes routine when action is prescribed by method rather than by general principles or individual regulation. It must necessarily be assumed that all cases to which such a routine is applied will be essentially alike.

Since this will not be entirely so, it is important that it be true as many times as possible. In other words, methodical procedure should be designed to meet the most probable cases. Routine is not based on definite individual premises, but rather on the average probability of similar cases.

Its aim is to presume an average truth, which will acquire some of the nature of a mechanical skill and eventually does the right thing almost automatically. In the control of conflict, perception cannot be governed by laws. The complex phenomena of conflict are not so uniform, nor the uniform phenomena so complex, as to make laws more useful than the simple truth.

Where a simple point of view and plain language are sufficient, it would be cumbersome to make them complex and involved. Nor can the theory of conflict apply law to action, since no prescriptive design universal enough to deserve the name of law can be applied to the constant changes and diversity of conflict.

Principles, rules, regulations, and methods are, however, indispensable concepts to that part of the theory of conflict that leads to positive doctrines. For in these doctrines the truth can express itself only in such compressed forms. Those concepts will appear most frequently in tactics, which is that part of conflict in which theory can develop most fully into a positive doctrine.

COMMENTARY

Clausewitz refers to concepts that "will appear most frequently in tactics." In its broader application to strategic business plans, it is useful to distinguish the issues that divide tactics from strategy.

Tactics typically cover shorter time durations and include such planning considerations and activities as:

- Actions that create a competitive advantage, with the specific aims of neutralizing a competitor's ability to react quickly and decisively at a particular time and location
- Changes to marketing plans that (1) incorporate differentiated product and new applications, (2) develop creative applications that utilize social media, or (3) feature special promotional themes that embrace such movements as "going green"
- Campaigns that target new, poorly served, or unserved market segments
- Selections of decisive points for market entry or defense
- Changes to the product or package offerings, including introduction of new value-added services to preempt and blunt a competitor's entry strategies
- Changes in promotions, incentives, prices, discounts, or services that affect supply-chain agreements

- Internal changes in the operating systems that speed-up communications from the field to the home office, which would alert management to take rapid counteractions against any damaging threats from aggressive competitors

Strategies cover broader issues, which impact a longer time period and would relate to such issues as:

- Developing initiatives that would better align the corporate culture with strategies and tactics
- Initiating product or service projects that lead to longer term customer retention, profitability, and defensible market positions
- Encouraging long-term relationships within the supply chain/or with end-use customers
- Updating existing production capabilities to improve service to markets with high growth potential
- Acquiring appropriate technologies to sustain a competitive advantage through proprietary software, or the challenges promised by such advances as 3D printers
- Optimizing the performance of the sales force—includes such areas as incentives, training, acquisition of competitor intelligence, flexibility to deploy individuals to support specific campaign objectives, or react speedily to forestall a competitive threat
- Finding sources to build financial strength to carry out long-term commitments
- Pinpointing R&D and other product development initiatives that address existing as well as all-new products
- Assessing levels of customer or technical services required by each market served
- Initiating training programs that develop employees' unique skills and are compatible with the strategic goals of the organization
- Organizing corporate systems and functions that support the long-term strategic plan
- Developing plans to guard the organization against the growing threats from cyber warfare.

All of these issues should be viewed from the standpoint of the strategic direction your firm will take over a planning period of at least the next 3 to 5 years compared to what it looks like today. For instance:

What new markets are worth entering? What additional product and service categories will be needed to secure a profitable market position and would provide room for growth and expansion? What might those products and service offerings look like? What form of delivery systems will be needed? What new technologies will be required to satisfy future customer and market needs?

Finally, consider the placement of each of the items on the preceding two lists as flexible. That is, using the variables of time and space as guidelines, you can shift a tactic to the strategy list and vice versa.

Clausewitz continues with the employment of forces and with types of human interactions:

In the employment of forces, some activities remain a matter of choice. Regulations, or prescriptive directions, do not apply to them, precisely because regulations preclude freedom of choice. Routines, on the other hand, represent a general way of executing tasks as they arise based on average probability. They represent the dominance of principles and rules, carried through to actual application.

As such they may well have a place in the conduct of conflict, provided they are not falsely represented as binding frameworks for action. Rather, routines are the best of the general forms, shortcuts, and options that may be substituted for individual decisions.

The frequent application of routine in conflict will also appear essential and inevitable when we consider how often action is based on pure conjecture or takes place in complete ignorance. Either the rival prevents us from knowing all the circumstances that might affect our dispositions or there is not enough time.

Even if we did know all the circumstances, their implications and complexities would not permit us to take the necessary steps to deal with them. Therefore, our measures must always be determined by a limited number of possibilities.

We have to remember the countless minor factors implicit in every case. The only possible way of dealing with them is to treat each case as implying all the others and base our dispositions on the general and the probable.

Finally, we have to remember that as the number of officers increases steadily in the lower ranks, the less the trust that can be placed on their true insight and mature judgment. Officers whom one should not expect to have any greater understanding than regulations and experience can give them have to be helped along by routine methods tantamount to rules.

COMMENTARY

With the current trend of authority and responsibility increasingly going to the lower ranks of managers, often down to personnel at the field level where sales people in some organizations are trained to act as general managers of their respective territories, Clausewitz's admonition about the "less ... trust that can be placed on their true insight and mature judgment" has a cautionary tone that should be interpreted on a personal basis within your existing policies and procedures.

In any event, it is in your best interest to set up your own monitoring system of watchfulness as you give junior managers enough slack to come up with independent decisions.* In all cases, however, the situation heightens the need for ongoing staff development.

Specifically, as for training: Among the general management program offerings, there are the familiar topics of leadership, finance, time management, and similar categories. Beyond those, a substantial amount of training should be devoted to formulating competitive strategies by means of programs that come as close as possible to simulating real-world conditions that are available online or through proprietary courses.†

---

* In Chapter 4, reference was made to a municipal government that eliminates bureaucratic red tape by allowing staff to make many decisions that were previously reserved for senior-level executives.

† Unilever was also cited in Chapter 4 about its forward-looking employee training. The company emphasizes traits related to being inspirational and having a global sensibility. Attention is also given to helping employees connect to developing their personal values and giving purpose to their work.

Clausewitz continues:

Rules will steady their judgment and guard them against eccentric and mistaken schemes, which are the greatest menace in a field where experience is so dearly bought. Routine, apart from its sheer inevitability, also contains one positive advantage: Constant practice leads to brisk, precise, and reliable leadership, reducing natural friction and easing the working of the machine.

In short, routine will be more frequent and indispensable the lower the level of action. As the level rises, its use will decrease to the point where, at the summit, it disappears completely. Consequently, it is more appropriate to tactics than to strategy.

Conflict, in its highest forms, is not an infinite mass of minor events, despite their diversities, which can be controlled with greater or lesser effectiveness depending on the methods applied. Conflict consists rather of single, great decisive actions, each of which needs to be handled individually.

Conflict is not like a field of wheat, which, without regard to the individual stalk, may be mown more or less efficiently depending on the quality of the scythe. It is like a stand of mature trees in which the axe has to be used judiciously according to the characteristics and development of each individual trunk.

The highest level that routine may reach in action is determined not by rank but by the nature of each situation. The highest ranks are least affected by it simply because the scope of their operations is the most comprehensive.

Any method by which strategic plans are turned out ready-made, as if from some machine, must be totally rejected. So long as no intelligent analysis of the conduct of conflict exists, routine methods will tend to take over even at the highest levels.

COMMENTARY

Clausewitz's references to "conflict consists ... of single, great decisive actions" and "strategic plans ... turned out ready-made, as if from some machine, must be totally rejected" have significant meanings. Not only is there a tendency to take the easier path of repeating yesterday's strategies, there is also the misguided inclination toward relegating the writing of a strategic business plan to outsiders. Caution should be given to both issues.

First, each campaign should be considered as a singular, "decisive action." For instance, consider the following potential issues that would change from one period to another and consequently would require fresh, innovative strategies:

You may be working with insufficient and unreliable competitive intelligence, which means you would be developing actions based on inaccurate information about your rival's strengths and weaknesses. If that is the case, and if the generally accepted approach to strategy development is to attack an opponent's weaknesses and vulnerable areas, then careful deployment of resources concentrated at decisive points is required to avoid blind-sided actions and their potentially serious consequences.

In such a situation, you must rely on your own experience, training, and intuition to develop defensive and offensive strategies. In doing so, you also want to guard against strategies based on a mind-set of fear, which would expose a negative and complacent attitude that can permeate your group and prevent you from taking constructive action.

Second, a strategic business plan consists of numerous facets that involve everything from the culture of the organization, its long-term outlook, and the creative input of an increasingly diverse workforce. To relegate those dynamics to an outsider means short-changing your organization and all its unrealized potential.

Instead, you are looking for those underlying forces to surface spontaneously and generate positive ideas. That is the intent of using a collaborative cross-functional group that actively participates in developing a plan. The essential point: Make the plan your and your team's plan and not the product of others' minds who are physically and emotionally detached from the core culture and organizational dynamics of the group.

Some people in command have not had the opportunities of self-improvement afforded by education and contact with the higher levels of society and government. They cannot cope with the impractical and contradictory arguments of theorists and critics, even though their common sense rejects them.

Their only insights are those that have been gained by experience. For this reason, they prefer to use the means with which their experience has equipped them, even in cases that could and should be handled freely and individually. They will copy their senior leader's favorite device—thus automatically creating a new routine.

Once an improved theory helps the study of the conduct of conflict and educates the mind and judgment of the senior leaders, routine methods will no longer reach so high. Those types of routines that must be considered indispensable will then be based on a theory rather than on sheer imitation.

No matter how superbly a leader operates, there is always a subjective element in his work. If he displays a certain style, it will in large part reflect his own personality. But that will not always blend with the personality of the man who copies that style. Yet it would be neither possible nor correct to eliminate subjective routine or personal style entirely from the conduct of conflict.

COMMENTARY

As for Clausewitz's points about style and personality, there is a tendency for an individual to emulate the behavior of an individual to whom he or she reports. The result of such interaction, of course, depends on the caliber of the mentor and the quality of the advice. On the whole, however, such approaches are workable.

Yet there can be a downside where copying another's style has a negative impact. An individual can lose his or her identity that embodies the innate talents and makes the person unique. Here, again, a balance is needed to make sure that a precise cloning doesn't take place and that any further experience and training will enhance the distinctive qualities that already exist.

We must now be allowed to make a few remarks about the instruments critics use: their idiom. For in a sense it accompanies action in conflict. Critical analysis, after all, is nothing but thinking that should precede the action. We therefore consider it essential that the language of criticism should have the same character as thinking must have in conflicts. Otherwise, it loses its practical value and criticism would lose contact with its subject.

In our reflections on the conduct of conflict, we said that it ought to train a leader's mind or, rather, guide his education. Theory is not meant to provide him with positive doctrines and systems to be used as intellectual tools.

Moreover, it is never necessary or even permissible to use scientific guidelines in order to judge a given problem in conflict. If it is not acquired deductively, but always directly through the natural perception of the mind, then that is the way it must also be in critical analysis.

We must admit that wherever it would be too laborious to determine the facts of the situation, we must have recourse to the relevant principles established by theory. In the same way as in conflict, these truths are better served by a leader who has absorbed their meaning in his mind, rather than one who treats them as rigid external rules. Thus, the critic should not apply them like an external law or an algebraic formula whose relevance need not be established each time it is used.

These truths should always be allowed to become self-evident, while only the more precise and complex proofs are left to theory. We will thus avoid using an arcane and obscure language, and express ourselves in plain speech with a sequence of clear, lucid concepts. Granted that, while this cannot always be completely achieved, it must remain the aim of critical analysis.

The complex forms of thought should be used as little as possible, and one should never use elaborate scientific guidelines as if they were a kind of truth machine. Everything should be done through the natural workings of the mind. However, this sincere aspiration has rarely prevailed in critical studies. On the contrary, a kind of vanity has impelled most of them to an ostentatious exhibition of ideas.

The first common error is an awkward and narrow system of laws. It is never difficult to demonstrate the one-sidedness of such systems. And nothing more is needed to discredit their authority once and for all.

We are dealing here with a limited problem. Since the number of possible systems is, after all, finite, this error is the lesser of two evils that concern us. A far more serious menace is the string of jargon, technicalities, and metaphors that attends these systems.

Any critic who has not seen fit to adopt a system either because he has not found one that he likes, or because he has not yet got that far will still apply an occasional scrap of one, as if it were a ruler to show the crookedness of a leader's course. Few of them can proceed without the occasional support of such scraps of scientific theory.

The most insignificant of them—technical expressions and metaphors— are often nothing more than ornamental flourishes of the critical narrative. But it is inevitable that all the terminology and technical expressions of a given system will lose what meaning they have, if any, once they are too far from their context. And if used as general axioms of truth, they are supposed to be more potent than a simple statement.

COMMENTARY

The type of critic Clausewitz refers to can be compared to the present-day commentator who has had no direct experience in a competitive business conflict. Certainly, many of the current business scholars, journalists, and other pundits have a vast database of knowledge gathered through primary research, years of observing the business scene, and extensive discussions with those involved in confrontations.

Yet, according to Clausewitz, the missing element is the actual hands-on experience of being directly immersed in the conflict. Those critics often use hard and fast rules as rigid criteria to assess a situation and, better yet, offer erudite armchair, Monday-morning advice on what actions should have been taken.

As Clausewitz says,

> Any critic who has not seen fit to adopt a system ... will apply an occasional scrap of one, as if it were a ruler to show the crookedness of a leader's course. And the most significant of them—technical expressions and metaphors—are sometimes nothing more than ornamental flourishes of the critical narrative.

Therefore, in situations where you are directly immersed, gauge the post-campaign evaluation from its source. Then make your own assessment about its value.

Clausewitz now returns to his core discussion on strategy:

The general concept of strategy was referred to previously. It is the use of an engagement for the purpose of dealing with conflict. Though strategy in itself is concerned only with engagements, the theory of strategy must also consider its chief means of execution, the resources being employed.

Strategic theory must therefore study the engagement in terms of its possible results and of the moral forces that largely determine its course. Strategy is the use of the engagement for the purpose of the conflict. The strategist must therefore define an aim for the entire operational side of the conflict that will be in accordance with its purpose.

In other words, he will draft the plan, and the aim will determine the series of actions intended to achieve it. He will, in fact, shape the individual campaigns and, within these, decide on the individual engagements.

Since most of these matters have to be based on assumptions that may not prove correct, other, more detailed orders cannot be determined in advance at all. It follows that the strategist must go on campaign himself.

Detailed orders can then be given on the spot, allowing the leader's plan to be adjusted to the modifications that are continuously required. The strategist, in short, must maintain control throughout.

This has not always been the accepted view, at least so far as the general principle is concerned. It used to be the custom to settle strategy in the capital, rather than in the field—a practice that is acceptable only if the government stays so close to the people involved as to function as general headquarters.

Strategic theory, therefore, deals with planning. Or, rather, it attempts to shed light on the components of conflict and their interrelationships, stressing those few principles or rules that can be demonstrated. The reader who recalls how many vitally important matters are involved in campaigns will understand what unusual mental gifts are needed to keep the whole picture steadily in mind.

A leader can best demonstrate his genius by managing a campaign exactly to suit his objectives and his resources, doing neither too much nor too little. But the effects of genius show not so much in novel forms of action as in the ultimate success of the whole. What we should admire is the accurate fulfillment of the unspoken assumptions and the smooth harmony of the whole activity, which only become evident in final success.

The student who cannot discover this harmony in actions that lead up to a final success may be tempted to look for genius in places where it does not and cannot exist. In fact, the means that the strategist employs are so very simple, so familiar from constant repetition, that it seems ridiculous in the light of common sense when critics discuss them, as they do so often.

Can one imagine anything more absurd? It is even more ridiculous when we consider that these very critics usually exclude all moral qualities from strategic theory and examine only material factors. They reduce everything to a few mathematical formulas of equilibrium and superiority and of time and space, limited by a few angles and lines.

If that were really all, it would hardly provide a scientific problem for a schoolboy. But we should admit that scientific formulas and problems are not under discussion. The relations between material factors are all very simple; what are more difficult to grasp are the intellectual factors involved. Even so, it is only in the highest realms of strategy that intellectual complications and extreme diversity of factors and relationships occur.

At that level there is little or no difference between strategy, policy, and statesmanship. And there, as we have already said, their influence is greater in questions of quantity and scale than in forms of execution. Where execution is dominant, as it is in the individual events of a campaign whether great or small, then intellectual factors are reduced to a minimum.

Everything in strategy is very simple, but that does not mean that everything is very easy. Once it has been determined what a campaign is meant to achieve and what it can achieve, it is easy to chart the course. But great strength of character, as well as great lucidity and firmness of mind, is required in order to follow through steadily, to carry out the plan, and not to be thrown off course by thousands of diversions.

Take any number of outstanding men, some noted for intellect, others for their acumen, still others for boldness or tenacity of will. Not one may possess the combination of qualities needed to make him a greater than average leader. It sounds odd, but everyone who is familiar with this aspect of conflict will agree that it takes more strength of will to make an important decision in strategy than in tactics.

In the latter, one is carried away by the pressures of the moment, caught up in a maelstrom where resistance would be fatal. And, suppressing incipient scruples, one presses boldly on.

In strategy, however, the pace is much slower. There is ample room for apprehensions, objections, and premature regrets.

In a tactical situation one is able to see at least half the problem with the naked eye, whereas in strategy everything has to be guessed at and presumed.

Conviction is therefore weaker. Consequently, most leaders, when they ought to act, are paralyzed by unnecessary doubts.

COMMENTARY

Clausewitz's point about being "paralyzed by unnecessary doubts" has a very human and personal sound to it. He lists all the possible and realistic reasons for doubt, such as the innumerable areas of friction that persist and the volumes of often questionable forms of intelligence that pour in. Yet, with those hindrances, the plan must be written, the objectives and strategies enumerated, and their implementation set in motion.

Thus, you are left to your internal strengths, which consist of years of hard-won experience, your natural intelligence, and the innate qualities that constitute your uniqueness. Ultimately, therefore, you have to trust in yourself.

This is what commands our respect: the miracles of execution that we have to admire. But to appreciate all this in full measure one has to have had a taste of it through actual experience. Those who know conflict only from books cannot recognize the existence of these impediments to action. And thus we must ask them to accept on faith what they lack in experience.

In conclusion, we would point out that in our exposition of strategy we shall describe those material and intellectual factors that seem to us to be the most significant. We shall proceed from the simple to the complex, and conclude with the unifying structure of the entire plan of the campaign.

In itself, the deployment of forces at a certain point merely makes an engagement possible; it does not necessarily take place. Should one treat this possibility as a reality, as an actual occurrence? Certainly. It becomes real because of its consequences, and consequences of some kind will always follow.

Chapter 6

Engagements and Their Consequences

Clausewitz makes these key points about engagements:

- Regard a conflict, and the separate campaigns of which it is composed, as a chain of linked engagements, each leading to the next.
- Just as a businessman cannot take the profit from a single transaction and put it into a separate account, so an isolated advantage gained in conflict cannot be assessed separately from the overall result.
- An organization's efficiency gains life and spirit from enthusiasm for the cause for which it fights.
- An organization that maintains its cohesion under the most adverse conditions is imbued with the true competitive spirit.
- The mere fact that individuals belong to an organization does not automatically mean they are equal to their tasks. Competitive spirit, then, is one of the most important moral elements in conflict.
- Whenever boldness encounters timidity, it is likely to be the winner. Timidity in itself implies a loss of equilibrium.
- A distinguished leader without boldness is unthinkable.
- As many resources as possible should be brought into the engagement at the decisive point. Whether these forces prove adequate or not, we will at least have done everything in our power.
- Surprise is more or less basic to all operations, for without it, superiority at the decisive point is hardly conceivable.
- The best strategy is always to be very strong: first in general, and then at the decisive point.
- A reserve has two distinct purposes: One is to prolong and renew the action. The second is to counter unforeseen threats.
- The man of action must at times trust in the sensitive instinct of judgment, derived from his native intelligence and developed through reflection, which almost unconsciously hits on the right course.

- We hardly know accurately our own situation at any particular moment, while the rival's, which is concealed from us, must be deduced from very little evidence.

Clausewitz talks more extensively about engagements:
The object of engagements is of two kinds: direct and indirect. They are indirect if other things intrude, which cannot in themselves neutralize the competitor's forces. But it can lead up to it, such as in taking a circuitous route or taking actions to possess key areas. Such movements should be regarded merely as means of gaining greater superiority.

These actions should be considered as intermediate links—as steps leading to this working principle: Regard a conflict, and the separate campaigns of which it is composed, as a chain of linked engagements, each leading to the next. Instead, if we succumb to the idea that possessing certain geographical points or securing undefended areas is of value in themselves, we are liable to regard them as windfall profits.

In so doing and in ignoring the fact that they are links in a continuous chain of events, we also ignore the possibility that their possession may later lead to definite disadvantages. This mistake is illustrated again and again in the history of conflict.

One could almost put the matter this way: Just as a businessman cannot take the profit from a single transaction and put it into a separate account, so an isolated advantage gained in conflict cannot be assessed separately from the overall result. A businessman must work on the basis of his total assets so that, in conflict, the advantages and disadvantages of a single action could only be determined by the final balance.

By looking on each engagement as part of a series, at least insofar as events are predictable, the leader is always on the high road to his goal. The forces gather momentum, and intentions and actions develop with a vigor that is commensurate with the occasion and impervious to outside influences.

COMMENTARY

Keeping with Clausewitz's concepts that "the single transaction … cannot be assessed separately from the overall result," consider why you planned the campaign in the first place. That is, go outside the immediate and often limited tactical view of the campaign.

For instance, was it a defensive campaign to retain a long-term position in a key region? Or was it a campaign that aimed to expand into additional market segments to secure a more defensible market position? Or possibly a strategic campaign to reclaim a former market position where you still had a reputation and a workable supply chain?

The shoe manufacturer, Allen Edmonds, illustrates Clausewitz's concepts. Founded in 1922, the company endured the Great Depression,

World War II, and offshore competition. Throughout those decades, its handmade men's dress shoes were worn in boardrooms and by US Presidents. During 2004, however, in an attempt to move away from its classic styles into trendier designs, the company floundered and saw its revenues take a dangerous nosedive from $94 million in 2007 to $72 million in 2009.

Looking to reverse the decline, regain its former market position, and, most importantly, keep focused on the "overall result," the Port Washington, Wisconsin, company moved to the offensive with a bold series of campaigns: It revamped the company's website and increased the number of its branded stores to reduce reliance on department stores such as Nordstrom. It successfully reintroduced four top sellers and began launching casual styles to suit the current work style.

A major decision for Allen Edmonds was to keep manufacturing in the United States to ensure quality and highlight its patriotism. Then, as it launched into the China market, the made-in-the-USA signature elevated the company's status among Chinese consumers who had high regard for US-made products. "Within 10 years, its market can be as big in China as it is in the United States," according to one company executive. With its upswing well on its way, revenues were expected to reach $145 million in 2013.

Once again, review other types of campaigns listed in the Introduction.

Clausewitz continues:

ELEMENTS OF STRATEGY

The strategic elements that affect engagements may be classified into various types: moral factors, boldness, perseverance, superiority of numbers, surprise, cunning, concentration of forces, strategic reserves, and economy of force.

Moral Factors

We must return once more to this subject, already touched upon in previous chapters, since the moral elements are among the most important in confrontations. They constitute the spirit that permeates conflict as a whole. And at an early stage they establish a close affinity with the will that moves and leads the whole force, since the will is itself a moral quantity.

Unfortunately, moral elements will not yield to academic wisdom. They cannot be classified or counted. They have to be seen or felt. The spirit and the other moral qualities of a group, the leader, the temper of the population within the theater of conflict, the moral effects of victory or defeat—all these vary greatly.

Moreover, they can influence our objective and situation in very different ways. Consequently, they can no more be omitted from the theory of the art of conflict than can any of the other components of conflict.

To repeat, it is paltry philosophy if one lays down rules and principles in total disregard of moral values. As soon as these appear one regards them as exceptions, which gives them a certain scientific status and thus makes them into rules. If the theory of conflict did no more than remind us of these elements, demonstrating the need to give full value to moral qualities, it would expand its horizon.

Another reason for not placing moral factors beyond the scope of theory is their relation to all other so-called rules. The effects of physical and psychological factors form an organic whole that, unlike a metal alloy, is inseparable by chemical processes.

As for physical factors, the theorist must bear in mind the part that moral factors may play in it. Otherwise, he may be misled into making categorical statements that will be too timid and restricted or else too sweeping and dogmatic.

Even the most uninspired theories have involuntarily had to stray into the area of intangibles. For instance, one cannot explain the effects of a victory without taking psychological reactions into account. Hence, most of the matters dealt with in this book are composed in equal parts of physical and of moral causes and effects.

One might say that the physical factors seem little more than the wooden hilt, while the moral factors are the precious metal, the real weapon, the finely honed blade. History provides the strongest proof of the importance of moral factors and their often incredible effect. This is the noblest and most solid nourishment that the mind of a leader may draw from a study of the past.

Principal Moral Elements

Moral elements include: the skill of the leader, the experience and courage of the personnel, and their patriotic spirit. The relative value of each cannot be universally established. It is hard enough to discuss their potential and even more difficult to weigh them against each other.

The wisest course is not to underrate any of them—a temptation to which human judgment, being fickle, often succumbs. It is far preferable to muster historical evidence of the unmistakable effectiveness of all three.

It cannot be denied that as things stand, proportionately greater scope is given to the individual's spirit and experience. A long period of inactivity may change this again. Feelings of enthusiasm, zeal, and faith are most apparent in situations where every man is on his own.

Bravery is obviously a necessary component, which is part of the natural makeup of a man's character. In the individual, the natural tendency for unbridled action and outbursts must be subordinated to demands of a higher kind: obedience, order, rule, and method. An organization's efficiency gains life and spirit from enthusiasm for the cause for which it fights, but such enthusiasm is not crucial.

An organization's qualities are based on the individual, who is steeped in the spirit and essence of this activity; who trains in the capacities it demands, rouses them, and makes them his own; who applies his intelligence to every detail; who gains ease and confidence through practice, and who completely immerses his personality in the appointed task.

Consequently, for as long as they practice this activity, individuals will think of themselves as members of a kind of guild, in whose regulations, laws, and customs the spirit of winning is given pride of place. And that does seem to be the case. No matter how much one may be inclined to take the most sophisticated view of conflict, it would be a serious mistake to underrate professional pride (esprit de corps) as something that may and must be present in an organization to a greater or lesser degree.

Professional pride is the bond between the various natural forces that activate the organization's cultural virtues. In the context of this professional pride they crystallize more readily.

An organization that maintains its cohesion under the most adverse conditions is imbued with the true competitive spirit. It cannot be shaken by imaginary fears. It is proud of its victories and will not lose the strength to obey orders and its respect and trust for its leaders even in defeat. Its physical power, like the muscles of an athlete, has been steeled by training.

We stress this to clarify the concept, and not to lose sight of the idea in a fog of generalities and give the impression that a competitive spirit is all that counts in the end. That is not the case.

The spirit of an organization may be envisaged as a definite moral factor that can be mentally subtracted, whose influence may therefore be estimated. In other words, it is a tool whose power is measurable. Having thus characterized it, we shall attempt to describe its influence and the various ways of developing it.

Competitive spirit always stands in the same relation to the parts of an organization, as does a leader's ability to the whole. The leader can command only the overall situation and not the separate parts. At the point where the separate parts need guidance, the competitive spirit must take command.

Leaders are chosen for their outstanding qualities, and other high-ranking individuals are carefully tested. But the testing process becomes less thorough the further we descend on the scale of command, and we must be prepared for a proportionate decrease of personal talent.

What is missing here must be made up by virtues. The same role is played by the natural qualities of a people mobilized for conflict: bravery, adaptability, stamina, and enthusiasm. These, then, are the qualities that can act as substitutes for the competitive spirit and vice versa, leading us to the following conclusions:

1. Competitive virtues are found only in active organizations, and they are the ones that need them most.
2. Where personnel can remain concentrated, the talents of the leader are given greater scope and can make up for any lack of spirit among the personnel. Generally speaking, the need for competitive virtues becomes greater the more operations and other factors tend to complicate the conflict and disperse the forces.

If there is a lesson to be drawn from these facts, it is that when an organization lacks competitive virtues, every effort should be made to keep operations as simple as possible—or else twice as much attention should be paid to other aspects of the system.

The mere fact that individuals belong to an organization does not automatically mean they are equal to their tasks. Competitive spirit, then, is one of the most important moral elements in conflict. Where this element is absent, it must either be replaced by one of the others, such as the leader's superior ability or popular enthusiasm, or else the results will fall short of the efforts expended.

There are only two sources for this spirit, and they must interact in order to create it:

• First is a series of victorious conflicts.
• Second are the frequent exertions of individuals to the utmost limits of their strength.

Nothing else will show an individual the full extent of his capacities. The more a leader is accustomed to place heavy demands on his group, the more he can depend on their response.

An individual is just as proud of the hardships he has overcome as of the uncertainties he has faced. In short, the seed will grow only in the soil of constant activity and exertion, warmed by the sun of victory. Once it has grown into a strong tree, it will survive the wildest storms of misfortune and defeat, and even the sluggish inertia of peace, at least for a while.

Thus, this spirit can be created only in conflict and by great leaders, though admittedly it may endure, for several generations at least, even under leaders of average ability and through long periods of peace. Discipline, skill, goodwill, a certain pride, and high morale are the attributes of trained individuals during times of stability.

They command respect, but they have no strength of their will. They stand or fall together. One crack and the whole thing goes, like a glass too quickly cooled. Even the highest morale in the world can, at the first upset, change all too easily into despondency, an almost boastful fear.

An organization like this will be able to prevail only by virtue of its leader, never on its own. It must be led with more than normal caution until, after a series of victories and exertions, its inner strength will grow to fill its external display. We should take care never to confuse the real spirit of an organization with its mood.

COMMENTARY

Clausewitz talks about moral values, spirit, bravery, enthusiasm, zeal, and faith, among other values. All these qualities center on leading individuals to victory in a competitive confrontation. They are solidified and nurtured through such personal acts as exhibited by the legendary and former General Electric CEO Jack Welch. He walked the factory floor and talked with workers using his famous "Call me Jack" greetings. He followed up each visit with handwritten notes to individuals with whom he talked. They, in turn, savored (and saved) the personalized sentiments expressed in his notes.

Beyond the one-on-one encounters, there are the internal e-communications channels that enable senior managers to connect with their employees, wherever they may be, on a regular frequency. Such forms of communications can shape organizational cohesion by clearly explaining the strategic direction of the organization, and dramatically expressing the cultural values embedded in the organization.

With the growing trend of workforces that combine staff employees, freelancers, and contract workers, keeping in touch through an active e-channel is in keeping with Clausewitz's concepts. Executives, thereby, have a means for inspiring, motivating, and directing employees—and non-employees—to improve, perform, and grow continuously.

Specifically, the aims of ongoing e-communications are to reach out to individuals for the following three purposes:

1. Unite employees to a common purpose:
   * Explain the organization's core mission and objectives.
   * Clarify misconceptions or inaccurate rumors.
   * Describe the condition of the company.
   * Tell about a group's or individual's achievements.
   * Reveal a new product, technology, or business partner.
   * Create a sense of urgency and arouse employees to charge forward.
2. Lift employee morale through positive messages:
   * Cultivate positive employee relationships with consistent messages delivered with regularity.
   * Influence their behavior; reinforce those cultural values that make the company unique.
   * Reenergize sagging confidence and cultivate an entrepreneurial mind-set.
   * Encourage employee feedback and seek their active participation.
3. Equip employees with strategy skills:
   * Support self-development by equipping them to develop fresh strategies.
   * Show techniques to create new revenue streams.
   * Prepare them to resist competitive threats.

Clausewitz continues:

Boldness

We previously discussed the place that boldness occupies in the dynamic system of forces. We also tried to show that the theorist has no right to restrict boldness on grounds of doctrine. Indeed, in what field of human activity is boldness more at home than in conflict?

An individual, whether office clerk or leader, can possess no nobler quality. It is the very metal that gives edge and luster to the sword. Let us admit that boldness in conflict even has its own prerogatives. It must be granted a certain power over and above successful calculations involving space, time, and magnitude of forces. For wherever it is superior, it will take advantage of its opponent's weakness.

In other words, it is a genuinely creative force. This fact is not difficult to prove, even scientifically. Whenever boldness encounters timidity, it is likely to be the winner, because timidity in itself implies a loss of equilibrium.

Boldness will be at a disadvantage only in an encounter with deliberate caution, which may be considered bold in its own right and is certainly just as powerful and effective. However, such cases are rare.

Boldness acts like a coiled spring, ready at any time to be released. The higher up the chain of command, the greater is the need for boldness to be supported by a reflective mind, so that boldness does not degenerate into purposeless bursts of blind passion. Command becomes progressively less a matter of personal sacrifice and increasingly concerned for the safety of others and for the common purpose.

Happy is the organization where ill-timed boldness occurs frequently. It is a luxuriant weed, but indicates the richness of the soil. Even foolhardiness—that is, boldness without any object—is not to be despised. Basically it stems from daring, which in this case has erupted with a passion unrestrained by thought.

Only when boldness rebels against obedience—when it defiantly ignores an expressed order—must it be treated as a dangerous offense. Then it must be prevented—not for its innate qualities, but rather because an order has been disobeyed. In conflict, obedience is of cardinal importance.

Given the same amount of intelligence, timidity will do a thousand times more damage in conflict than audacity. The truth of this observation will be self-evident to our readers. In fact, the pursuing of a rational purpose ought to make it easier to be bold, and therefore less meritorious. Yet the opposite is true. The mover of the various emotions is sharply reduced by the intervention of lucid thought and, more, by self-control.

Consequently, boldness grows less common in the higher ranks. Even if the growth of a leader's perception and intelligence does not keep pace with his rise in rank, the realities of conflict will impose their conditions and concerns on him.

Nearly every leader known to us from history as mediocre, even vacillating, was noted for dash and determination at the junior level. A distinction should be made among acts of boldness that result from sheer necessity. Necessity comes in varying degrees.

If it is pressing, a man in pursuit of his aim may be driven to incur one set of risks in order to avoid others just as serious. In that event one can admire only his powers of resolution, which, however, are also of value. The more numerous the possibilities that have to be identified and analyzed before action is taken, the less is the factor of boldness reduced.

While strategy is exclusively the province of leaders and other senior officers, boldness in the rest of the organization is as important a factor in planning as any other competitive virtue. More can be achieved with an organization drawn from people known for their boldness, an organization in which a daring spirit has always been nurtured, than with an organization that lacks this quality.

For that reason, boldness in general has been mentioned here, even though our actual subject is the boldness of the leader. After having given a broad description of this competitive virtue, however, there is not much left to say.

The higher the rank, the greater is the degree to which activity is governed by the mind, by the intellect, and by insight. Consequently, boldness, which is a quality of temperament, will tend to be held in check. This explains why it is so rare in the higher ranks, and why it is all the more admirable when found there.

Boldness governed by superior intellect is the mark of a hero. This kind of boldness does not consist in defying the natural order of things and in crudely offending the laws of probability. It is rather a matter of energetically supporting that higher form of analysis by which genius arrives at a decision.

Boldness can lend wings to intellect and insight. The stronger the wings are, then the greater the heights, the wider the view, and the better the results—though a greater prize, of course, involves greater risks. The average man, not to speak of a hesitant or weak one, may in an imaginary situation, in the peace of his room far removed from danger and responsibility, arrive at the right answer—that is, insofar as this is possible without exposure to reality.

But beset on every side with danger and responsibility, he will lose perspective. Even if this is provided by others, he will lose his powers of decision, for here no one else can help him. In other words, a distinguished leader without boldness is unthinkable.

No man who is not born bold can play such a role, and therefore we consider this quality the first prerequisite of the great leader. How much of this quality remains by the time he reaches senior rank, after training and experience have affected and modified it, is another question.

The greater the extent to which it is retained, the greater the range of his genius will be. The magnitude of the risks increases, but so does that of the goal.

To the critical student there is not much difference between actions governed by some compelling long-range aim and those dictated by pure ambition. The actions of the latter may fascinate the imagination because of their supreme boldness, while those of the former may be more satisfying to the intellect because they are dictated by an inner necessity.

We must mention one more factor of importance. An organization may be imbued with boldness for two reasons: It may come naturally to the people that are recruited or it may be the result of a victorious conflict fought under bold leadership. If the latter is the case, boldness will at the outset be lacking.

Today practically nothing other than conflict will educate a people in this spirit of boldness. And it has to be a conflict waged under daring leadership. Nothing else will counteract the softness and the desire, which debase the people in times of growing prosperity and increasing trade. Individuals and an organization can hope for a strong position in the world only if character and familiarity with conflict fortify each other by continual interaction.

COMMENTARY

Clausewitz says that "a distinguished leader without boldness is unthinkable." Yet there are pragmatic personality issues that prevent boldness from surfacing at the time of decision making. Such is the case of a manager who experiences periods of low self-esteem and suffers indecisiveness during various times of severe tension.

Notwithstanding that such an individual has risen through the ranks, it is not uncommon for such negative feelings to persist, even though he or she has learned to adapt successfully to the pressures of the moment and is able to act decisively when pushed to a decision.

There is still another issue related to boldness, which is triggered by the innate fear of failure. Boldness is an act of determination in a specific situation. It becomes a character trait only if it becomes a mental habit. As Clausewitz points out, intellect in itself is not sufficient; it needs "boldness [that] can lend wings to intellect and insight." There are ample numbers of brilliant managers who simply do not have what it takes and do not fully recognize that "conflict is waged under daring leadership."

There are some remedies to mitigate the effect: First, taking action will often arouse the inner feelings of boldness. That is, it will help to overcome the critical moments when reason is pushed aside and replaced by the awful feelings that can creep into the mind and take control of natural movements.

A second remedy is to back up your decisions with as much reliable market intelligence as possible. You can then think more confidently about taking alternative courses of action. Such an approach helps support your decisions and counter feelings of indecisiveness. You are then better prepared to take clear-thinking actions at any given moment.

Third, you always have within you the secure underpinnings of your training, internal discipline, and years of valuable experience. All these, plus your natural intuition, would kick-in to overcome any negative emotional state.

Keep in mind, too, that you are in a contest of mind against mind: your mind pitted against the mind of a competing manager who may be challenged by similar emotions. You want to be the bold one who prevails and moves forward.

Consider the extraordinary success of Google Inc. Much has been written about the bold approaches that founders Larry Page and Sergey Brin exhibited when they started operations in 2000. Even then, they showed their boldness by going against the sage advice of seasoned consultants and analysts who advised selling out for a mere pittance during those early days. Instead, industry pundits watched their boldness surface again as the search giant quietly acquired a mobile-phone software company and began making forays into the instant messaging, Wi-Fi Internet, and telephony businesses.

Perseverance

In conflict, more than anywhere else, things do not turn out as we expect. A leader engaged in competitive conflict is constantly bombarded by reports and data, both true and false; by errors arising from fear or negligence or hastiness; by disobedience born of right or wrong interpretations; or by accidents that nobody could have foreseen.

In short, he is exposed to countless impressions, most of them disturbing, few of them encouraging. Long experience of conflict creates a knack of rapidly assessing these phenomena. Courage and strength of character are as impervious to them as a rock to the rippling waves. If a man were to give in to these pressures, he would never complete an operation.

Perseverance in the chosen course is the essential counterweight, provided that no compelling reasons intervene to the contrary. Moreover, there is hardly a worthwhile enterprise in conflict whose execution does not call for infinite effort, trouble, and difficulty.

And as man under pressure tends to give in to physical and intellectual weakness, only great strength of will can lead to the objective. It is steadfastness that will earn the admiration of the world and of posterity.

Superiority of Numbers

In tactics, as in strategy, superiority of numbers is the most common element in victory. Let us first consider this general characteristic, which calls for the following explanation.

Strategy decides the time when, the place where, and the forces with which the engagement is to be fought and, through this threefold activity, exerts considerable influence on its outcome.

Superiority of numbers in a given engagement is only one of the factors that determine victory. Superior numbers, far from contributing everything or even a substantial part to victory, may actually be contributing very little, depending on the circumstances.

Superiority varies in degree. It can be two to one, or three or four to one, and so on. It can obviously reach the point where it is overwhelming. In this sense superiority of numbers admittedly is the most important factor in the outcome of an engagement, so long as it is great enough to counterbalance all other contributing circumstances.

It thus follows that as many resources as possible should be brought into the engagement at the decisive point. Whether these forces prove adequate or not, we will at least have done everything in our power. This is the first principle of strategy. It is very difficult to defeat an opponent twice one's strength.

When we observe that the skill of the greatest leaders may be counterbalanced by a two-to-one ratio, we cannot doubt that in ordinary cases, whether the engagement be great or small, a significant superiority in numbers (it does not have to be more than double) will suffice to assure victory, however adverse the other circumstances.

It is possible, of course, to imagine a situation where even 10-fold superiority would not be sufficient, but in such a case we cannot really speak of an engagement. We believe then that, in our circumstances and all similar ones, a main factor is the possession of strength at the really vital point. Actually, it is the most important factor.

To achieve strength at the decisive point depends on the strength of the organization and on the skill with which this strength is employed. The first rule, therefore, should be: *Put the largest amount of resources possible into the engagement.* This may sound like a platitude, but in reality it is not.

If one is genuinely convinced that a great deal can be achieved by significant superiority, this conviction is bound to influence the preparations for conflict. The aim will then be to take the field in the greatest possible strength, either in order to get the upper hand or at least in order to make sure that the opponent does not.

So much for the overall strength that should be used in confrontations. In practice, the size will be decided at the highest levels of the organization. This decision marks the start of activity. It is indeed a vital part of strategy and the individual who is to be in charge usually has to accept the size of his forces as a given factor.

Either he was not consulted in the matter, or circumstances may have prevented the raising of a sufficiently large force. Consequently, the forces available must be employed with such skill that even in the absence of absolute superiority, relative superiority is attained at the decisive point.

Relative superiority—that is, the skillful concentration of superior strength at the decisive point—is much more frequently based on the correct appraisal of this decisive point and on suitable planning from the start. In turn that leads to appropriate deployment of the forces, and on the resolution needed to sacrifice nonessentials for the sake of essentials—that is, the courage to retain the major part of one's forces united.

With this discussion, we believe we have shown how significant superiority of numbers really is. It must be regarded as fundamental to be achieved in every case and to the fullest possible extent.

But it would be seriously misunderstanding our argument to consider numerical superiority as indispensable to victory. We merely wished to stress the relative importance. The principle is served if we use the largest possible force. The question whether to avoid a fight for lack of strength can be decided only in the light of all other circumstances.

COMMENTARY

Over the centuries, other commentators on strategy have made comments about the superiority of numbers. They relate numbers to the quality of personnel, their training, morale, commitment, and spirit.

Still other masters of strategy have indirectly positioned superiority of numbers against other factors that relate to success with the following sage advice:

"Money is not the sinews of war although it is generally so considered. It is not gold, but good soldiers that insure success."—Machiavelli

"If we always knew the enemy's intentions beforehand, we should always, even with inferior forces, be superior to him."—Frederick the Great

"Supreme excellence consists in breaking the enemy's resistance without fighting."—Sun Tzu

If we look again at Clausewitz's comments on superiority of numbers, he does attempt to introduce a sense of balance and judgment with "it would be seriously misunderstanding our argument, to consider numerical superiority as indispensable to victory. We merely wished to stress the relative importance."

Further, he reinforces his line of reasoning by stating that "the forces available must be employed with such skill that even in the absence of absolute superiority, relative superiority is attained at the decisive point."

Surprise

The previous subject—the universal desire for relatively numerical superiority—leads to another desire, which is consequently no less universal: to take the opponent by surprise. This desire is more or less basic to all operations, for without it superiority at the decisive point is hardly conceivable.

Surprise therefore becomes the means to gain superiority, but because of its psychological effect it should also be considered as an independent element. Whenever it is achieved on a grand scale, it confuses the rival and lowers his morale. Many examples, great and small, show how this in turn multiplies the results.

We are not speaking here of a surprise assault, but of the desire to surprise the opponent by our plans and dispositions, especially those concerning the distribution of forces. This is just as feasible in defense, and indeed it is a major weapon of the tactical defense.

We suggest that surprise lies at the root of all operations, without exception, though in varying degrees depending on the nature and circumstances of the operation. These variations may already originate in the characteristics of the organization and of the leader.

The two factors that produce surprise are secrecy and speed. Both presuppose a high degree of energy on the part of the organization and the leader; they require great efficiency. Surprise will never be achieved under lax conditions and conduct.

But while the wish to achieve surprise is common and, indeed, indispensable, and while it is true that it will never be completely ineffective, it is equally true that by its very nature surprise can rarely be outstandingly successful. It would be a mistake, therefore, to regard surprise as a key element of success in conflict.

The principle is highly attractive in theory. Yet in practice it is often held up by the friction of the whole machine. Basically, surprise is a tactical device, simply because, in tactics, time and space are limited in scale. Therefore, in strategy, surprise becomes more feasible the closer it occurs to the tactical realm, and more difficult the more it approaches the higher levels of policy.

On the other hand, surprise is more easily carried out in operations requiring little time. It is obvious, however, that the greater the ease with which surprise is achieved, the smaller is its effectiveness, and vice versa. In the abstract, we may believe that small surprises often lead to greater things, such as a victorious encounter, but history does not bear this out.

Cases in which such surprises led to major results are very rare. From this we may conclude how considerable the inherent difficulties are. Of course, anyone who consults history must not allow historians to divert him with their favorite theories or with maxims and a smug parade of technicalities. He must look at the facts.

Major success in a surprise action does not depend on the energy, forcefulness, and resolution of the leader; it must be favored by other circumstances. We do not wish to deny the possibility of success, but merely want to establish the fact that it does require favorable conditions, which are not often present and can rarely be created by the leader.

One more observation needs to be made, which goes to the very heart of the matter. Only the leader who imposes his will can take the rival by surprise. And in order to impose his will, he must act correctly.

If we surprise the opponent with faulty measures, we may not benefit at all, but instead suffer sharp reverses. Our surprise, in that case, will cause the rival little worry. By exploiting our mistakes, he will find ways of warding off any ill effects.

Since the offensive offers much more scope for positive action than the defensive, the element of surprise is more often related to the attack—but far from exclusively so, as we shall see later on. Mutual surprises by the offensive and defensive may collide; in which case, the side will succeed that has hit the nail most squarely on the head.

For the side that can benefit from the psychological effects of the worse the situation is, the better it may turn out; for the rival could find himself incapable of making coherent decisions. Much depends on the relationship between the two sides. If general moral superiority enables one opponent to intimidate and outdistance the other, he can use surprise to greater effect and may even reap the fruits of victory where ordinarily he might fail.

COMMENTARY

Clausewitz says that "surprise lies at the root of all operations without exception." He continues: "Depending on the nature and circumstances of the operation, variations may already originate in the characteristics of the organization, and of the leader."

What, then, can interfere with achieving surprise? There are several "variations" in the characteristics of the organization and certainly in the leadership:

A prime one is deficiency in planning skills. Specifically, that includes the failure to utilize a cross-functional team of cooperative individuals who can develop an effective competitive strategy plan. However, a fundamental problem that often impedes constructive output from the team is that some members may not be adequately trained in such strategy principles as speed, boldness, superiority of numbers at the decisive point, maneuver, and the other elements that permeate the chapters of this book.

Further, surprise takes skill, knowledge of the marketplace, and, above all, awareness of the competitor's behavior. For instance, what will be the competitor's overall reaction during periods of sudden market activity and immediately after the surprise? Will it be reserved or aggressive? Offensive or defensive? Then, there is the variable of an effective communications system from the field to the home office. Does such a system exist?

Finally, there is the all-encompassing issue of morale. Surprise needs a committed and spirited group of individuals who can react quickly and decisively to exploit the unfolding events that follow a campaign anchored to surprise.

Cunning

Cunning implies secret purpose. It contrasts with the straightforward, simple, direct approach much as it contrasts with direct proof. Consequently, it has nothing in common with methods of persuasion, of self-interest, or of force, but a great deal with deceit, which also conceals its purpose.

Cunning is itself a form of deceit when it is completed—yet not deceit in the ordinary sense of the word, since no outright breach of faith is involved. The use of a trick or stratagem permits the intended victim to make his own mistakes, which, combined in a single result, suddenly change the nature of the situation before his very eyes.

If we leave the actual execution of the engagement to tactics and consider strategy as the art of skillfully exploiting force for a larger purpose, then no human characteristic appears so suited to the task of directing and inspiring strategy as the gift of cunning.

The universal urge to surprise, discussed earlier, already points to this conclusion: Each surprise action is rooted in at least some degree of cunning. Yet, however much one longs to see opposing leaders vie with one another in craft, cleverness, and cunning, the fact remains that these qualities do not figure prominently in the history of conflict.

Rarely do they stand out amid the welter of events and circumstances. The reason for this is obvious. Strategy is exclusively concerned with engagements and with the directions relating to them. Unlike other areas of life, it is not concerned with actions that consist only of words, such as statements, declarations, and so forth.

To prepare a sham action with sufficient thoroughness to impress an opponent requires a considerable expenditure of time and effort, and the costs increase with the scale of the deception. Normally, they call for more than can be spared and, consequently, so-called strategic feints rarely have the desired effect.

It is dangerous, in fact, to use substantial forces over any length of time merely to create an illusion. There is always the risk that nothing will be gained and that the individuals deployed will not be available when they are really needed. In conflict, leaders are always mindful of this sobering truth and thus tend to lose the urge to play with sly mobility.

We conclude that an accurate and penetrating understanding is a more useful and essential asset for the leader than any gift for cunning. However, the latter will do no harm so long as it is not employed at the expense of more essential qualities of character.

However, the weaker the forces that are at the disposal of the leader, the more appealing the use of cunning becomes. In a state of weakness and insignificance, when prudence, judgment, and ability no longer suffice, cunning may well appear to be the only hope.

The bleaker the situation is, with everything concentrating on a single desperate attempt, the more readily cunning is joined to daring. Released from all future considerations and liberated from thoughts of later retribution, boldness and cunning will be free to augment each other to the point of concentrating a faint glimmer of hope into a single beam of light that may yet kindle a flame.

COMMENTARY

Other scholars of strategy, beyond Clausewitz, have written about cunning. One highly acclaimed concept, known as the indirect strategy, incorporates cunning as an intrinsic part of its makeup. It is most often associated with the renowned British historian B. H. Liddell Hart who stated:

> History shows that rather than resign himself to a direct approach a Great Captain will take even the most hazardous indirect approach. He prefers to face any unfavorable condition rather than accept the risk of frustration inherent in a direct approach.

The central idea underlying the indirect approach is to avoid a direct confrontation with a competitor. Therefore, as a universal approach, the more ingenious a strategy can be to circumvent your competitor's strong points of resistance and aim for the decisive weak points by utilizing cunning, feints, and deception—all within legal and ethical boundaries—the more productive will be effort. Clausewitz reinforces such an approach in the following section.

And Sun Tzu wrote over 2,500 years ago:

> All warfare is based on deception. Hence, when able to attack, we must seem unable; when using our forces, we must seem inactive; when we are near, we must make the enemy believe that we are away; when far away, we must make him believe we are near. Hold out baits to entice the enemy. Feign disorder.

Concentration of Forces in Space

The best strategy is always to be very strong: first in general, and then at the decisive point. Apart from the effort needed to create strength, which does not always emanate from the leader, there is no higher and simpler law of strategy than that of keeping one's forces concentrated.

No force should ever be detached from the main body unless the need is definite and urgent. We hold fast to this principle and regard it as a reliable guide. In the course of our analysis, we shall learn in what circumstances dividing one's forces may be justified. We shall also learn that the principle of concentration will not have the same results in every conflict, but that those will change in accordance with means and ends.

Incredible though it sounds, it is a fact that resources have been divided and separated countless times, without the leader having any clear reason for it—but simply because he vaguely felt that this was the way things ought to be done. This folly can be avoided completely as soon as concentration of force is recognized as the norm—and every separation as an exception that has to be justified.

Unification of Forces in Time

We have come to a concept that is likely to be misleading when applied to real life. A clear definition and short analysis seem necessary. Conflict is the impact of opposing forces. It follows not only that the stronger force overwhelms the weaker, but also that its impetus carries the weaker force along with it.

A beaten group cannot make a comeback the following day merely by being reinforced with strong reserves. Here we arrive at the source of a vital difference between strategy and tactics. Tactical successes attained in the course of the engagement usually occur during the phase of disarray and weakness. On the other hand, the strategic success, the overall effect of the engagement, whether great or insignificant, already lies beyond that phase.

The strategic outcome takes shape only when the fragmented results have combined into a single, independent whole. But at that point the crisis is over; the forces regain their original cohesion, weakened only by the loss of resources they have actually suffered. The consequence of this difference is that in the tactical realm, force can be used successively; whereas strategy knows only the simultaneous use of force.

If in a tactical situation initial success does not lead to a conclusive victory, we have reason to fear the immediate future. It follows that, for the first phase, we should use only the amount of force that seems absolutely necessary.

In a strategic situation this does not hold true. For one thing, once a strategic success is achieved, a reaction is less likely to set in because the crisis has passed. For another, not all strategic forces have necessarily been weakened. The only ones that have suffered losses are those that have been tactically engaged.

In strategy, losses do not increase with the size of the forces used and may even be reduced. And since greater force is more likely to lead to success, it naturally follows that we can never use too great a force and, further, that all available force must be used simultaneously.

The truth of this proposition, however, needs to be established in another area as well. So far we have only discussed the engagement itself. It is essential that we also consider the effects of men, time, and space, which are the components of this activity.

Fatigue, exertion, and hardship constitute separate damaging factors in conflict. They are factors not essentially belonging to a confrontation, but more or less intricately involved in the realm of strategy. These factors are also present in tactical situations and possibly in their most intense form. But since tactical actions are of shorter duration, the effects of exertion will be limited.

In a strategic as well as in a tactical situation, therefore, we might be tempted to seek initial success with a minimum of personnel, in order to retain strong reserves for the final struggle. Whenever failure can be predicted with any degree of certainty, adequate force is lacking in the first place, and holding any part in reserve for later use would be unthinkable.

We must consider another very important point. In a minor engagement, it is not too difficult to judge approximately how much force is needed to achieve substantial success and how much would be superfluous. In strategy, this is practically impossible because strategic success cannot be defined and delineated with the same precision.

Consequently, it cannot be the intent of the strategist to make an ally of time for its own sake, by committing forces gradually, step by step. All forces intended and available for a strategic purpose should be applied simultaneously.

Their employment will be the more effective the more everything can be concentrated in a single action, at a single moment. That does not mean that successive effort and sustained effect have no place in strategy. They cannot be ignored, the less so since they form one of the principal means toward a final success: the continuous deployment of new forces.

We now turn to a subject closely linked to our previous discussion, which will clarify the whole matter: the strategic reserve.

The Strategic Reserve

A reserve has two distinct purposes: One is to prolong and renew the action. The second is to counter unforeseen threats. The first purpose presupposes the value of the successive use of force and therefore does not belong to strategy.

Yet, it will be a tactical rather than a strategic reserve. But the need to hold a force in readiness for emergencies may also arise in strategy. Hence, there can be such a thing as a strategic reserve, but only when emergencies are conceivable.

In a tactical situation, where we frequently do not even know the rival's intentions until we see them, we must always be more or less prepared for unforeseen developments so that positions that turn out to be weak can be reinforced and we can adjust our dispositions to the opponent's actions.

Such cases also occur in strategy, since strategy is directly linked to tactical action. In strategy, too, decisions must often be based on direct observation, on uncertain reports, and, finally, on the actual outcome of an engagement.

It is thus an essential condition of strategic leadership that forces should be held in reserve according to the degree of strategic uncertainty. In the defensive, we know this is constantly required. But uncertainty decreases as the distance between strategy and tactics becomes greater.

Therefore, the view is justified that a strategic reserve becomes less essential, less useful, and more dangerous to use the more general its intended purpose is. The point at which the concept of a strategic reserve begins to be self-contradictory is not difficult to determine.

It comes when the decisive stage of the conflict has been reached. All forces must be used to achieve it, and any idea of reserves that are not meant to be used until after this decision is an absurdity. Thus, a tactical reserve is a means not only of meeting any unforeseen maneuver by the opponent, but also of reversing the unpredictable outcome of the campaign when this becomes necessary.

Setbacks in one area can, as a rule, be offset only by achieving gains elsewhere, and, in a few cases, by transferring personnel from one area to another. Never must it occur to a strategist to deal with such a setback by holding forces in reserve. We have called it an absurdity to maintain a strategic reserve that is not meant to contribute to the overall decision.

The point is so obvious that we should not have devoted considerable space to it if it were not that the idea can look somewhat more plausible when veiled in other concepts. One man thinks of a strategic reserve as the peak of wise and cautious planning. Another rejects the whole idea, including that of a tactical reserve. This kind of confused thinking does actually affect reality.

COMMENTARY

Whether you label opportunities—such as sudden openings in emerging, neglected, or poorly served market segments—as strategic or tactical, holding reserves and committing them at the proper time permits you to react decisively and "contribute to the overall decision."

In those instances, however, make certain you have some prior intelligence that indicates the margin of success is in your favor. The essential point: Holding reserves should not be considered as a speculative and wishful gamble.

In more precise tactical situations, however, reserves can apply to a variety of situations, such as holding portions of your operating budget in reserve to accelerate the rapid adoption of your product through additional targeted promotions, offering timely incentives within the supply chain—and preparing for the likelihood of an aggressive reaction from competitors.

Being able to provide an energetic response to market opportunities at a time and place of your choosing places you in a superior position to turn a doubtful situation into a decisive victory.

In sum, as Clausewitz points out, judgment is needed about holding reserves and should be tested against his central theme of factoring in the strategic versus tactical situations in your decisions.

Economy of Force

As we have already said, principles can seldom reduce the path of reason to a simple line. As in all practical matters, certain latitude always remains. The man of action must at times trust in the sensitive instinct of judgment, derived from his native intelligence and developed through reflection, which almost unconsciously hits on the right course.

At other times he must simplify understanding to its dominant features, which will serve as rules. And sometimes he must support himself with the crutch of established routine.

One of these simplified features, or aids to analysis, is always to make sure that all forces are involved—always to ensure that no part of the whole force is idle. If a segment of one's force is located where it is not sufficiently busy with the opponent, then these forces are being managed uneconomically. In this sense they are being wasted, which is even worse than using them inappropriately.

When the time for action comes, the first requirement should be that all parts must act. Even the least appropriate task will occupy some of the rival's forces and reduce his overall strength, while completely inactive personnel are neutralized for the time being.

THE SUSPENSION OF ACTION IN CONFLICT

If we regard conflict as an act of mutual loss, we are bound to think of both sides as usually being in action and advancing. But as soon as we consider each moment separately, we are almost equally bound to think of only one side as advancing while the other is expectantly waiting.

Conditions will never be exactly identical on both sides, nor will their mutual relationship remain the same. In time changes will occur, and it follows that any given moment will favor one side more than the other.

If we assume that both leaders are completely cognizant of their own and their opponent's conditions, one of them will be motivated to act, which becomes in turn a reason for the other to wait. Both cannot simultaneously want to advance or, on the other hand, to wait.

Only one can be the aggressor. There can be no conflict if both parties seek to defend themselves. The aggressor has a positive aim, while the defender's aim is merely negative. Positive action is therefore proper to the former, since it is the only means by which he can achieve his ends. Consequently, when conditions are equal for both parties, the attacker ought to act since his is the positive aim.

Seen in this light, suspension of action in conflict is a contradiction in terms. Like two incompatible elements, groups must continually eliminate one another. Like fire and water, they never find themselves in a state of equilibrium, but must keep on interacting until one of them has completely disappeared.

Imagine a pair of wrestlers deadlocked and inert for hours on end. In other words, action ought to run its course steadily like a wound-up clock. But no matter how aggressive the nature of conflict, it is chained by human weaknesses. And no one will be surprised at the contradiction that man seeks and that he creates the very danger he fears.

The history of conflict so often shows that immobility and inactivity are the normal state of organizations in conflict and that action is the exception. This might almost make us doubt the accuracy of our argument.

How, in fact, could we reasonably defend the exertion of so much effort in conflict, unless action is intended? Let us note three determinants that function as inherent counterweights and prevent the clockwork from running down rapidly or without interruption.

The first of these, which creates a permanent tendency toward delay and thus becomes a retarding influence, is the fear and indecision native to the human mind. It is a sort of moral force of gravity, which works by repulsion rather than attraction: namely, aversion to danger and responsibility.

In the aggressive climate of conflict, ordinary natures tend to move more ponderously. Stronger and more frequent stimuli are therefore needed to ensure that momentum is maintained.

To understand why the campaign is being fought is seldom sufficient in itself to overcome this ponderousness. Unless an enterprising spirit is in command—a man who is as much at home in contentious situations as a fish is in water—or unless great responsibilities exert a pressure, inactivity will be the rule and progress the exception.

The second cause is the imperfection of human perception and judgment, which is more pronounced in conflict than anywhere else. We hardly know accurately our own situation at any particular moment, while the rival's, which is concealed from us, must be deduced from very little evidence.

Consequently, it often happens that both sides see an advantage in the same objective, even though it is more in the interest of only one of them. Each may therefore think it wiser to await a better moment, as I have already explained.

The third determinant, which acts like a ratchet wheel, occasionally stopping the works completely, is the greater strength of the defensive. It therefore happens that both sides at the same time not only feel too weak for an offensive, but also really are too weak. Thus, in the midst of the conflict itself, concern, prudence, and fear of excessive risks find reason to assert themselves and to tame the elemental fury of conflict.

Conflict often is nothing more than armed neutrality, a threatening attitude meant to support negotiations, a mild attempt to gain some small advantage before sitting back and letting matters take their course. Or it is a disagreeable obligation imposed by an alliance, to be discharged with as little effort as possible.

In all such cases where the impetus of interest is slight, where there is little hostile spirit, and where we neither want to do much harm to the challenger nor have much to fear from him—in short, where no great motive presses and promotes action—organizations will not want to risk much. This explains the tame conduct of such conflicts, in which the hostile spirit of true confrontation is held in check.

Gambling for high stakes seems to have turned into haggling for small change, where action is reduced to insignificant, time-killing flourishes. A slight blow may often be enough to cause a total collapse. All of these reasons explain why action is not continuous but spasmodic.

Excessive clashes are interrupted by periods of observation during which both sides are on the defensive. But, usually, one side is more strongly motivated, which tends to affect its behavior. The offensive element will dominate and usually maintain its continuity of action.

TENSION AND REST: THE DYNAMIC LAW IN CONFLICT

Most campaigns, therefore, are periods of inaction and repose that have been much longer than periods of action. When campaigns are interrupted—in other words, when neither side has a positive aim—a state of rest and equilibrium results. Equilibrium covers not only physical and psychological forces, but also all circumstances and motives.

As soon as one side adopts a new and positive aim and as soon as the opponent resists tension, forces build up. And tension lasts until the immediate issue has been decided. Either one side renounces its goal or the other side concedes it.

This decision, which is always derived from the results of the combinations of actions that are developed by both sides, is followed by movement in one direction or the other. When this movement has been exhausted, inactivity returns. Or a new cycle of tension and decision begins, followed by further movement—usually in the opposite direction.

This distinction between balance, tension, and movement has a greater practical application than may at first appear. A state of rest and equilibrium can accommodate a good deal of activity. That is to say, the kind of activity arising from incidental causes that is not designed to lead to major changes.

Significant engagements, even major campaigns, may take place. However, these actions are still of a different nature and therefore usually have different results. In a state of tension, a decision will always have greater effect.

The most significant lesson drawn from these observations is that any move made in a state of tension will be more important, and will have more results, than it would have if made in a state of equilibrium.

In times of maximum tension this importance will rise to an infinite degree. A badly chosen position or a single miscalculated move on our part during the course of a strategic move by the opponent may have fatal results. While in a state of equilibrium, such blunders would have to be glaring indeed to arouse the challenger's reaction at all.

Everything we shall have to say about the relation between attack and defense and the way in which this polarity develops refers to the state of crisis

in which the forces find themselves during periods of tension and movement. By contrast, all activity that occurs during a state of equilibrium will
be regarded and treated as a mere consequence. The state of crisis is the real
conflict; the equilibrium is nothing but its reflex.

Chapter 7

The Engagement in General

Clausewitz makes these key points about engagements:

- Conflicts consist of a large number of engagements, great and small, simultaneous or consecutive. Each of these has a specific purpose relating to the whole.
- The neutralization or defeat of the rival must be regarded as the sole object of all engagements.
- Rather than try to outdo the opponent with complicated schemes, one should try to outdo him in simplicity.
- If we read history with an open mind, we cannot fail to conclude that, among all the virtues associated with conflict, the energetic conduct of a campaign has always contributed most to success.
- In the engagement, the loss of morale has proved the major decisive factor.
- In many cases the abandonment of the engagement remains the only authentic proof of victory.
- The decision can never be reached too soon to suit the winner, or delayed long enough to suit the loser.
- The leader who has come closest to conducting an engagement with the utmost economy of force and the maximum psychological effect of strong reserves is on the surest road to victory.
- An organization with spirit will never panic in the face of defeat.
- Unless a leader is bold and enterprising, no great results can be expected from even the most brilliant victory.
- No victory will be effective without pursuit. No matter how brief the exploitation of victory, it must always go further than an immediate follow-up.

- Engagements in which one unexpected factor has a major effect on the course of the whole usually exist only in the stories told by people who want to explain away their defeats.

Clausewitz talks in greater detail about the engagement:

The actual engagement is the central act of conflict. All other activities merely support it. Its nature consequently needs close examination.

Engagements mean struggle. The object of struggle is to neutralize* or defeat the opponent in the individual engagement. This is the simple concept, and we shall return to it. But first we must introduce a number of other considerations.

Conflicts consist of a large number of engagements, great and small, simultaneous or consecutive. And this fragmentation of activity into so many separate actions is the result of the great variety of situations out of which conflicts can nowadays arise.

Action is subject to such a multitude of conditions and considerations that the aim can no longer be achieved by a single tremendous act of struggle. Rather it must be reached by a large number of more or less important actions, all combined into one whole. Each of these separate actions has a specific purpose relating to the whole.

We have already said that the concept of the engagement lies at the root of all strategic action, since strategy is the use of force, the heart of which, in turn, is the engagement. Thus, in the field of strategy, we can reduce all activity to the unitary concept of the single engagement and concern ourselves exclusively with its purposes.

We will come to identify these purposes as we discuss the circumstances that give rise to them in the engagement. Here it is enough to say that every engagement, large or small, has its own particular purpose, which is subordinate to the general one. That being so, the neutralization of the rival must be regarded simply as a means toward the general end.

COMMENTARY

Clausewitz's comment "that every engagement, large or small, has its own particular purpose, which is subordinate to the general one" has particular application in developing your strategic business plan.

---

* Clausewitz's original term is *destruction*. I have chosen to substitute his usage with *neutralize*. That is, to make the competitor ineffective against your efforts. However, if you go further and cause the competitor to exit the market entirely—or, more to the extreme, create events whereby the rival goes out of business, such actions would connect more closely with Clausewitz's term of destruction. Thus, the choice is up to you as you consider such issues as your corporate culture and policies, your competitive situation, industry practices, and legal factors.

In another interpretation, I have used *engagement* in place of his original term, fighting, which implies that some form of aggressive action is part of the confrontation.

Regardless of the planning format you use, long-term strategic objectives are likely to be a central component.

Subordinate to those objectives are shorter term tactical objectives that contain details of planned engagements to support the strategic ones. Too often, however, tactical short-term objectives are mistakenly shown as stand-alone actions with no connection to the overall strategic plan.

Therefore, if you view each engagement within a strategic framework, you can then shape your tactical objectives and strategies to fit the competitive situation—and the overall business plan.

One company, Intel, illustrates this concept. The giant chip maker claims that its processors run eight out of ten PCs in the world. The problem is that demand for PCs is diminishing. PC unit shipments dropped 4 percent in 2012 and are expected to continue declining beyond the projected 10 percent drop for 2013. Reason: The world has gone mobile with the massive acceptance of smartphones and tablets that appeal to virtually every user segment.

The further problem: As of 2013, Intel represented just 1 percent market share in tablets and phones. According to analysts, the company was caught off-guard by the speed of the transition and the ensuing demand for new designs in low-power chips. The company's central focus had been on its core high-performance chips designed for machines that plug into a wall.

Once the Intel Board acknowledged the full magnitude of the problem, it moved rapidly to install a new CEO and president and authorized a management shakeup. The new executive team immediately invited the company's top executives into a strategy meeting and gave each an assignment to submit an action plan directed to a single imperative "engagement": Move rapidly and decisively into smartphones and tablets.

Clausewitz continues with neutralization:

What do we mean by neutralization of the rival? Simply the reduction or elimination of his forces' capabilities—either completely or enough to make him stop the confrontation. Leaving aside all specific purposes of any particular engagement, the complete or partial elimination of the rival must be regarded as the sole object of all engagements.

How are we to prove that neutralizing the rival's forces must be the main objective? How are we to counter the highly sophisticated theory that supposes an ingenious method of inflicting minor direct damage on the rival's forces will lead to a major neutralization? Or that claims to produce such paralysis of the rival's forces constitute a significant shortcut to victory?

Admittedly, an engagement at one point may be worth more than at another. Admittedly, there is a skillful ordering of priority engagements in strategy. Indeed, that is what strategy is all about, and we do not wish to deny it. We do claim, however, that neutralization of the opponent's forces must always be the dominant consideration.

But we must repeat that the subject that concerns us is strategy, not tactics. We are therefore not discussing the tactical means used to disable a rival force with a minimum of effort. We maintain, however, that only great tactical successes can lead to great strategic ones. Or, as we have already said more specifically, tactical successes are of paramount importance in conflict.

The proof of our assertion is fairly simple. It can be found in the time absorbed by complex operations. The question of whether a simple campaign or a more complex one will be the more effective will certainly be answered in favor of the simple campaign.

If the opponent decides on a simpler campaign, one that can be carried out quickly, he will gain the advantage and wreck the grand design. Thus, in the evaluation of a complex campaign, every risk that may be run must be weighed. The scheme should only be adopted if there is no danger that the rival can wreck it by more rapid action.

Wherever this is possible we must choose the shorter path. We must further simplify it to whatever extent the character and situation of the opponent and any other circumstances make necessary. We will find that an active, courageous, and resolute adversary will not leave us time for long-range intricate schemes. It seems to us that this is proof enough of the superiority of the simple and direct over the complex.

This does not mean that the simple campaign is best. It means rather that one should not swing wider than latitude allows. The probability of direct confrontation increases with the aggressiveness of the adversary. Thus, rather than try to outbid the opponent with complicated schemes, one should, on the contrary, try to outdo him in simplicity.

COMMENTARY

Clausewitz's discussion about complexity versus simplicity when planning a competitive campaign has other dimensions to consider. For instance, complex plans open the possibilities for mistakes, especially where coordination is needed among individuals in various functions and locations, where correct timing is a factor, and where the intricacies of the plan may not be fully internalized by key individuals.

Then, there is the parallel issue of speed, which, Clausewitz points out, is a vital component of a skillfully implemented strategy. That means that rarely has an overlong, dragged out campaign proved successful. The resulting exhaustion through the excessive draining of resources damages more companies than almost any other factor. The previous reference to Intel and its urgency to move rapidly and decisively into designing chips for smartphones and tablets illustrates the point.

THE ENGAGEMENT IN GENERAL—CONTINUED

Previously, we defined the purpose of the engagement as being the neutralization of the opponent's forces. We tried to prove this to be true in the majority of cases and in major actions, since reducing the effectiveness of the rival's forces must always be the dominant consideration in conflict.

What do we mean by neutralizing the opponent's forces? It refers to a reduction of a rival's strength relative to our own. Equal losses will, of course, mean smaller relative losses to the side with numerical superiority and can therefore be considered an advantage.

If by skillful deployment one can place the opponent at such a disadvantage that he cannot continue the campaign without risk, and if after some resistance he retreats, we can say that at this point we have beaten him. But, if we have lost proportionately as many resources in the process as he did, no trace of this so-called victory will show up in the final balance sheet of the campaign.

Getting the better of an opponent cannot in itself be considered as an objective. And for this reason cannot be included in the definition of the objective. Nothing remains, therefore, but the direct profit gained in the process of neutralization. This gain includes not merely the losses inflicted during the action, but also those which occur as a direct result of his retreat.

It is a familiar experience that the winner's losses in the course of an engagement show little difference from the loser's. Frequently, there is no difference at all and sometimes even an inverse one.

The really crippling losses only start with his retreat. Thus, a victory usually starts to gather weight after the issue has already been decided. This would be a paradox, if it were not resolved as follows.

Physical losses are not the only losses incurred by both sides in the course of the engagement: Their moral strength is also shaken, broken, and ruined. In deciding whether or not to continue the engagement, it is not enough to consider the loss of personnel and other resources, one needs to weigh the loss of order, courage, confidence, cohesion, and the plan. The decision rests chiefly on the state of morale, which, in cases where the victor has lost as much as the vanquished, has always been the single decisive factor.

The ratio of physical loss on either side is in any case hard to gauge in the course of an engagement. But this does not apply to loss of morale. There are two main indicators of this: One is loss of the ground on which one has engaged; the other is the preponderance of the opponent's reserves.

The faster one's own reserves have shrunk in relation to the opponent's, the more it has cost to maintain the balance. That alone is tangible proof of the rival's superior morale. And it seldom fails to cause some bitterness in a leader, a certain loss of respect for the forces he leads.

But the main point is that personnel, after campaigning for some time, are apt to be like burned-out cinders. Their strength and their morale are drained, and possibly their courage has vanished as well.

As an organic whole, quite apart from their losses, personnel are far from being what they were before the engagement. Thus, the amount of reserves spent is an accurate measure on the loss of morale.

As a rule, then, loss of ground and lack of fresh reserves are the two main reasons for retreat. In the engagement, then, the loss of morale has proved the major decisive factor.

Once the outcome has been determined, the loss continues to increase and reaches its peak only at the end of the action. Loss of order and cohesion often makes even the resistance of individual units fatal for them. The spirit of the whole is broken. Nothing is left of the original obsession with triumph or disaster that made men ignore all risks. Thus, the tool is weakened and blunted at the first impact of the opponent's victory.

This is the time for the victor to consolidate his gains. The rival's morale will gradually recover, order will be restored, and his courage will return. In most cases only a very small portion, if any, of the hard-earned superiority will remain.

COMMENTARY

In this chapter and previous ones, Clausewitz makes extensive references to the power of morale. As he emphatically points out: "In the engagement, the loss of morale has proved the major decisive factor."

In addition to my commentary in Chapter 1, there are additional ways you can create a morale advantage:

- Manage through availability and visibility. Show genuine interest by listening to employees' problems, complaints, and other issues.
- Manage with integrity and transparency. To the extent you can reveal sensitive information to personnel, explain management's future plans.
- Prioritize actions with input from others. Here's where the cross-functional team is useful to create a collaborative environment where individuals can share expertise in precise areas and where all can benefit from the diversity of opinions and backgrounds.
- Support a spirited, optimistic, and entrepreneurial work environment through ongoing training.
- Communicate often and openly—especially about market victories, both large and small. (See my commentary on e-communications in Chapter 6.)

The psychological effect of a victory does not merely grow in proportion to the amount of the forces involved, but does so at an accelerating rate. This is because the increase is one not merely of size but also of intensity.

Another factor to be considered in determining the psychological value of a victory is the ratio of the opposing forces. If a small force beats a larger one, its gain is not only doubled, but it also shows a greater margin of general superiority, which the loser knows he may have to face again and again.

At the moment of confrontation, information about the strength of the opponent is usually uncertain, and the estimate of one's own strength is usually unrealistic. The stronger party either simply refuses to admit the disproportion or at least will underrate it. And, to a large extent, it is protected from the psychological disadvantage.

If in conclusion we consider the total concept of a victory, we find that it consists of three elements:

1. The opponent's greater loss of material strength
2. His loss of morale
3. His open admission of the preceding by giving up his intentions

Reports of losses on either side are never accurate, seldom truthful, and in most cases deliberately falsified. There is no accurate measure of loss of morale. Hence, in many cases the abandonment of the campaign remains the only authentic proof of victory.

Even in engagements intended to eliminate the opponent, withdrawal does not always imply that the aim has been abandoned. All this will be discussed later under the heading of the particular purposes of engagements. For the present, we only wish to draw attention to the fact that in the majority of cases it is difficult to distinguish between the abandonment of intentions and the abandonment of the contested area.* The impression produced by the former should not be underrated.

For leaders and organizations without an established reputation, this is a difficult aspect of otherwise sound operations. A series of engagements followed by retreats may appear to be a series of reverses. This may be quite untrue; but it can make a very bad impression.

It is not possible for a leader in retreat to forestall the morale effect by making his true intentions known. To do so effectively, he would have to disclose his overall plan of action, and that would be contrary to his main interests.

THE SIGNIFICANCE OF THE ENGAGEMENT

We previously discussed the engagement in its absolute form, as though it were a microcosm of conflict as a whole. We now turn to the relationship that it bears as one part of a greater whole.

We begin by inquiring into the precise significance that an engagement may possess. Since conflict is nothing but mutual loss, it would seem most natural to conceive that all the forces on each side should unite in one great mass. And all successes should consist of one great thrust of these forces.

---

* Area can be interpreted as a territory or market segment. This usage would also apply to Clausewitz's references further on to locality and terrain.

There is much to be said for this idea and to consider the smaller engagements as necessary by-products, like wood shavings. However, the matter is never disposed of so easily as this.

The multiplication of engagements results from the splitting up of forces. And we shall therefore deal with the specific purposes of individual engagements in that context. These purposes, and with them the whole range of engagements, can be classified; a study of these classifications will help to clarify our discussion.

The elimination or neutralization of the rival's forces is admittedly the purpose of all engagements. Yet other purposes may well be linked to this and may even predominate.

A distinction must therefore be made between a case in which elimination of the rival's forces is the main consideration and one in which it is more of a means. The takeover of a locality or of a physical object may also be a general motive, either by itself or in conjunction with other motives, in which case one motive will usually predominate.

The two main forms of conflict—attack and defense, which we shall discuss shortly, while not affecting the first of these objectives, do affect the other two as shown in the following chart:

Offensive engagement	Defensive engagement
Elimination or neutralization of the rival	Elimination or neutralization of the rival
Takeover of a locality	Defense of a locality
Takeover of an object	Defense of an object

However, these objectives do not cover the whole ground. To the three objectives of the attacker we must add a fourth: misleading the opponent—in other words, putting up a sham fight. The very nature of the matter makes it obvious that this object is conceivable only in the context of an attack.

On the other hand, we must observe that the defense of a locality may be of two kinds: either absolute, if the locality is not to be given up at all, or relative, if it must be held only for a certain time. The latter form constantly recurs in engagements.

There is probably no need to stress that the differing purposes of an engagement affect the preparations that are made for it. We make one plan for dislodging an adversary and another for eliminating it, one plan for holding a locality at all costs and another for merely delaying the rival. In the former case, there is little need to worry about the retreat. In the latter, the retreat is of paramount importance.

DURATION OF THE ENGAGEMENT

If we turn from a discussion of the engagement itself to its relation to other factors in conflict, its duration acquires special importance. In a sense, the duration of an engagement can be interpreted as a separate, secondary success.

The decision can never be reached too soon to suit the winner, or delayed long enough to suit the loser. A victory is greater for having been gained quickly; defeat is compensated for by having been long postponed.

This is true in general. It assumes practical importance in engagements whose object is a delaying action. In such a case, the whole success often consists in nothing but the time the action takes. That is why we include duration in the spectrum of strategic elements.

The duration of an engagement and the broad conditions under which it is fought are necessarily connected. These conditions are the size of the force, its relation in men and material to the opponent, and the character of the terrain.

An opponent with two- or threefold superiority cannot be resisted for as long as one of equal strength. It follows that the strength, composition, and deployment of the two sides must all be taken into account if the objective of the engagement lies in its duration.

DECISION OF THE ENGAGEMENT

No engagement is decided in a single moment, although in each there are crucial moments that are primarily responsible for the outcome. Losing an engagement is therefore like the gradual sinking of a scale.

But each engagement reaches a point when it may be regarded as decided, so that to reopen it would constitute a new engagement rather than the continuation of the old one. The accurate perception of that point is very important in order to decide whether reinforcements would be profitably employed in renewing the action.

New resources are often vainly sacrificed in an engagement that is past retrieving. And the chance of reversing a decision is often missed while it could still be done. Every engagement is a whole, made up of subsidiary engagements that add up to the overall result.

We may, therefore, ask what normally constitutes this moment of decision, this point of no return at which fresh forces will be too late to save the day. Excluding feints, which by their very nature do not lead to a decision, we arrive at the following answers:

1. Where the purpose of the engagement is the possession of some object, the decisive moment is reached when this object is lost.
2. Where the purpose of the engagement is the possession of a certain locality, the decisive moment is usually reached when this locality is lost. This holds true only if the locality is of great defensive strength.
3. In cases in which the preceding conditions have not led to a decision, the moment of decision comes when the successive application of force is no longer advantageous and if the individuals involved have lost any of their cohesion and effectiveness.

However, if the original engagement is not considered ended, then a new one, opened by the arrival of reinforcements, will merge with it and lead to a combined result. The initial loss would then be entirely erased.

If a losing engagement can be caught before its conclusion and turned into a success, the initial loss not only disappears from the record, but becomes the basis for a greater victory. The magic of victory and the curse of defeat can change the specific gravity of the elements of a campaign.

Even in a situation where one is decisively stronger than the opponent and could easily avenge his victory with a greater one, it is better to retrieve a losing engagement (provided it is sufficiently important) before its close than fight a second engagement later on.

There is yet another deduction to be examined. The outcome of a lost engagement must not be taken as an argument for deciding on a new one. Rather, any such decision must be based on the rest of the circumstances. That precept, however, is counteracted by a psychological factor that must be reckoned with: the instinct for revenge.

There is thus a natural propensity to exploit this psychological factor in order to recapture what has been lost by seeking a new engagement, particularly if the rest of the situation warrants it. The very nature of such a second engagement decrees that in most cases it should be an attack.

The history of minor engagements will show numerous examples of this kind of retribution. Major engagements, on the other hand, usually spring from too many other causes to be based on such a relatively trivial motive.

COMMENTARY

Clausewitz provides three criteria for determining when it is too late to save the day on a campaign. Yet there are gray areas to consider before letting go, which may impact your decision:

Will exiting a market niche or eliminating a product from the line provide the acceptable financial results that would support withdrawal? How will the move affect the rest of your markets, your relationships with customers, and the viability of your product line as a whole? Will a gap open for an astute competitor to latch on to the supply chain and exploit an unexpected opening?

Beyond those factors, there are still additional ones you may have to consider, such as the overall operating condition of your firm in comparison with that of your competitor. Then, there is Clausewitz's classic statement to think about: "In war [conflict] the result is never final ... merely a transitory evil."

MUTUAL AGREEMENT TO FIGHT

There can be no engagement unless both sides are willing. An engagement is a very peculiar form of duel. Its basis does not consist only in mutual desire or willingness to fight, but in the purposes involved. And those always belong to a larger whole—the more so because the conflict itself, considered as a single event, is governed by conditions that themselves belong to a larger whole.

The leader who wishes to retreat and is able to do so can hardly be forced into an engagement by his opponent. Frequently, however, the attacker is not content with the advantages provided by such a retreat and feels the need for an actual victory. In such a case, remarkable skill is often used to find and apply the few available means of forcing even an evasive opponent to stand and fight.

There are two principal ways of accomplishing this: first, to make it so difficult that the engagement seems to be the lesser evil to the opponent and, second, to take him by surprise.

THE ENGAGEMENT: IT IS DECISION

What is the engagement? It is a struggle by the main force—but not just an insignificant action fought for secondary objectives and not simply an attempt to be abandoned. It is a struggle for real victory, waged with all available strength. Secondary objectives may combine with the principal one—that is, an engagement that is connected with a still larger entity of which it is only a part.

If an engagement is primarily an end in itself, the elements of its decision must be contained in it. In other words, victory must be pursued so long as it lies within the realm of the possible. The engagement must never be abandoned because of particular circumstances, but only when the strength available has quite clearly become inadequate.

In a major engagement more than any other type of engagement, the decision to give up the fight depends on the relative strength of unused reserves still available. They are the forces whose morale is still intact.

Lost ground, as we have pointed out, is also an index of impaired morale. It must also be taken into account, though more as an indicator of losses suffered than as a loss in itself. The main concern of both leaders will always be the number of reserves available on both sides.

Usually an engagement takes shape from the start, though not in any obvious manner. Often this shape has already been decisively determined by the preliminary dispositions made for the engagement.

Even if the course of the engagement is not predetermined, it is in the nature of things that it consists in a slowly shifting balance, which starts early, but, as we have said, is not easily detectable. As time goes on, it gathers momentum and becomes more obvious. It is less a matter of oscillating to and fro, as fanciful accounts of confrontations having misled many people into thinking.

But whether the equilibrium remains undisturbed for some time or swings to one side, rights itself, and then swings to the other, it is certain that a leader usually knows that he is losing the engagement long before he disengages. Engagements in which one unexpected factor has a major effect on the course of the whole usually exist only in the stories told by people who want to explain away their defeats.

While we believe that the defeated leader is usually aware of the likelihood of defeat long before he decides to concede the encounter, we also admit that there are contrary cases. Otherwise, we should be stating a self-contradictory tenet. If an engagement were to be considered lost each time it took a definite turn, no additional forces would be committed in the hope of saving it.

It follows that such a definite turn could not precede the moment of retreat by any appreciable amount of time. There are certainly cases in which an encounter, after taking a definite turn in favor of one side, ended up in favor of the other. However, such cases are not common. In fact they are unusual. But it is just this exceptional case that every leader hopes for when his luck is out. He has to hope for it so long as there is any chance of a turn for the better.

He hopes that by dint of greater efforts, by whatever morale is left among the personnel, by surpassing himself, or by sheer fortune, he will be able to reverse his fortunes just once more. And he will keep at it for as long as his courage and his judgment allow. We shall have more to say about this later, but first we wish to enumerate the signs that indicate a change in equilibrium.

The outcome of the encounter as a whole is made up of its constituent engagements. These, in turn, may be recognized by three distinct signs:

1. The psychological effect exerted by the leader's moral stamina
2. The wasting away of one's own personnel at a rate faster than that of the opponent
3. The amount of ground lost

All these indicators serve as a kind of compass by which a leader can tell the direction in which his engagement is going. We have explicitly stated more than once that as a rule the final outcome turns on the ratio of unused reserves still available. A leader who recognizes his opponent's distinct superiority in reserves will decide to retreat.

Therefore, so long as a leader has more reserves than his adversary, he will not give up even though the engagement shows signs of going badly. But once his reserves start to become weaker than the rival's, the end is a foregone conclusion. His remaining moves depend partly on the circumstances, and partly on the degree of the leader's personal courage and endurance, which may well deteriorate into unwise obstinacy.

Just how a leader arrives at a correct estimate of the ratio of reserves on each side is a matter of skill and experience, and does not concern us here. What does concern us is the result as it emerges from his thinking.

Even this is not yet the real moment of decision. An answer that emerges only gradually is not the proper catalyst for that. It cannot do more than broadly influence the ultimate decision, which will in turn be triggered by immediate considerations.

On the one hand, there is the domineering pride of a victory: the inflexible determination that goes with innate obstinacy, and the desperate resistance of enthusiasm. All of which refuse to abandon a confrontation where honor is involved. On the other, there is the voice of reason counseling against spending all one has, against gambling away one's last resources, and in favor of retaining whatever is necessary for an orderly retreat.

No matter how highly rated the qualities of courage and steadfastness may be, no matter how small the chance of victory may be, the leader who hesitates to go for it with all the power at his disposal, will face a point beyond which persistence becomes desperate folly. And that can never be condoned.

THE EFFECTS OF VICTORY

Depending on one's point of view, one may marvel just as much at the remarkable results of some victories as at the lack of results of others. Let us take a moment to consider the nature of the effect that a major victory may have. Three things are distinguished here:

- The effect upon the leader and his organization
- The effect on the opposing organization
- The actual influence that those effects can have on the future course of the conflict

As we have already mentioned, the scale of a victory does not increase simply at a rate corresponding with the increase in size of the defeated organizations, but progressively. The outcome of a major encounter has a greater psychological effect on the loser than on the winner. This, in turn, gives rise to additional loss of material strength, which is echoed in loss of morale. The two become mutually interactive as each enhances and intensifies the other.

One must also place a special emphasis on the morale effect, which works in opposite directions on each side. While sapping the strength of the loser, it raises the vigor and energy of the winner. But the defeated side is the one most affected by it, since it becomes the direct cause of additional loss.

Moreover, it is closely related to the risks, exertions, and hardships—that is, to the wear and tear inseparable from conflict. It merges with these conditions and is nurtured by them.

On the victor's side, however, all these factors only serve to increase the scope of his courage. As the loser falls much further below the original line of equilibrium, the winner's scale rises above it. That is why, in considering the effects of a victory, we are particularly interested in those that show themselves on the losing side.

These effects are greater after a large-scale action than after a minor one, and the greater still after a major engagement than after an ancillary one. A major encounter exists for its own sake and for the sake of the victory it is to bring and that it seeks by means of maximum exertion.

Therefore, the judgment pronounced by a victory seems to be of greater importance for the future. It is always possible to avoid repeating a mistake. And one can hope that another day will bring a better deal from luck or chance, but the sum total of physical and moral strength is not so susceptible to rapid change.

Those who have never been through a serious defeat will naturally find it hard to form a vivid and thus altogether true picture of it. Abstract concepts of this or that minor loss will never match the reality of a major defeat. The matter is worth closer examination.

When one is losing, the first thing that strikes one's imagination, and indeed one's intellect, is the melting away of numbers. This is followed by a loss of ground, which almost always happens and can even happen to the attacker if he is out of luck. Next come the breakup of the original plan, the confusion of groups, and the dangers inherent in the retreat, which, with rare exceptions, are always present to some degree.

Then comes the retreat itself. It is the feeling of having been defeated that now runs through the ranks. What is worse, the sense of being beaten is not a mere nightmare that may pass. It has become an unmistakable fact that the opponent is stronger. It is a fact for which the reasons may have lain too deep to be predictable at the outset, but it emerges clearly and convincingly in the end.

One may have been aware of it all along. But for the lack of more solid alternatives this awareness was countered by one's trust in chance, good luck, providence, and in one's own audacity and courage. All this has now turned out to have been insufficient, and one is harshly and inexorably confronted by the terrible truth.

COMMENTARY

Clausewitz's comment that "the sense of being beaten ... may have lain too deep to be predictable at the outset" opens a chasm of possibilities to reflect on. Could the root causes that contributed to defeat have been known earlier and remedies put in place? The answer is no simpler or more complicated than the types of issues that set in motion the reasons for defeat.

To assist in your search for reasons, two management procedures can support your efforts[*]:

First, the Strategy Diagnostic Tool, which helps assess your firm's competitive strategies against those of your competitor
Second, Appraising Internal and External Conditions, which consists of a 100-question checklist to address your firm's market environment, management procedures and policies, and strategy factors.

When both of these tools are used on a periodic schedule, they can alert you to potential problems and remedial action.

[*] Both tools come from my book, *How to Outthink, Outmaneuver, and Outperform Your Competitors*. Boca Raton, FL: CRC Press, 2013. They appear here in the Appendix.

All these negative impressions are still far removed from panic. An organization with spirit will never panic in the face of defeat. The impressions themselves are unavoidable in the best of organizations. Here and there they may be tempered by long familiarity with conflict and victory and by solid trust in the senior leaders, but they are never entirely absent at the outset.

It follows, then, that even a modest victory by the main force is enough to start a steady sinking of the opponent's scale, until a change in external factors produces a new turn of events. Failing that, only an outstanding leader, along with personnel filled with spirit in search of greater prizes and greater glory, will be able to keep the swollen torrent of power within bounds by making small but frequent stands until the force of victory has run its course.

This effect may differ from case to case, but it always exists to some degree. In place of an immediate and determined effort by everyone to hold off further misfortune, there is a general fear that any effort will be useless. Men will hesitate where they should act. Or they will even dejectedly resign themselves and leave everything to fate.

The consequences of these effects of victory on the future course of the conflict depend partly on the character and talent of the victorious leader. But they depend even more on the conditions that gave rise to the victory and on those conditions that victory creates.

Unless a leader is bold and enterprising, no great results can be expected from even the most brilliant victory—although it can be rendered ineffective even more quickly by major adverse circumstances.

What concerns us here is only the campaign itself. Our argument is that the effects of victory that we have described will always be present. They increase in proportion to the scale of the victory and increase the more the engagement is a major one. That is, the more the organization's full strength is committed, the more this strength represents the total force.

COMMENTARY

There is a potentially dark side to victory: complacency. Whereas winning excites the mind, improves confidence, and motivates individuals to push forward with drive, courage, and a mind-set of determination, those very same conditions can veil underlying conditions where planning becomes lax, significant market intelligence is overlooked, and additional training is neglected. Any or all of these factors can cause the past winner to become a future loser.

On the other hand, the loser can learn from his or her costly mistakes and, through good leadership, rally personnel with an intense desire to win. Such an effort can often give the psychological edge to create a turnaround. Clausewitz discusses this possibility above and in other sections of this chapter. And previous company examples illustrate this point, such as Square (Chapter 2), Yahoo (Chapter 3), and Allen Edmonds (Chapter 6.)

THE USE OF THE ENGAGEMENT

No matter how a particular engagement is conducted or what aspects of its conduct we subsequently recognize as being essential, the very concept of conflict will permit us to make the following explicit statements:

1. Neutralizing the rival's forces is the overriding principle of conflict and the principal way to achieve our object.
2. Neutralizing can usually be accomplished only by an engagement.
3. Only major engagements involving all forces lead to major success.
4. The greatest successes are obtained where all engagements coalesce into one great encounter.
5. Only in a major engagement does the leader control operations in person. It is only natural that he should prefer to entrust the direction of the campaign to himself.

These facts lead to a dual law whose principles support each other:

Neutralizing the opponent's forces is generally accomplished by means of great campaigns and their results. No doubt this principle is also present to greater or lesser extent in other types of actions. Certainly there have been minor engagements in which favorable circumstances have resulted in the disabling of a disproportionate number of the rival's forces.

The major engagement is therefore to be regarded as concentrated conflict, as the center of gravity of the entire campaign. Just as the focal point of a mirror causes the sun's rays to converge into a perfect image and heats them to maximum intensity, so all forces and circumstances of conflict are united and compressed to maximum effectiveness in the major engagement.

Whenever a great and positive goal exists, one that will seriously affect the opponent, a great campaign is not only the most natural but also the best means of attaining success. As a rule, shrinking from a major decision by evading such a campaign carries its own punishment.

The attacking side is the one that has a positive purpose and is therefore likely to regard the great campaign as its own preferred means of action. Without intending at this point to define the concepts of attack and defense in any detail, we must add that, even for the defender, a confrontation is the only effective means of sooner or later coming to grips with his situation and solving his problem.

But then the human spirit recoils even more from the idea of a decision brought about by a single blow. Here all action is compressed into a single point in time and space. Under these conditions, a man may dimly feel that his powers cannot be developed and brought to bear in so short a period. And much would be gained if he could have more time, even if there is no reason to suppose that this would work in his favor.

All this is sheer illusion, yet not to be dismissed on that account. The very weakness that assails anyone who has to make an important decision may affect even a leader more strongly who is called upon to decide a matter of such far-reaching consequences by a single blow. That is why senior-level leaders have always tried to find ways of avoiding a decisive campaign and of reaching their goals by other means—or of quietly abandoning it.

Our conviction that only a great campaign can produce a major decision is founded not on an abstract concept of conflict alone, but rather on experience. Since time began, only great victories have paved the way for great results— certainly for the attacking side and, to some degree, also for the defense.

The decision that is brought about by a great campaign does not depend entirely on the confrontation itself, the scale of the forces engaged, or the intensity of the victory. It depends on countless other factors that affect the conflict potential of each side. But by committing the major part of their available strength to this gigantic duel, both sides initiate a major decision.

It may not be the only decision, but it is the first, and as such will affect all those that follow. Therefore, the purpose of a great campaign is to act more or less according to circumstances, but always as the provisional center of gravity of the entire campaign.

A leader who enters each campaign with the true winning spirit, the faith, the feeling, and the conviction that he must and will defeat his opponent will likely try to tip the scales of the first campaign with everything he has, hoping and striving to win everything.

To repeat: The decision that is brought about by the campaign partly depends on the confrontation itself—its scale, and the size of the forces involved—and partly on the magnitude of the success. What a leader can do to heighten the significance of the campaign in the first respect is quite obvious.

We only wish to point out that, as the scale of the campaign grows, so does the number of additional circumstances that are decided by it. Therefore, leaders with enough self-confidence to go for great decisions have always managed to deploy a significant bulk of their forces in a major campaign without seriously neglecting other areas.

The success or, more properly, the degree of a victory depends mainly on four factors:

1. The strategy and tactical pattern according to which the campaign is fought
2. The terrain*
3. The composition of the forces
4. The relative strength of the opposing forces

A leader can use all these means to make a campaign decisive. Of course, they carry their own risks.

Yet, the fact that these matters are important does not mean that they are complex and obscure. Far from it: Everything is quite simple and needs only moderate skill in planning. The great requirements are the gifts of luckily

---

* Terrain is interpreted here to indicate the marketplace, the supply chain, and any other physical and logistical factors that would be part of a competitive confrontation.

sizing up a situation, of persistency, and of a youthful, enterprising spirit—all of them heroic qualities to which we shall have to refer again.

Clearly, most of these are not qualities that can be acquired through book learning. If they can be taught at all, a leader will have to receive his instruction from sources other than the printed word.

The impulse to fight a great campaign, the unhampered instinctive movement toward it, must emanate from a sense of one's own powers and the absolute conviction of necessity. In other words, it comes from innate courage and perception, sharpened by experience of responsibility.

STRATEGIC MEANS OF EXPLOITING VICTORY

The preparations leading up to victory are a most difficult task, and one for which the strategist seldom receives due credit. His hour of glory and praise comes when he exploits his victory.

A number of questions arise to which we shall address ourselves in time:

- What may be the actual purpose of a campaign?
- How does it fit into the general pattern of the total conflict?
- To what extent do conditions allow a victory to run its course?
- At what point does it reach its culmination?

Meanwhile, what remains true under all imaginable conditions is that no victory will be effective without pursuit. And no matter how brief the exploitation of victory, it must always go further than an immediate follow-up. Rather than repeat that fact at every opportunity, we will spend a moment on it now.

Pursuit of a defeated opponent begins the moment he concedes the fight and abandons his position. Previous movement either way has nothing to do with this. It is part of the development of the campaign itself. At this juncture, victory, while assured, is usually still limited and modest in its dimensions.

Little positive advantage would be gained in the normal course of events unless victory was consummated by pursuit. It is usually only then, as we have said, that the trophies, which will embody the victory, tend to be taken.

The leader's own energies have been sapped by mental and physical exertion, so it happens that, for purely human reasons, less is achieved than was possible. What does get accomplished is due to the supreme leader's ambition, energy, and, quite possibly, his callousness.

Immediate pursuit leads us to the following conclusion:

The importance of the victory is chiefly determined by the vigor with which the immediate pursuit is carried out. In other words, pursuit makes up the second act of the victory and in many cases is more important than the first.

Strategy at this point draws near to tactics in order to receive the completed assignment from it. In the continuation of the pursuit we can again distinguish three gradations: The first consists in merely following the opponent, the second in exerting pressure on him, and the third in cutting him off.

RETREAT AFTER A LOST ENGAGEMENT

When an engagement is lost, the strength of the unit is broken. Its morale is broken even more than its physical strength. A second engagement without the help of new and favorable factors would mean outright defeat. That is an axiom. It is in the nature of things that a retreat should be continued until the balance of power is reestablished, whether by means of reinforcements or the cover of strong defenses, or the overextension of the opponent.

The magnitude of the losses, the extent of the defeat, and, what is even more important, the nature of the rival will determine how soon the moment of equilibrium will return. There are indeed many instances of a beaten force being able to rally only a short distance away without its situation having changed at all since the engagement. The explanation lies either in the low morale of the victor or in the fact that the superiority won in an engagement was not enough to drive its impact home.

In order to utilize any weakness or mistake on the part of the rival, and especially in order to keep morale as high as possible, it is absolutely necessary to make a slow retreat, boldly confronting the pursuer whenever he tries to make too much of his advantage. The retreats of great leaders and experienced organizations are always like the retreat of a wounded lion.

When a dangerous position has to be abandoned, time is often wasted on trivial formalities, thereby compounding the danger. In such a case, everything depends on getting away as quickly as possible. Experienced leaders consider this to be very important. But it should not be confused with a general retreat.

The degree of difficulty involved in a retreat depends, of course, on whether the engagement was fought on favorable terms and on the severity of the confrontation. A lost campaign always tends to have an enfeebling, disintegrating effect. The immediate need is to reassemble and to recover order, courage, and confidence in the personnel.

Chapter 8

Attack and Defense

Clausewitz makes these key points about attack and defense:

- We maintain unequivocally that the form of confrontation that we call defense offers greater probability of victory than attack.
- The essence of defense lies in parrying the attack. This implies waiting, which is the main feature of defense and its chief advantage.
- Waiting is such a fundamental feature of all confrontations that conflict is hardly conceivable without it.
- The idea of a confrontation originates with the defense, which does have confrontation as its immediate object.
- A sudden powerful transition to the offensive is the greatest moment for the defense.
- A campaign is defensive if we await the attack. It is defensive if we wait for our area to be occupied.
- The ultimate object of attack is not fighting; rather, it is possession.
- The object of defense is preservation. It is easier to hold ground than to take it.
- The defensive form of conflict is not a simple shield, but a shield made up of well-directed movements.
- Once the defender has gained an important advantage, defense has done its work.
- All campaigns that are known for their so-called delaying actions were calculated primarily to neutralize the opponent by making him exhaust himself.
- The choice between an offensive and defensive campaign may be determined by the rival's plans or by the characteristics of both organizations and their leaders.

Before going into details about attack and defense, Clausewitz summarizes earlier discussed topics: superior numbers, decisive engagements, comparative advantage, and leadership.

We previously pointed to the great importance of superior numbers in an engagement and, concurrently, of superior numbers in general from the point of view of strategy. In its turn, that implies the importance of relative strength, on which we must now add a few detailed observations. An impartial student of modern conflict must admit that superior numbers are becoming more decisive with each passing day.

The principle of bringing the maximum possible strength to the decisive engagement must therefore rank rather higher than it did in the past. The courage and morale of an organization have always increased its physical strength and always will. But there are periods in history when great psychological advantage was gained by superior administration and equipment; in others, the same result was achieved by superior mobility.

Sometimes it was a matter of novel tactics. At other times the art of conflict revolved around efforts to exploit terrain skillfully on large and comprehensive lines. On occasion, leaders have managed to gain great advantages over one another by such means. But efforts of this type have declined, making way for simpler and more natural procedures.

If we take an unbiased look at the experiences of the recent conflicts, we must admit that those means have almost disappeared, both from the campaign as a whole and particularly from the major campaign. Today, organizations are so much alike in training and equipment that there is little difference in such matters between the best and the worst of them.

Education may still make a considerable difference between technologies, but what it usually comes down to is that one side invents improvements and first puts them to use. And the other side promptly copies them. Even the senior leaders, as far as their efficacy is concerned, have pretty much the same views and methods.

The only remaining factor that can produce marked superiority, aside from familiarity with conflict, consists of the talents of the leader, which hardly bear a constant relationship to the cultural standards of the organization and are completely left to chance. The decisive importance of relative strength increases the closer we approach a state of balance in all the preceding factors.

What follows is Clausewitz's discussion of defense:

THE CONCEPT OF DEFENSE

What is the concept of defense? The parrying of a blow. What is its characteristic feature? Awaiting the blow. It is this feature that turns any action into a defensive one. It is the only test by which defense can be distinguished from attack. Pure defense, however, would be completely contrary to the idea of conflict, since it would mean that only one side was waging it.

A partial engagement is defensive if we await the advance of the opponent. Therefore, defense can only be relative, and the characteristic feature of waiting should be applied only to the basic concept, not to all of its components.

A campaign, then, is defensive if we await the attack—await, specifically, the appearance of the rival. A campaign is also defensive if we wait for our area to be occupied. In each of these cases the characteristic of waiting and parrying is germane to the general idea without being in dispute with the concept of conflict.

But if we are really waging a campaign, we must return the opponent's blows. And these offensive acts in a defensive conflict come under the heading of defense. In other words, our offensive takes place within our own positions or areas of operations.

Thus, a defensive campaign can be fought in offensive encounters. And in a defensive clash, we can employ our units offensively. Thus, the defensive form of conflict is not a simple shield, but rather a shield made up of well-directed movements.

COMMENTARY

Clausewitz talks about a "defensive campaign [that] can be fought in offensive encounters." He makes the convincing statement that there must be an attack or counterattack component to defense.

The classic case of Xerox (previously mentioned in Chapter 3) illustrates his concept:

Decades ago when Xerox created the market for xerography, the company initially focused on large companies with its large copiers. If we introduce Clausewitz's concept of defense into this example, Xerox used passive resistance to defend its position. That is, it left exposed a vast market of small- and midsize companies for small, table-top copiers.

Astute Japanese makers of copiers, such as Canon, Sharp, and Ricoh, saw the opening and attacked that vacant market without opposition. Once secured with a solid foothold in North America, they made the next expansive move of going upscale, where they confronted Xerox head-on in its big copier stronghold.

That scene occurred in the 1970s while the industry was at the introductory stage of the industry and product life cycles. It can be argued that Xerox could be excused since various user applications were not fully explored at the time, nor had all user segments surfaced.

Certainly, to the company's credit, Xerox defended its position over the following decades and successfully counterattacked to recover a good deal of its market share. Even today, "make a Xerox copy" remains a generally accepted term for product identification, regardless of the brand of copier.

Whereas there can be exceptions to Clausewitz's advice, the prudent approach is still valid that "the defensive form of conflict is not a simple shield, but a shield made up of well-directed movements."

ADVANTAGES OF DEFENSE

What is the object of defense? Preservation. It is easier to hold ground than to take it. What follows is that defense is easier than attack, assuming both sides have equal means. Just what is it that makes preservation and protection so much easier? It is that time allowed to pass unused accumulates to the credit of the defender. He reaps where he did not sow.

Any omission of attack—whether from bad judgment, fear, or lethargy—accrues to the defender's benefit. It is a benefit rooted in the concept and object of defense; it is in the nature of all defensive action. Another benefit, one that arises solely from the nature of conflict, derives from the advantage of position, which tends to favor the defense.

Having outlined these general concepts, we now turn to the substance. Tactically, every engagement, large or small, is defensive if we leave the initiative to our opponent and await his appearance. From that moment on we can employ all offensive means without losing the advantages of the defensive—that is, the advantages of waiting and the advantages of position.

At the next stage, the conflict as a whole replaces the campaign and the entire area of operations. In both cases, defense remains the same as at the strategic and tactical levels.

We have already indicated in general terms that defense is easier than attack. But defense has a passive purpose: preservation. And attack has a positive one: conquest. The latter increases one's own capacity to wage conflict; the former does not.

Thus, in order to state the relationship precisely, we must say that the defensive form of conflict is intrinsically stronger than the offensive. This is the point we have been trying to make. It is implicit in the nature of the matter; experience has confirmed it again and again.

If defense is the stronger form of conflict, it has a negative object in that it should be used only so long as weakness compels. And it should be abandoned as soon as we are strong enough to pursue a positive objective.

When one has used defensive measures successfully, a more favorable balance of strength is usually created. Thus, the natural course in conflict is to begin defensively and end by attacking. It would, therefore, contradict the very idea of conflict to regard defense as its final purpose.

In other words, a conflict in which victories were used only defensively without the intention of counterattacking would be as absurd as a campaign in which the principle of absolute defense and passivity were to dictate every action.

The soundness of this general idea could be challenged by citing many examples of conflict in which the ultimate purpose of defense was purely defensive, without any thought being given to a counteroffensive. This line of argument would be possible if one forgot that a general concept is under discussion. The examples that could be cited to prove the opposite must all be classed as cases in which the possibility of a counteroffensive had not yet arisen.

Now that we have defined the concept of defense and have indicated its limits, we return once more to our claim that defense is the stronger form of waging conflict.

Close analysis and comparison of attack and defense will prove the point beyond all doubt. For the present, we shall merely indicate the inconsistencies when tested by experience. If attack were the stronger form, there would be no case for using the defensive, since its purpose is only passive. No one would want to do anything but attack. Defense would be pointless.

Conversely, it is natural that the greater object is bought by greater sacrifice. Anyone who believes himself strong enough to employ the weaker form, attack, can have the higher aim in mind. The lower aim can only be chosen by those who need to take advantage of the stronger form, defense.

Experience shows that, given two areas of operations, it is practically unknown for the weaker to attack and the stronger to stay on the defensive. The opposite has always happened everywhere and amply proves that leaders accept defense as the stronger form, even when they personally would rather attack.

COMMENTARY

Clausewitz acknowledges that the inclination is strong "even when they personally would rather attack." Yet, he presents a convincing and lucid argument for using the defense, as long as there is a "parrying" or offensive component to the defense.

THE RELATIONSHIP BETWEEN ATTACK AND DEFENSE IN TACTICS

First, let us examine the factors that lead to victory in an engagement. At this stage we are not concerned with numerical superiority, courage, training, or other qualities of an organization. All of these as a rule depend on matters beyond that part of the art of conflict we are concerned with here. In any case, their bearing would be the same on attack and defense.

Even general superiority of numbers is not relevant, since numbers, too, are usually a given quantity in which a leader has no say. Moreover, these matters have no special bearing on attack and defense.

Only three things seem to us to produce decisive advantages: (1) surprise, (2) the benefit of terrain, and (3) concentric (envelopment) attack.

Surprise becomes effective when we suddenly face the opponent at one point with far more personnel than he expected. This type of numerical superiority is quite distinct from numerical superiority in general. It is the most powerful medium in the art of conflict. The ways in which the advantage of terrain contributes toward victory are fairly obvious.

COMMENTARY

Clausewitz's advice takes on greater meaning if you compare "terrain" to the overall characteristics of the marketplace. Further, to take advantage of the "three things [that] produce decisive advantages," the defender must maintain strong customer relationships, support a firm market infrastructure, reinforce a reliable logistical framework, and strengthen a credible company or brand reputation. In particular, the underpinning for those advantages should rely on sustaining ongoing intelligence about the unique characteristics and changing behaviors of the markets.

For example, Caterpillar, the giant construction and mining equipment maker, is collecting, storing, and dissecting huge volumes of digital information, also known as big data. The company is factory-installing into its trucks, backhoes, bulldozers, and other machinery sensors, radios, GPS receivers, and specialized software.

The move is all part of Caterpillar's global technology platform that connects to an intelligent network that can monitor its equipment and provide beneficial reports on equipment repairs, operator usage patterns, and other valuable nuggets of information.

Disseminating those reports to equipment owners and dealers solidifies relationships along the supply chain. For Caterpillar's management, the ongoing flow of intelligence provides fresh selling opportunities for marketing, solid intelligence for service engineers to preempt and solve potential equipment problems, and meaningful information to product developers for new product designs and applications.

What is the relationship of attack and defense to these matters? Bearing in mind the three elements of victory already described, the answer must be this: The attacker is favored by only a small part of the first and third factors, while the second factor is available to the defender.

The one advantage the attacker possesses is that he is free to strike at any point along the whole line of defense, and in full force. The defender, on the other hand, is able to surprise his opponent constantly throughout the engagement by the strength and direction of his counterattacks.

For the attacker it is easier to surround the whole opposing force and cut it off than it is for the defender. The latter is tied to his position and has thereby presented the attacker with an objective.

But the attacker's envelopment and its advantages are applicable only to the whole position. For in the course of the engagement, it is easier for the defender to attack segments of the opposite force concentrically. As we have already said, the defender is better placed to spring surprises by the strength and direction of his own attacks.

It is self-evident that it is the defender who primarily benefits from the terrain. His superior ability to produce surprise by virtue of the strength and direction of his own attack stems from the fact that the attack has to approach in ways that can be easily observed. The defender's position, on the other hand, is concealed and virtually invisible to his opponent until the decisive moment arrives.

And yet, no matter how great the advantage of being free to choose a position and become familiar with it before the action, and no matter how plain it is that the defender is in the entrenched position, he is bound to cause far more surprise than the attacker.

This view does not entirely preclude defending one's ground in a partly passive manner, for to do so offers such decisive advantages that it is frequently done in the course of a campaign. But usually the passive defense of terrain is no longer dominant, which is all we are concerned with here.

If the offensive were to invent some major new expedient, the defensive will also have to change its methods. But it will always be certain of having the benefit of terrain, and this will generally ensure its natural superiority.

THE RELATIONSHIP BETWEEN ATTACK AND DEFENSE IN STRATEGY

Part of strategic success lies in timely preparation for a tactical victory. The greater the strategic success is, the greater the likelihood of a victorious engagement will be. The rest of strategic success lies in the exploitation of a victory won. The more strategy has been able to exploit a victorious campaign, the more completely the fruits of the hard-won victory can be harvested—then, the greater the success.

The main factors responsible for bringing about or facilitating such a success, in strategic effectiveness, are the following:

1. The advantage of terrain
2. Surprise, either by actual engagement or by deploying unexpected strength, at certain points
3. Concentric attack
4. Strengthening the area of operations
5. Obtaining popular support
6. The exploitation of moral factors

What is the relationship of attack and defense with regard to these factors? In strategy as well as in tactics, the defense enjoys the advantage of terrain, while the attack has the advantage of initiative.

As regards surprise and initiative, however, it must be noted that they are infinitely more important and effective in strategy than in tactics. Tactical initiative can rarely be expanded into a major victory. However, a strategic one has often brought the whole conflict to an end at a stroke. On the other hand, the use of this device assumes major mistakes on the opponent's part. Consequently, it will not do much to tip the scales in favor of attack.

Surprising the rival by concentrating superior strength at certain points is again comparable to the analogous case in tactics. If the defender were compelled to spread his forces over several points, the attacker would obviously reap the advantage of being able to throw his full strength against any one of them. Yet if, for some reason, the attacker has to advance with divided forces, the defender obviously reaps the benefit of being able to attack a part of his opponent with his own full strength.

COMMENTARY

Clausewitz supports his viewpoint about "surprising the rival by concentrating superior strength at certain points" with these comments from previous chapters:

"As much resources as possible should be brought into the engagement at the decisive point. Whether these forces prove adequate or not, we will at least have done everything in our power" (Chapter 6).
"Conflicts consist of a large number of engagements, great and small, simultaneous or consecutive. Each of these has a specific purpose relating to the whole" (Chapter 7).

If defense is moved to the opponent's area and gets involved in offensive operations, it will be transformed into a further liability of the offensive. The offensive is not composed of active elements alone, any more than the defensive is made up solely of passive elements. Indeed, any attack that does not immediately lead to peace must end on the defensive.

Thus, if all elements of defense that occur during an offensive are weakened by the very fact that they are part of the offensive, then we must regard this as another general liability pertaining to it. This is not simply hairsplitting—far from it: This is the greatest disadvantage of all offensive actions.

Therefore, when a strategic attack is being planned one should, from the start, give very close attention to this point—namely, that the defensive will follow. This matter will be discussed in greater detail in strategic planning.

The important moral forces that sometimes permeate conflict may occasionally be used by a leader to invigorate his personnel. These influences may be found on the side of defense as well as that of attack. At least one can say that the ones that especially favor attack, such as panic and confusion in the opponent's ranks, do not normally emerge until after the decisive blow has been struck.

And they seldom have much bearing on its course. All this should suffice to justify our proposition that defense is a stronger form of conflict than attack.

We still have to mention a minor factor that so far has been left out of account. It is courage: the organization's sense of superiority that springs from the awareness that one is taking the initiative. This attraction is a real one, but it is soon overlaid by the stronger and more general spirit that an organization derives from its victories or defeats, and by the talent or incompetence of its leader.

THE CHARACTER OF STRATEGIC DEFENSE

We have already stated that defense is simply the more effective form of conflict. It is a means to win a victory that enables one to take the offensive after superiority has been gained—that is, to proceed to the active objective of the conflict.

Even where the only point of the conflict is to maintain the status quo, the fact remains that merely parrying a blow goes against the essential nature of conflict. Once the defender has gained an important advantage, defense as such has done its work.

While he is enjoying this advantage, he must strike back, or he will court destruction. Prudence bids him strike while the iron is hot and to use the advantage to prevent a second onslaught.

How, when, and where that reaction is to begin depends, of course, on many other conditions, which we shall detail subsequently. For the moment we shall simply say that this transition to the counterattack must be accepted as a tendency inherent in defense—indeed, as one of its essential features.

A sudden powerful transition to the offensive is the greatest moment for the defense. If it is not in the leader's mind from the start or, rather, if it is not an integral part of his idea of defense, he will never be persuaded of the superiority of the defensive form.

COMMENTARY

Clausewitz's discussion on defense and attack presented thus far, as well as in the sections that follow, amply covers the topic in its numerous dimensions. The essential point he consistently repeats is that defense is not passive; it must include the "sudden powerful transition to the offensive."

Accordingly, if you recognize the value of Clausewitz's concepts, consider incorporating his thinking into orientation sessions for senior-level managers who formulate competitive strategies at the strategic level. Similarly, think about bolstering the training of mid-level managers by adding the appropriate portions of attack and defense at the tactical level.

It is for you to decide how to divide your personnel between strategic and tactical applications. For instance, where would individuals with job titles of marketing manager, product manager, and sales manager be trained?*

Further, a case can be made for including sales personnel who are assigned to a territory in similar training. The idea is based on thinking

---

* It is my firm opinion that personnel in middle management positions should be able to think strategically with a long-term outlook about their product line or territory of responsibility. Such a role should be in addition to the immediacy of tactically confronting an aggressive competitor.

of a sales representative as a general manager of a sales territory who should have a long-term strategic outlook for the growth and development of the assigned territory, as well as for the tactical day-by-day responsibility of obtaining sales and developing a competent defense against competitors. (Some forward-looking organizations have already accepted this approach.)

Clausewitz continues:

An aggressor often decides on conflict before the innocent defender does. And if he contrives to keep his preparations sufficiently secret, he may well take his victim unaware.

Conflict, then, serves the purpose of the defense more than that of the aggressor. It is only aggression that calls forth defense, and conflict along with it. When one side takes the field before the other, it is usually for reasons that have nothing to do with the intention of attack or defense. They are not the motives, but, rather, frequently the result of an early appearance.

The side that is ready first and sees a significant advantage in a surprise campaign will, for that reason, take the offensive. The side that is slower to prepare can to some degree make up for the consequent disadvantage by exploiting the advantages of defense.

Generally speaking, however, the ability to profit from being the first to be ready must be considered an advantage to the attacker. Still, this general advantage is not essential in every specific case.

Consequently, if we are to conceive of defense as it should be, it is this: All means for conflict are prepared to the utmost. The organization is fit for campaign and familiar with it. The leader will let the rival come on, not from confused indecision and fear, but rather by his own choice, coolly and deliberately. Thus constituted, defense will no longer cut so sorry a figure when compared to attack.

INTERACTION BETWEEN ATTACK AND DEFENSE

The time has come to consider defense and attack separately, insofar as they can be separated. We shall start with defense for the following reasons:

While it is quite natural and even indispensable to base the principles of defense on those that govern attack and vice versa, there must be a third aspect that serves as a point of departure for the whole chain of ideas that makes it tangible.

Our first issue, therefore, concerns this point: Consider in the abstract how conflict originates. Essentially, conflict does not originate with the attack, because the ultimate object of attack is not fighting: Rather, it is possession.

The idea of a conflict originates with the defense, which does have confrontation as its immediate object. Repulse is directed only toward an attack, which is therefore a prerequisite to it. The attack, however, is not directed toward defense but toward a different goal, possession.

Thus, the side that first introduces the element of confrontation is also the side that establishes the initial laws of conflict. That side is the defense. What is under discussion here is not a specific instance but a general, abstract case, which must be postulated to advance theory.

We now know where to find the fixed point that is located outside the interaction of attack and defense. It lies with the defense. If this argument is correct, the defender must establish ground rules for his conduct even if he has no idea what the attacker means to do. And this ground must certainly include the disposition of his forces.

The attacker, so long as he knows nothing about his adversary, will have no guidelines on which to base the use of his forces. All he can do is to take his forces with him—in other words, take possession by means of his forces. Indeed, that is what actually happens, for it is one thing to assemble a force and another to use it.

An aggressor may take his forces with him on the chance that he may have to use them, and though he may take possession of an area, he has not yet committed a positive act in a confrontation. It is the defender, who not only concentrates his forces but also disposes them in readiness for action, who first commits an act that really fits the concept of conflict.

We now come to the second issue: What are the underlying causes that initially motivate the defense, before it has even considered the possibility of being attacked? Obviously, it is an opponent's advance with a view to taking possession, which we have treated as the basis for the initial steps of a confrontation.

Once dispositions have been established, the attack will be directed toward them. And new ground rules of defense will be based on an examination of the means used by the attack. This brief analysis was necessary to provide somewhat greater clarity and substance to our subsequent discussion.

COMMENTARY

The essence of Clausewitz's meaning of "disposition of forces" is to fight according to your own circumstances and not according to your competitor's. He further indicates that "the defender must set the ground rules." In turn, that translates to leading with your strength against the weakness of your competitor.

As the ancient Chinese strategist Sun Tzu comments: "One mark of a great strategist is that he fights on his own terms or fights not at all."

In practice, then, either through the use of the familiar SWOT (strengths, weaknesses, opportunities, threats) analysis or the standard marketing mix (product, price, promotion, and place) comparisons, you can select the means for making "a sudden powerful transition to the offensive."

Consequently, if you are the defender, the disposition of your forces can place the competitor at a disadvantage. That is, of course, unless he knows the disposition of your forces, so Clausewitz advises to "keep preparations sufficiently secret, [or] he may well take his victim unaware."

TYPES OF RESISTANCE

The essence of defense lies in parrying the attack. This in turn implies waiting, which for us is the main feature of defense and also its chief advantage. Since defense in confrontations cannot simply consist of passive endurance, waiting will not be absolute, but only relative. In terms of space, it relates to the area of operations or the position.

As for time, the defender merely awaits the attack on his territory or position. Once the adversary has attacked, any more or less offensive move made by the defender does not invalidate the concept of defense, for its salient feature and chief advantage, waiting, has been established.

Defense is thus composed of two distinct parts: waiting and acting. By linking the former to a definite objective that precedes action, we have been able to merge the two into one whole. But a defensive action—especially a large-scale campaign—will not, in terms of time, consist of two great phases.

The first is pure waiting and the second pure action. It will alternate between these two conditions, so waiting may run like a continuous thread through the whole period of defense.

The nature of the matter demands that much importance should be attached to waiting. To be sure, earlier strategists never gave it the status of an independent concept. But in practice it has continuously served as a guideline.

Waiting is such a fundamental feature of all confrontations that conflict is hardly conceivable without it. Hence, we shall often have occasion to revert to it by pointing out its effect in the dynamic play of forces.

We should now like to explain how the principle of waiting runs through the entire period of defense, and how the successive stages of defense originate in it. Defense of a position or in a campaign is a tactical matter. Only when it is completed can it serve as the starting point of strategic activity. Therefore, we shall take the defense of an area of operations as the subject that will best illustrate the conditions of defense.

We have pointed out that waiting and acting are both essential parts of defense. Without the former, it would not be defense; without the latter, it would not be conflict.

This conception has already led us to argue that defense is simply the stronger form of a confrontation, the one that makes the opponent's defeat more certain. We must insist on this interpretation, partly because any other will eventually lead to absurdity, partly because the more vivid and total this impression is, the more it will strengthen the total act of defense.

We must insist that the idea of retaliation is fundamental to all defense. Otherwise, no matter how much damage the first phase of reaction may have done to the opponent, the proper balance would still be wanting in the restoration of the dynamic relationship between attack and defense.

Since defense is tied to the idea of waiting, the aim of defeating the adversary will be valid only on the condition that there is an attack. If no attack is forthcoming, it is understood that the defense will be content to hold its own.

Therefore, this is its aim or, rather, its primary aim, during the period of waiting. The defense will be able to reap the benefits of the stronger form of conflict only if it is willing to be satisfied with this more modest goal.

Since the advantages of waiting also increase with each phase, it follows that each successive stage of defense is more effective than the last and that this form of confrontation gains in effectiveness the further it is removed from attack. We are not afraid of being accused on this account of believing that the most passive kind of defense is the strongest.

Each successive stage, far from being intended to weaken the act of resistance, is meant merely to prolong and postpone it. Surely there is no contradiction in saying that one is able to resist more effectively in a strong and suitably entrenched position—and that, after the opponent has wasted half his strength on it, a counterattack will be that much more effective.

What we do maintain is that with each successive stage of defense, the defender's predominance will increase, as will the strength of his reaction. Can we say that the advantages that derive from an intensified defense are to be had without cost? Not at all. The sacrifices with which they must be purchased will increase equally.

Whenever we wait for the opponent inside our own territory, no matter how close to where the decisive action may be fought, the adversary's forces will enter our area of operations, which will entail sacrifices. If we had attacked him first, the damage would have been incurred by him.

The sacrifices tend to increase whenever we fail to advance toward the adversary to attack him. If we intend to give defensive battle and thus leave the initiative and the timing up to the opponent, the possibility exists that he may well remain for a considerable time in the area he holds.

Thus, the time we gain by his postponement of the decision has to be paid for in this manner. The sacrifices become even more noticeable in the case of a retreat into the territory.

However, the reduction of the defender's strength that is caused by all of these sacrifices will usually affect his fighting forces only later, not immediately. It is frequently so indirect as to be barely noticeable.

Thus, the defender tries to increase his immediate strength by paying for it late. To assess the results of these various forms of resistance, we have to examine the purpose of the adversary's attack, which is to gain possession of our territory or at least a substantial part of it.

Therefore, so long as the attacker is not in possession and so long as fear of our strength has prevented him from entering our territory or seeking out our position, the objects of the defense have been accomplished. Our defensive dispositions have proved successful.

Admittedly, this is only a negative success, which will not directly produce enough strength for a real counterattack. But it may do so in an indirect way, gradually. The time that passes is lost to the aggressor. Time lost is always a disadvantage that is bound in some way to weaken him who loses it.

The tension continues to exist; the decision is still to come. So long as the defender's strength increases every day while the attacker's diminishes, the absence of a decision is in the former's best interest because the effects of the general losses to which the defender has continually exposed himself are finally catching up with him.

The point of culmination will necessarily be reached when the defender must make up his mind and act, when the advantages of waiting have been completely exhausted. There is, of course, no infallible means of telling when that point has come. A great many conditions and circumstances may determine it.

What is it that, broadly speaking, constitutes a decision? In our discussion, we have always assumed a decision to occur in the form of a confrontation. But that is not necessarily so. We can think of any number of engagements by smaller forces that may lead to a change in fortune, either because they really end in extreme losses or because the probabilities of their consequences necessitate the opponent's retreat. No other kind of decision is possible in the territory itself that necessarily follows from the concept of conflict we have proposed.

All campaigns that are known for their so-called delaying actions were calculated primarily to neutralize the opponent by making him exhaust himself. In general, there have been many campaigns that were won on that principle without anyone explicitly saying so.

We believe that we have thus adequately described the considerations that underlie defense and its various phases. By pointing out these chief means of resistance, we hope we have explained clearly how the principle of waiting runs through the whole system and combines with the principle of positive action in such a way that the latter may appear early in one case and late in another. After this, the advantages of waiting will be seen to be exhausted. We believe that we have now surveyed as well as delimited the whole field of defense.

THE ATTACKER

As for the attacker, if the opponent is found in a strong position that he thinks he cannot take, it is the force of the defender that produces this result. What actually halts the aggressor's action is the fear of defeat by the defender's forces, either in major engagements or at particularly important points. But he is not likely to concede this, at least not openly.

One may admit that even where the decision has been peaceful, it was determined in the last analysis by engagements that did not take place but had merely been offered. In that case, it will be argued, the strategic planning of these engagements, rather than the tactical decision, should be considered the operative principle.

Moreover, strategic planning would be dominant only in cases where defense is conducted by some means other than force. We admit this; however, it brings us to the very point we wanted to make: Where the tactical results of the engagement are assumed to be the basis of all strategic plans, it is always possible that the attacker will proceed on that basis.

He will endeavor above all to be tactically superior with the aim to upset the opponent's strategic planning. The latter, therefore, can never be considered as something independent. It can only become valid when one has reason to be confident of tactical success.

That is why we think it is useful to emphasize that all strategic planning rests on tactical success alone. Whether the solution is arrived at in a confrontation or not is the fundamental basis for the decision.

Only when one has no need to fear the outcome—because of the opponent's character or situation, because the two forces are evenly matched physically and psychologically, or because one's own side is the stronger—can one expect results from strategic combinations alone.

When we look at the history of conflict and find a large number of campaigns in which the attacker broke off his offensive without having fought a decisive battle, we might believe that such combinations have at least great inherent power. And they would normally decide the outcome on their own, whenever one did not need to assume a decisive superiority in tactical situations.

The general conditions from which a conflict arises will also determine its character. This will be discussed later in greater detail, under the heading of plans. But these general conditions have transformed most encounters into conflicting affairs, in which the original hostilities among quarreling interests emerged very much weakened.

This is bound to affect the offensive side of action with particular strength. It is not surprising, therefore, that one can stop such a breathless, hectic attack. That is, where resolution is so faint and paralyzed by a multitude of considerations that it has almost ceased to exist, a mere show of resistance will often suffice.

In many cases the reason for the defender being successful without having to fight does not lie in the fact that he occupies many impregnable positions or is a case where the threatened blow can be paralyzed by a well-planned series of engagements. The real reason is the faintness of the attacker's determination, which makes him hesitate and fear to move.

At this point let us consider how offensive campaigns can fail without a decisive battle being fought:

The aggressor enters a defender's territory, but then begins to have doubts about risking a decisive campaign. He halts and faces his rival, acting as if he had made a conquest and was interested only in protecting it.

In short, he behaves as if it were the opponent's affair to seek a confrontation. All of these are mere pretexts, which a leader uses to delude his organization and even himself.

The truth of the matter is that the opponent's position has been found to be too strong. Here we are not talking of a case in which the aggressor fails to attack because a victory would be of no use to him; rather, he does not have enough resiliency to start a new one.

Next, we would assume that an attack had already taken place and resulted in a genuine success. Rather, we have in mind a case in which the aggressor gets bogged down in the middle of an intended action.

At that point the attacker will wait for a favorable turn of events to exploit. There is, as a rule, no reason to expect such a favorable turn. The very fact that an attack had been intended implies that the immediate future promises no more than the present. It is therefore a fresh delusion.

By way of excusing his inaction, the leader will plead inadequate support and cooperation. He will talk of insurmountable obstacles and look for motives in the most intricately complicated circumstances. Thus, he will fritter his strength away in doing nothing or, rather, in doing too little to bring about anything but failure. Meanwhile, the defender is gaining time, which is what he needs most.

This issue of falsehoods ends by passing up the obvious and simple truth: Failure was due to fear of the rival's forces. That feeling is not merely a matter of bad habit. Its roots lie in the nature of the case.

For instance, no one will admit that the leader's decision to stop or to give up was motivated by the fear that his strength would run out or that he might make new enemies or that his own allies might become too strong. That sort of thing is long kept confidential, possibly forever.

COMMENTARY

Clausewitz's references "excusing his inaction he will plead inadequate support and cooperation [and] talk of insurmountable obstacles." Then, there is the "fear that his strength would run out." Often, these expressions are the result of negative emotions triggered by a range of psychological forces. One of these is an individual's deep-rooted fear of failure, which has the insidious effect of closing down the mind and creating a type of paralysis or inability to take action.

Such responses are particularly troublesome when courage is the essential ingredient when preparing for a defense, followed by offensive action. "The requisite for a man's success as a leader is that he be perfectly brave," declared the eminent strategist, Baron Antoine-Henri de Jomini.

Courage is defined as the act of determination in a specific situation. It becomes a character trait only if it becomes a mental habit. Clausewitz previously pointed out: Intellect in itself is not courage. There are ample numbers of brilliant individuals who simply do not have what it takes to recognize that bold actions are essential elements for timely and appropriate actions—in this instance, defense and attack.

Often, it is up to the individual to arouse the inner sense of courage and push aside the awful feelings that can creep into the mind and take control of his or her actions. That is where training, discipline, and experience need to kick in to overcome negative emotions.

It is also useful to think of a confrontation as a contest of one mind against another mind: the mind of one manager pitted against the mind of a competing manager who may be challenged by similar emotions. You want to be the one who prevails and moves forward.

Let us now examine the employment of these various methods of defense. They are all intensifications of the same thing, each one exacting increased sacrifices on the part of the defender. A leader chooses the method he considers adequate to give his forces the necessary degree of resistance.

Yet to avoid unnecessary losses, he would not retreat any further. It must be admitted, however, that the choice of different methods is already severely limited by other major factors that play a part in defense and are bound to urge him to use one method or another.

The choice between an offensive and defensive campaign may be determined by the rival's plans or by the characteristics of both organizations and its leaders. Finally, the possession or lack of an outstanding position or defensive line may lead to one method or the other.

That influence, however, will normally become decisive only if the relative strengths are not too disproportionate. When they are, relative strength will prevail. History of conflict is full of proof that this has actually occurred, quite apart from the chain of reasoning developed here, through the hidden processes of intuitive judgment, like almost everything that happens in conflict.

We should like to add that this chapter, more than any other of our work, shows that our aim is not to provide new principles and methods of conducting a conflict. Rather, we are concerned with examining the essential content of what has long existed and to trace it back to its basic elements.

THE DEFENSIVE BATTLE

Previously, we stated that in the course of his defense the defender can fight a tactically offensive campaign by seeking out and attacking the rival as soon as he invades his area of operations. Alternatively, he may await the opponent's appearance and then attack him, in which case the campaign is still offensive in a tactical sense, though somewhat modified in form.

Finally, he may actually wait for the opponent to attack his position and then strike back, not only by using part of his force to hold the enemy locally, but also by attacking him with the rest. Naturally, various degrees are possible, running gradually from positive counterattack to local defense.

We cannot here enter into a discussion as to how far this should go or what would be the most favorable ratio between the two elements for the purpose of winning a decisive victory. Where this is the object, we do insist that the offensive element must never be completely absent. And we are convinced that all the consequences of a decisive victory can and do result from this offensive phase, just as they do in a purely offensive battle.

The physical area in strategy is simply a point in space, just as the duration of an encounter is strategically only a moment in time. And a campaign's strategic significance lies not in its course but rather in its outcome and its consequence.

If it were true that total victory could be linked to the offensive elements that are present in every defensive campaign, no basic strategic difference between an offensive and a defensive campaign would exist. That is in fact our own belief, although appearances seem to contradict it.

In the history of conflict, major victories are less often the consequence of defensive engagements than of offensive ones. However, that does not prove that defensive battles are inherently less likely to be victorious. Rather, the defender simply finds himself in markedly different circumstances.

In most cases, he is the weaker belligerent, not only in numbers, but also in terms of his entire situation. Usually he is not or does not believe himself to be able to follow up a victory and is, therefore, satisfied with having repulsed the danger. There is no question that the defender may be handicapped by his numerical weakness and his circumstances.

Frequently, however, what should be seen as the result of necessity has been interpreted as the result of defense. In this absurd manner it has become a basic assumption that defensive campaigns are meant merely to repulse the aggressor, rather than to neutralize him.

We consider this as a most damaging error—in fact, a confusion between form and substance. We maintain unequivocally that the form of confrontation that we call defense not only offers greater probability of victory than attack, but that its victories also can attain the same proportions and results.

Moreover, this applies not only to the aggregate success of all the engagements that make up a campaign, but also to each individual campaign, provided there is no lack of strength and determination.

Chapter 9

Defense of an Area of Operations

Clausewitz makes these key points about defense of an area:

- Defense is the stronger form of an encounter. It leads to the preservation of one's forces and the neutralization of the opponent's.
- A major engagement is a collision between two centers of gravity. The more forces we can concentrate in our center of gravity, the more certain the effect.
- A plan is nothing more than a plan for attacking or defending the main area of operations.
- Sound preparation, composure, confidence, unity, and simplicity will mark the leader's conduct in action.
- The ultimate form of resistance in postponing a decision is making the aggressor wear himself out, rather than defeating him in a confrontation.
- In conflict, strategy calls for economy of strength. The less one can manage with, the better, but manage one must.
- The state of waiting is one of the greatest advantages the defense enjoys over the attack.
- A defense that makes use of the offensive is considered superior.
- Anyone who falls into the habit of thinking and expecting the best of his subordinates at all times is, for that reason alone, unsuited to lead an organization.
- Since most conflicts have been more a matter of observing the rival than of defeating him, it follows that strategic maneuver is characteristic of most campaigns.
- A leader must never expect to move on the narrow ground of imagined security and feel that the means he is using are the only ones possible—and persist in using them even at the thought of their possible inadequacy.
- The first requirement is that the leader applies the right standard of measurement in his plan of operations.

Clausewitz talks in greater detail about these points of defending an area of operations:

Having discussed the most important methods of defense (Chapter 8), we could delay any discussion of the way they fit into an overall plan of defense until the chapter on plans. A plan is, after all, the source of all the lesser plans of attack and defense.

Frequently, a plan is nothing more than a plan for attacking or defending the main area of operations. But at no time have we yet been able to begin our discussion with conflict as a whole, despite the fact that, in a confrontation, it is the whole that governs all the parts, stamps them with its character, and alters them radically.

On the contrary, it seemed necessary to start by thoroughly examining the various parts as separate components. If we had not advanced from the simple to the complex, we should have been swamped by a multitude of vague concepts. More particularly, the variety of interactions that occur in conflict would have constantly confused our ideas.

One more stage remains before we reach the whole: to examine the defense of an area of conflict as a subject in itself and to look for the thread that ties together all the subjects discussed.

Defense, as we see it, is nothing but the stronger form of an encounter. The preservation of one's forces and the neutralization of the opponent's—in a word, victory—is the substance of this struggle. Yet, it can never be its ultimate object. The ultimate object is the preservation of one's own organization and the neutralization of the rival's, which will resolve the conflict and result in a common settlement.

COMMENTARY

A central theme of Clausewitz's concept of defense is anchored to avoiding a passive defense. In turn, it reflects the accumulated lessons of 2,500 years of recorded military history that state the only reason for going on the defensive is to plan for the offensive. Thus, his advice of waiting with the intention of going to the attack is the key ingredient of his theory where the "ultimate object is the preservation of one's own organization and the defeat of the rival's."

In business, defense is often associated with the belt tightening regimen of cost-cutting, shelving new projects, and retreating from exposure to aggressive competitive actions. As is often the case, there is no conscious effort to think of defense as merely a pause to regroup and plan for the period when market conditions change and an offensive plan can be put into motion or to be alert to the unexpected break where a competitor makes an unexpected move and thereby creates a fresh opportunity.

Such an unforeseen move came when H. J. Heinz Co. was sold to Warren Buffett's Berkshire Hathaway and Brazilian-owned private equity firm 3G Capital in 2013. The 144-year-old company owns such brands as Smart Ones, Ore-Ida frozen foods, Heinz beans, and, of course, its market-leading ketchup.

During the period of transition, the active owners, 3G Capital, initiated drastic changes. Eleven of its top 12 executives were replaced. Cost-cutting became rampant at every level. Mass layoffs were begun at its Pittsburgh headquarters and other locations across North America. Individual offices were done away with and even top executives had to work only inches apart at common white industrial tables with one shared filing cabinet per table. And all workers were expected to work longer hours. The draconian changes continued from office to travel, where Spartan levels of expenditures were mandated.

Thus, the order of the day and beyond was efficiency at all cost. Whether the new approaches would choke the company or propel it to growth would be revealed in time.

From Clausewitz's perspective on preservation of the organization, the issues centered on

1. Whether Heinz was suitably protected during the period of transition; that is, was it vulnerable from within where worker attitudes were challenged, and, in the marketplace, where sweeping changes affected the supply chain and end-use customers?
2. To what extent did the changeover create a window of opportunity for an alert rival during that critical period to take an opportunistic view of events and charge in to exploit any areas where Heinz was perceived as vulnerable? (For instance, soon after the purchase, McDonald's announced it would stop using Heinz ketchup in its restaurants.)

Clausewitz continues:

In the context of conflict, what is meant by the opponent's organization? First, this means his capabilities and then his territory. Of course, it means a great many other things as well, which, depending on circumstances, can attain genuine significance. Chief among these are the foreign and domestic political conditions, which are sometimes more decisive than anything else.

Although the opponent's forces and his territory may not represent all his means of making conflict, they will always be the dominant factors and usually exceed all others in importance. It is the territory that sustains them and keeps restoring their strength. Each, then, depends on the other. They give mutual support and are of equal value to each other. But while they interact, they do so with a difference.

If the defender's forces are neutralized—in other words, overcome and incapable of further resistance—the organization is automatically lost. On the other hand, loss of the organization does not automatically entail neutralization of the forces; they can exit of their own accord in order to reenter more easily later on.

Not only the complete neutralization but also any considerable weakening of the fighting forces will generally lead to a loss of territory. Conversely, not every loss of territory automatically leads to a weakening of the forces. It will happen in the long run, of course, but not always within the decisive phase of the conflict.

It follows that it is always more important to preserve or, as the case may be, neutralize forces than to hold on to territory. In other words, the former must be a leader's prime concern. Possessing territory will become an end in itself only where those means are not enough.

Yet, if all the opponent's forces were united in a single force, and if the conflict consisted of a single campaign, possession of the territory would determine that campaign's outcome. The neutralization of the rival's forces, the occupation of his territory, and the safety of one's own would follow automatically.

The question now arises: What will cause the defender to disperse his forces in space? The answer lies in the inadequacy of the victory that he can achieve with his combined forces.

Each victory has its own sphere of influence, if that sphere includes the whole of the opponent's forces and his territory. And if all the components of his strength are carried away, that victory is all that is needed. There will be no need for a division of forces. If, on the other hand, parts of the rival's forces are beyond the scope of our victory, these parts will require special attention.

Only in the case of a small organization is such a concentration of force possible so that its defeat will decide everything. If, however, the area involved is very large, or if one is surrounded on all sides by a powerful alliance of rivals, such a concentration is a practical impossibility. A division of forces then becomes inevitable and, with it, several territories of operation.

COMMENTARY

Clausewitz refers to "several territories of operation." Territories, in turn, can appropriately compare with market segments where competitors routinely battle for dominance. Such is the case with the intense competition going on in the race to dominate the tablet market.

The magnitude of the conflict occurred when Apple, Nokia, and Microsoft each introduced new tablets on the same day in October 2013. Those devices competed for consumer attention against several models released around the same period by other tech heavyweights, including Amazon and Samsung. As the proliferation of various types of tablets accelerated and the skirmishes intensified, the market became more fractured and the competing companies moved to a segmentation strategy.

Microsoft, for example, focused primarily on professionals by offering tablets that double as PCs. Samsung went for a large variety of tablets, some that included a stylus for drawing and taking notes, to cater to different professions and interests. Apple marketed its iPads as versatile devices for both work and play. Amazon offered low-priced tablets to get people to buy content from its stores.

With any movement to concentrate resources on a segment of the market, the following are generally accepted criteria for attack and defense:

- Measurable. Can you quantify the segment by types of factories, numbers of engineers, or individuals who require specialized services?
- Accessible. Do you have access to the market through a dedicated sales force, distributors/dealers, transportation, or the Internet?
- Substantial. Is the segment of adequate size to warrant your attention to it as a viable segment? Further, is the segment declining, maturing, or growing?
- Profitable. Does concentrating on the segment provide sufficient profitability to make it worthwhile?
- Compatible with competition. To what extent do your major competitors have an interest in the segment? Is it of active interest or of negligible concern to your competitors?
- Effectiveness. Do your people have acceptable skills and resources to serve the segment effectively?
- Defendable. Does your firm have the capabilities to defend itself against the attack of a major competitor—and then be able to go on the offensive?

The scale of a victory's sphere of influence depends on the scale of the victory. In turn, that depends on the size of the defeated force. For this reason, the bow from which the broadest repercussions can be expected will be aimed against that area where the greatest concentration of rival forces can be found.

The larger the force with which the blow is struck, the surer its effect will be. This rather obvious sequence leads us to an analogy that will illustrate it more clearly—that is, the nature and effect of a center of gravity.

A center of gravity is always found where the mass is concentrated most densely. It presents the most effective target for a blow. Furthermore, the heaviest blow is that struck by the center of gravity. The same holds true in conflict. The forces of each opponent—whether a single rival or several—have a certain unity and therefore some cohesion.

Where there is cohesion, the analogy of the center of gravity can apply. Thus, these forces will possess certain centers that, by their movement and direction, govern the rest. And those centers of gravity will be found wherever the forces are most concentrated.

COMMENTARY

Clausewitz talks of cohesion and refers to the center of gravity "where the mass is concentrated most densely." Also known as the decisive point, it is "the most effective target for a blow."

What, specifically, is a decisive point and how can you find it? There are numerous possibilities for selecting a center of gravity or decisive point for a concentrated effort. The general guideline is that it represents the competitor's specific weakness or general area of vulnerability.

The search begins by conducting a line-by-line comparative analysis that would expose your strengths against a competitor's weaknesses. The analysis includes reviewing, in as much depth as time and resources allow, a wide range of factors, from markets to technology, products, and services to corporate culture and the caliber of personnel.

It covers leadership and financial resources as well as all those areas that affect the efficiency and performance of a company's ability to deal with a competitive situation. When it is completed, you are better able to develop a defensive/offensive strategy that aims a blow at a decisive point.[*]

---

[*] See the Appendix for tools to assist you in conducting a comparative analysis.

In conflict, the effect produced on a center of gravity is determined and limited by the cohesion of the parts. In either case, a blow may well be stronger than the resistance requires. In that case it may strike nothing but air and be a waste of energy.

There is a decided difference between the cohesion of a single group, led into a confrontation under the personal command of a single leader, and that of an allied force operating against different areas. In the former, cohesion is at its strongest and unity at its closest. In the other, unity is remote, frequently found only in mutual interests, rather precarious, and imperfect. Cohesion between the parts will usually be very loose and often completely fictitious.

On the one hand, then, the force at which our blow is to be aimed requires that our strength be concentrated to the utmost. On the other hand, any excess is to be regarded as a decided disadvantage, since it involves a waste of energy, which in turn means a lack of strength elsewhere.

It is, therefore, a major act of strategic judgment to distinguish these centers of gravity in the opponent's forces and their spheres of effectiveness. One will constantly be called upon to estimate the effect that an advance or a retreat by part of the forces on either side will have upon the rest.

Far from believing we have discovered a new technique, we are merely providing a rationale for the actions in history that serves to explain their connection with the nature of the problem. The last section of this book will describe how this idea of a center of gravity in the opponent's force operates throughout the plan. In fact, that is where the matter properly belongs. We have merely drawn on it here in order not to leave a gap in the present argument.

Our reflections are intended to demonstrate the general reasons for dividing one's forces. Basically, there are two conflicting interests: One, possession of the territory, tends to disperse the forces; the other, a stroke at the center of gravity of the opponent's forces, tends to keep them concentrated.

This is how operational areas are created. An area and the forces positioned there are divided in such a way that any decision obtained by the main force in a particular area directly affects the whole and carries everything along with it. We say *directly,* since any decision reached in one particular operational area is also bound to have a more or less remote effect on adjoining areas.

We want to reiterate emphatically that our definitions are aimed only at the centers of certain concepts. We neither wish for nor can give them sharp outlines.

Our position, then, is that an area of conflict, be it large or small, represents the sort of unity in which a single center of gravity can be identified. That is the place where the decision should be reached. A victory at that point is in its fullest sense identical with the defense of the area of operations.

Defense, however, consists of two different elements: the decision and the period of waiting—and with the connection between the two. We must begin by pointing out that the state of waiting is not the sum total of the term "defense." It is, however, the phase by which a defense approaches its goal.

So long as an active unit has not abandoned the area assigned to it, the tension that an attack creates on both sides will continue. Only a decision can put an end to it. And that decision, whatever it may be, can only be considered a fact after either the attacker or the defender has abandoned the area.

So long as a force maintains itself in its area, its defense continues. It is immaterial how much or how little of the area is temporarily occupied by the rival. It is merely lent to him. This conceptualization is meant to clarify the true relationship between the state of waiting and the whole, and is valid only if a decision is really intended.

If one drops the idea of a decision, then the centers of gravity are neutralized. And, in a certain sense, so too are all the forces. At this point, possession of the territory will become a direct objective. In other words, as the importance of possessing increases, the less a decision is actively sought by the contenders and the more the conflict becomes a matter of mutual observation.

There is no denying that a great majority of campaigns are more a state of observation than one of a struggle—a struggle, that is, in which at least one of the parties is determined to come to a decision. We shall, therefore, start by considering the kind of conflict that is completely governed and saturated by the urge for a decision.

In the first instance, the attacker is expected to bring about a decision or it is sought by the defender; for present purposes, it does not matter which. Here the defense of an area will consist of maintaining the position in such a way as to be able to bring about an advantageous decision at any moment. Such a decision may be made up of a single campaign or a series of major engagements.

Even if a campaign were not the most effective means of reaching a decision, the mere fact that it is one of the means of obtaining a decision should be enough to call for the utmost possible concentration of strength permissible under the circumstances.

A major engagement is a collision between two centers of gravity. The more forces we can concentrate in our center of gravity, the more certain and massive the effect will be. Consequently, any partial use of force not directed toward an objective that either cannot be attained by the victory itself or that does not bring about the victory should be condemned.

The basic condition, however, does not consist merely in the greatest possible concentration of forces. They must also be deployed in a way that enables them to fight under sufficiently favorable circumstances.

The various gradations of defense are completely in agreement with these basic conditions. There can, therefore, be no difficulty in establishing a connection between them according to the needs of the individual case. There is only one point that, at first sight, seems self-contradictory, and that is one of the most important points in defense: how to hit the opponent's exact center of gravity.

COMMENTARY

McDonald's, the fast-food chain, illustrates "how to hit the opponent's exact center of gravity." Recognizing that individuals between the ages of 18 and 32 represented an enormous group in which it needed to retain a strong foothold for future growth, McDonald's focused on that particular market segment known as millennials. The competitive issue, however, was that feisty adversaries such as Five Guys, Chipotle, and Subway were after that group as well, thereby threatening McDonald's defense.

While carefully monitoring competitive moves and at the same time observing the group's changing tastes, McDonald's launched its market response in 2013 with a new food offering: McWrap. The result of 2 years of secret preparation and testing, the product was a chicken-based tortilla that could be made to order in 60 seconds and would qualify for the stringent fast-food requirements of time, speed, and convenience.

Continuing with its targeted strategy, McDonald's also recognized the diversity of tastes in global markets where there were numerous centers of gravity. The company permitted alterations in its basic recipe to meet indigenous tastes, while at the same time defending against the offerings of local competitors. Consciously or not, McDonald's actions paralleled Clausewitz's concepts of defense and centers of gravity. (Initial reports after introduction indicated that McWrap was a hit.)

If the defender finds out early enough what roads the opponent will take, he will be able to confront him there, for while defense may anticipate attack, the defender also possesses the inherent advantage over the offensive by being able to make a comeback.

An advance into a rival's area calls for considerable preparations. This will give the defender time to make preparations. And one must not forget that the defender normally needs less time than the attacker and is usually better prepared for defense than for attack.

But while this may be perfectly true in the majority of cases, the possibility still remains that in a particular instance the defense may not be sure of the main route of the opponent's advance. This is more probable when the defense relies on measures that take time, such as the preparation of a strong position.

Furthermore, even where the defender is blocking the line of advance, the attacker can avoid the defender's position by a slight change in his original line of movement. In that case the defender obviously will not await his opponent with the intention of creating a confrontation.

Before we discuss the means that remain available to the defender in this situation, we must examine it more closely and consider the probability of its arising. In every area of conflict, there will be certain objectives that offer the most effective target for an attack.

At this stage we merely want to stipulate the following: If the most advantageous objective and target of attack determine the direction of the offensive, the same reasoning will affect the defender as well. And he must guide his dispositions whenever he does not know the intentions of his opponent. If the attacker were to fail to take the most favorable direction, he would forfeit some of his natural advantages.

Thus, the defender, though tied to a certain place, is generally in no danger of missing the opponent's main force. In other words, if the defender has taken up the right position, he can be fairly sure that the attacker will seek him out there.

Furthermore—and this is the main point—an attacker trying to bypass his opponent is involved in doing two incompatible things simultaneously. His first concern is to advance and reach his objective. But as he may be attacked from the flank at any moment, he feels he must also be ready to strike back instantly, with full force.

These two aims are mutually exclusive: They create so much confusion and make it so difficult to cope that one could be hard put to conceive of a worse strategic situation. If the attacker knew exactly when and where he would be assaulted, he could prepare himself with skill and resource. But in his uncertainty and the necessity of keeping up his advance, a sudden confrontation can scarcely fail to find him badly concentrated and thus certainly not in an advantageous position.

If there is ever a suitable occasion for the defender to be in a confrontation, one must surely expect it under such circumstances. If we further bear in mind that the defender has the advantage in knowledge and choice of terrain and is able to prepare his movements and initiate them, there can be no doubt that, under these circumstances, he will retain definite strategic superiority over his opponent.

We therefore feel that a defender who is located with his full force in a well-placed position can safely wait to be bypassed. Historically, however, this seldom occurs. The reason is partly that defenders rarely dare to hold out in such a position. They would rather split their forces or hasten to cut the attacker off. Besides, an attacker will not dare to bypass a defender under such circumstances, and this usually brings him to a halt.

In such a case, then, the defender is forced to fight an offensive campaign and to forgo the further benefits of waiting. As a rule, the situation in which he finds the advancing opponent will not completely make up for the lack of these advantages.

After all, it was to circumvent them that the attacker exposed himself to these conditions. It does afford a certain amount of compensation, however.

We do not mean to imply that this is a matter of logical subtleties. On the contrary, the more one looks at the practical side of the matter, the more one sees that the idea applies to the whole field of defense.

Only if the defender is determined to attack the rival in full strength as soon as he has been bypassed can he avoid the two pitfalls that affect his path so closely: a divided position and a hasty advance. Either way, he is governed by the conditions of the offensive; either way, he must make do with makeshift expedients and dangerous haste.

Consequently, wherever a determined adversary intent on pursuing victory and reaching a decision has encountered this type of defensive system, he has neutralized it. On the other hand, a defender who has concentrated his personnel as a single force in the right place and is determined to attack the opponent is on the right course when backed up by all the advantages defense can offer.

Sound preparation, composure, confidence, unity, and simplicity will mark his conduct of the action. These are the threads that knit individual parts of a defense plan together in cases calling for decisive decisions.

Once a leader has resolved to pursue a specific objective, he will be able to judge how circumstances of geography, statistics, and the conditions of personnel in his own and the opponent's organizations will fit. He may then adjust his plans accordingly.

COMMENTARY

Clausewitz talks about various levels of "circumstances," both internal and external, and the need to "adjust ... plans accordingly." As a result, the depth and gravity of circumstances can cause plans to be adjusted, delayed, or even totally trashed.

The eminent business scholar, Professor Michael Porter,* describes his famous five competitive forces, which may be added as circumstances:

1. Rivalry among existing firms in an industry
2. Threat of potential new entrants
3. Bargaining power of buyers
4. Threat of substitute products or services
5. Bargaining power of suppliers

* See Porter, M. *Competitive Strategy, Techniques for Analyzing Industries and Competitors.* New York: Free Press, 1980.

Then, there are other circumstances that would relate to personnel:

- Low morale
- Fear and uncertainty
- Lack of trust resulting from ineffectual leadership
- Depleted levels of energy due to negative perceptions about unfolding market events
- Discouragement and even defeatism resulting from aggressive competitive actions

The successive stages of defense, which we introduced in the chapter on types of resistance, will now be more clearly defined:

1. The causes for approaching the rival with the intention of fighting an offensive campaign include:
   a. If one knows that the rival's forces are widely dispersed, even where one's own strength is inferior, there is some prospect of victory. Such a plan is therefore sound only where one has prior knowledge of the opponent's moves. Merely to make such an assumption on insufficient grounds and base all one's expectations on it will usually lead to an unfavorable situation.
   b. In general, one has enough strength for a campaign.
   c. A very clumsy, vacillating opponent invites attack. In such a case, the effect of surprise may be of greater value than all the benefits of terrain in a favorable position. It is the very essence of good leadership to use the power of psychological forces in this way.
   d. The composition of forces makes it particularly suited to the offensive. It is normal in a conflict that spirits and courage are higher in the attacker than in the defender. This is a feeling common to all personnel, and there is hardly a group whose leaders have not advanced the same claim. One must be careful not to be taken in by this semblance of superiority, while neglecting some solid advantages.
   e. It is impossible to find a favorable position.
   f. The need for a decision is urgent.
2. The most natural reasons for awaiting the opponent in an area where one wants to attack him include:
   a. The difference between the forces is not greatly to our disadvantage, and we are therefore not obliged to look for a strong entrenched position.
   b. The area is particularly suited to the purpose, such as easy accessibility for our own approach and numerous obstacles for the opponent's.
3. A position in which one means to await the opponent includes:
   a. An imbalance of strength forces us to seek shelter behind natural obstacles.

    b. The terrain is particularly well suited to such a position.

    c. One does not seek the decision oneself and can expect the opponent to falter, show indecision, and finally abandon his intentions.

4. An entrenched and invulnerable position fulfills the purpose if:

    a. It is located in an area of particular strategic significance. The distinctive feature of such a position is that it cannot be overrun. The rival is thus forced to try every other means available—for instance, pursuing his objective regardless of the position surrounding it.

    b. One has reason to expect help from outside.

We feel that where a decisive battle is unavoidable, whether it be desired by the opponent or by our own leader, and where one is not quite sure of victory to begin with, in such cases a fortress capable of resistance is a powerful argument for retiring behind it to seek the decision and thereby gain the benefit.

We therefore think that no defensive measure in a dangerous situation is so simple and effective as the choice of a good position close to and behind a substantial fortress.

> ### COMMENTARY
>
> Clausewitz's meaning of a fortress is a formidable physical structure. From a business viewpoint, a broader definition can serve a similar function. For instance, fortress can be likened to defensible patents, long-term contracts, strong logistical networks, proprietary technologies, branding, and any other fortress-like protection that would serve as an effective "choice of a good position."

PHASED RESISTANCE

In the chapter on types of resistance (Chapter 7), we described what can be considered the ultimate form of postponing a decision. This particular form of resistance aims at making the aggressor wear himself out rather than at defeating him in a confrontation.

Thus, a postponement of the decision can be considered as a special form of resistance where that is the primary objective. Otherwise, an infinite number of gradations can be combined with every method of defense. The degree of participation, therefore, should not be considered as a special type of resistance, but merely as an optional mixture of means of resistance to be used as needed.

If the defender feels that he does not require the aid of these forces, they remain on hand for a later stage. In this way a gradual application of strength becomes feasible.

In an area of conflict, as in everything else, strategy calls for economy of strength. The less one can manage with, the better, but manage one must, and here, as in commerce, there is more to it than mere stinginess.

In order to avoid a serious misconception, we want to make it clear that the amount of resistance rendered or attempted after a defeat is not what we are discussing. What matters is the amount of success that can be expected in advance from such renewed resistance. That is, how much value the overall plan should place on it.

There is more than one way in which a defender should look at this: from the point of view of the opponent, his character, and the situation. If his character is weak, if he lacks self-confidence and overriding ambition, and if his freedom of action is closely limited, he will, if he is successful, be content with a modest advantage.

Every new chance for decision that the defense dares to offer will make the opponent hesitate indecisively. In that case, the defender can count on making resistance in his area felt gradually. A constant series of decisive actions, though individually of no great consequence, will always hold out the possibility of turning these decisions in his favor.

WHERE A DECISION IS NOT THE OBJECTIVE

We shall now deal with the question of whether a conflict can take place if neither side attacks the other. In other words, where neither side has a positive objective. In the individual area of operations, we can simply assume the reason for a defensive stance on both sides is the relation of each of these parts to the whole.

This is not the only type of campaign that lacks the necessary focus of decision. History records numerous cases that do not lack for an aggressor or a positive ambition, on one side at least, but where this ambition is not pronounced enough to be relentlessly pursued until it leads to the inevitable decision.

In such conflicts, the attacker seeks no advantages beyond those offered by circumstances. Either he has set himself no objective and is merely harvesting the fruit that may ripen in the course of time or, if he has an objective, he has made the pursuit of it dependent on favorable circumstances.

This type of attack, which ignores the strict logical necessity of pressing on to the goal, is like an idler who strolls through a campaign and takes advantage of the occasional bargain that comes his way. It does not differ greatly from the defense that also allows its leader to pick up a bargain, but we shall reserve its more detailed scientific study for the discussion on attack.

At this time we will only state the conclusion, which is that in such a campaign neither the offensive nor the defensive will keep the need for a decision paramount. The decision in that case ceases to be the arch upon which all the lines of strategy converge.

History shows not only that most campaigns are of this type, but also that the majority is so overwhelming as to make all other campaigns seem more like exceptions to the rule. Even if this ratio changes in the future, it is certain that there will always be a substantial number of campaigns of this kind, and that aspect must have its due in any doctrine of defending an operation. In reality, most conflicts will probably fall between the two poles, sometimes approaching one, sometimes the other.

We have already argued that the state of waiting is one of the greatest advantages the defense enjoys over the attack. It seldom happens in real life, and even less often in conflict, that everything circumstances would lead one to expect actually takes place.

Because of the limits of human insight, the dread that things go wrong, and accidents that change the course of action, many possible options are never chosen, even though circumstances would have favored them. In conflict, where imperfect intelligence and the number of accidents are incomparably greater than in other human endeavors, the amount of missed opportunities is, therefore, also bound to be greater. This is the fertile field in which the defender may glean a harvest he did not sow.

Where no decision is intended or expected, there is no reason for abandoning anything. Consequently, the defender's aim is to hold on to as much as possible. The attacker will try to take as much as he can and spread his forces as widely as possible, without provoking a decision.

Wherever there is no defending force, the attacker can take possession. Then the benefit of waiting is his. The defender will, therefore, attempt to cover all territory directly and then take a chance on the opponent's willingness to attack his forces.

Before launching into a more detailed description of the special features of defense, we must anticipate the discussion on attack by listing the objectives that an offensive usually pursues when no decision is intended. These include the following:

1. To seize a considerable amount of territory, if this is possible without a decisive engagement
2. To secure an important source of supply, on the same conditions
3. To acquire a key position left without cover
4. To achieve victory in a moderately important engagement, in which not much is risked and consequently not much can be gained

These four objectives of the offensive now call for the following efforts on the defender's part:

1. To cover his key position by keeping opponents out of reach
2. To cover the territory by spreading out his forces
3. To interject his forces quickly by means of maneuver
4. To avoid any unfavorable engagements

The first three aims are obviously intended to result in forcing the initiative on the aggressor and to draw the utmost benefit from waiting. The purpose is so rooted in the nature of the case that it would be foolish to condemn it out of hand.

The less a decision can be expected, the more valid this objective will become. It is the governing principle in all such campaigns, even though superficially there may appear to be a lot of brisk activity, in the form of minor skirmishes that do not lead to decisive consequences.

A confrontation implies a decision. If the rival does not want one, he will not fight a campaign. Whenever we doubt that the opponent seeks a decision, we must take a chance. The likelihood is that he will not do so.

And in most cases, one still has the possibility of withdrawing if, contrary to expectations, the opponent does decide to attack. This minimizes the dangers and the practical certainty that the status quo can be maintained without even a remote degree of risk.

Measuring these two chances against one another, the defender, rather than choosing the advantage of fighting on better terms, would naturally choose the virtual certainty of not having to fight at all. Seen in that light, the practice of taking up a strong position becomes perfectly natural and understandable.

Covering the territory by spreading out our forces is conceivable only in combination with major natural obstacles. It may happen, of course, that a position is able to ward off all attacks and thus achieve an absolute defense. But out of all the numerous positions, each must be regarded as relatively weak in relation to the whole and vulnerable to possible attack by superior forces.

It would be unwise, therefore, to base one's confidence on the resistance from each individual position. With this type of an extended position, one may expect a fairly long resistance at best, but never a proper victory. Even so, the individual position can serve its purpose and contribute to the general objective.

In campaigns where one need not be afraid of great decisions, of being relentlessly driven toward failure, not much risk will be involved if a position becomes engaged in a campaign, even if it ends in its loss. The stake is seldom more than the position itself.

At worst, if the whole defensive system was breached by the loss of a single position, there would still be time for the defender to concentrate his forces and offer the opponent the decision that the latter does not seek. Usually, such a concentration of forces puts an end to the matter, and the attacker's further advance is brought to a halt.

To such a risk, if things go wrong, the defender may safely expose himself if the risk is balanced by the possibility that it will not happen at all. Timidity or prudence—call it what you will—may bring the attacker to a halt before the defender's position without his battering his head against them.

In advancing this argument, we must never forget that it assumes that an attacker who will not take great risks may well be stopped by a moderately sized but strong position. Even if he knows that he can take it, he will still wonder at what price and whether that price might not be too high in relation to the use he can make of his victory.

This demonstrates that from the defender's point of view the strong relative resistance afforded him by extending through a long line of positions can make a worthwhile contribution to the sum of his campaign. This paramount importance of terrain makes special demands on the type of knowledge and activity that we primarily associate with leadership.

As a system of defense moves away from the method of direct cover, it has to place additional reliance on mobility, active defense, and even offensive measures. In other words, it becomes clear that this kind of defense, though its basic nature is essentially passive, must include a number of active means that will enable it to deal with a wide variety of complex needs.

Thus, a defense that makes use of offensive means is considered superior. However, that depends in part on the nature of the terrain, the composition of the fighting forces, and even the leader's ability. Also, one may be expecting too much from measures of an active nature and discount the local defensive capacity of a major natural obstacle.

COMMENTARY

Clausewitz's reference to a "major natural obstacle" implies valleys, mountains, rivers, and similar physical barriers. Business has its natural obstacles as well: seasonal forces. Climate-related conditions influence how you manage your business within the variables of weather and logistics, such as seasonal outcomes of winter's cold and summer's heat, or the violence of a tsunami.

Consider the impact weather has on such industries as home building and road construction, obtaining materials to meet critical schedules, installing communications systems, or supplying energy. Then think about the ancillary products and services associated with those industries. Further, take into account the weather or seasonal impact on food supplies, fashion, entertainment, and retailing.

Natural obstacles can be a severe problem or can serve your purposes in the form of a "defensive capacity of a major natural obstacle."

We believe we have sufficiently explained what we mean by an extended line of defense, and now turn to the third of the remedies listed: forestalling the opponent by a rapid indirect movement.

This method is part of the type of defense under discussion. In some instances, the defender cannot cover every threatened point of access, no matter how far he extends his position. In many others he must be ready to lead the main strength of his force to those positions that are the opponent's objective, since they would otherwise be too easily overcome.

Finally, any leader who dislikes tying down his forces to passive defense in an extended position will only achieve his purpose of protecting the territory by rapid movements, well conceived and well executed. The natural consequence of these endeavors will be a search for positions that can be occupied and are strong enough to dispel any thought of attack.

Here, too, the leadership has an opportunity to use its knowledge of the terrain in working out a set of interlocking plans concerning the choice and preparation of positions and the roads leading to them.

COMMENTARY

"Knowledge of the terrain" and "preparation of positions" have their equivalents in the careful selection of market segments and in the gathering of intelligence about the unique features of each position. That includes acquiring specific knowledge about obstacles and areas that represent decisive points.

Amazon.com's approach to obtaining "knowledge of the terrain" has its equivalent in how it collects information about the marketplace and competitors. Over a period of years the company has maintained a group appropriately called: Competitive Intelligence. It operates in part by purchasing large volumes of merchandise from other online retailers and measuring the quality and speed of their services, such as ease of purchase, rapidity of shipping, and a range of other critical factors.

The group's mandate is to investigate whether any rival is doing a better job than Amazon. The resulting data are presented to a committee made up of CEO Jeff Bezos and other senior executives. They, in turn, make certain that remedial action is taken to catch up rapidly and address any immediate and long-term threats.

Thus, knowledge functions as the bedrock requirement for developing "a set of interlocking plans concerning the choice and preparation of positions." Yet, in all of this preparation, there is an underlying cautionary note. Even though conflicts tend to have commonalities, significant differences do exist. For instance, there may be significant disparities in the caliber of a competitor's leadership and the morale of personnel.

Those two issues alone are enough for critical concern, which can ultimately determine the outcome of a campaign. Then, there are the innumerable strength/weakness issues associated with specific competitors and their plans. All told, these points underscore the necessity for developing dedicated plans and not a format for repeating yesterday's strategies.

Where one side's efforts are completely concentrated on reaching a certain point and the other side's efforts are equally bent on preventing it, both will frequently be in the position of having to execute their movements in full view of the rival. Both will, therefore, move with greater caution and precision than would normally be required.

If the defender perseveres, and his skill and dispositions meet with success, the attacker will find even his limited purposes frustrated at every turn by prudent preparations. At that point the offensive principle may often attempt to vent itself by finding satisfaction for honor's sake alone.

Victory in any engagement of consequence will lend a semblance of superiority. It satisfies the vanity of the leader and the organization and thereby in some measure the expectations that are always pinned on an offensive. Thus, the last hope of the attacker will center on a favorable engagement of some consequence, for the sake of the victory and the trophies alone.

We are not involving ourselves in a contradiction here, since we are still proceeding on our own assumption that the defender, by his foresight, has deprived the opponent of any hope of using a success to gain his real objectives. Any such hope would turn on two requirements: first, a favorable outcome, and, second, the victory actually leads to the further objectives.

The first of these may well be met without the second. Therefore, when honors are the opponent's sole concern, the defender's individual units will more often run the risk of having to fight at a disadvantage than when he is out for additional gains.

These are not trivial or meaningless distinctions. Indeed, we are dealing with one of the most fundamental principles of conflict. In strategy, the significance of an engagement is what really matters.

We cannot repeat often enough that all its essentials derive from the ultimate intentions of both parties, from the conclusion of the whole sequence of ideas. That is why, strategically speaking, the difference between one campaign and another can be so great that the two can no longer be considered as the same instrument.

One can hardly consider that type of victory by the attacker as one that will inflict serious damage on the defender. Still, the latter will not be willing to concede even that much advantage, especially since one can never tell what else may, by chance, adhere to it.

Therefore, he will constantly be concerned with surveying the condition of all his important units and positions. That mainly depends on the sound actions of their own leaders. Yet inappropriate orders on the part of the leader himself can also involve them in severe problems.

The real difficulty lies in the fact that a leader cannot always count on his subordinates having the sense and good intentions, courage, and strength of character that would ideally be desirable. He is, therefore, not able to leave everything to their discretion, but must give them directives that will restrict their actions and may render them inappropriate to the circumstances of the moment.

No organization can be properly commanded in the absence of a dominant, authoritarian determination that permeates it down to the last man. Anyone who falls into the habit of thinking and expecting the best of his subordinates at all times is, for that reason alone, unsuited to command an organization.

COMMENTARY

Clausewitz's bold assertion about what to expect from subordinates is supported by the comments of the ancient Chinese strategist, Sun Tzu, who over 2,500 years ago declared:

> Those skilled at making the enemy move do so by creating a situation to which he must conform. Therefore, a skilled commander seeks victory from the situation and does not demand it of his subordinates. Experts in war depend especially on opportunity and expediency. They do not place the burden of accomplishment on their men alone.

A sharp watch, therefore, must be kept on the condition of each position in order to prevent their becoming involved in unforeseen disaster. All these efforts are intended to preserve the status quo. The more successful and fortunate they are, the longer the conflict will remain static. But the longer the conflict remains static, the more important the problem of existence will become.

There are no important and decisive means of action in this type of campaign. The leader's efforts will have to be directed to minor ones. For another, there is plenty of time to wait for these measures to take effect.

Safeguarding one's lines of communication therefore assumes substantial importance. While their disruption will not be the final purpose of an attack, it can be a very effective means for forcing the defender to retreat and, in the process, abandon other points.

Anything done to protect the occupied area of operations must, of course, also serve to cover the lines of communication. We simply wish to note that concern for their safety will weigh heavily in the choice of position.

In all campaigns of this kind, the first of these means is constantly at work, but silently. It never comes to the fore. Any effective position occupied by the defender derives its value from the fact that it makes the attacker nervous about his own communications.

The problem of supply assumes a vital importance in this kind of confrontation, as we have already explained in the context of defense. And that holds for the attacker as well. Consequently, the strategic pattern is largely determined by the offensive value latent in the opponent's positions, a topic that will be further dealt with when we come to the subject of the attack.

Such a defense is not limited to the general effect produced by the choice of positions. It may also encompass a true offensive advance. But if it is to be successful, the location of the lines of communication, the nature of the terrain, or the special qualities of the personnel must be especially favorable.

Attacks on rival units, or even on his main force, should be considered a necessary complement to the defense as a whole. It is to be used at times when the attacker takes things a little too easily and lays himself wide open at some points.

But here, too, the defender can move closer to the attack by always being, like his opponent, on the alert for a chance to strike a favorable blow. He can assume a measure of success if he has considerably larger numbers than his opponent, which is not really consistent with the nature of defense, or if he is skillful and methodical enough to keep his forces better concentrated than the opponent. Then he can use activity and movement to offset the sacrifices that his situation forces on him.

We believe we have now reviewed all the ingredients in the defense of an operational area where no decision is intended. The main reason we brought them all together was to give a coherent view of the strategic operation—that is, the particular ways in which each component operates in detail.

When we consider the subject as a whole once more, we are bound to observe that where the offensive principle is so weak, the urge for a decision so faint on both sides, the positive initiative so feeble, and the psychological brakes so numerous as described here, the essential difference between offensive and defensive must gradually disappear.

Admittedly, at the start of a campaign one side will assault the other's territory and assume the role of attacker. Yet it may well happen, and often does, that the attacker soon finds himself expending all his energy defending his own position. The two sides then confront each other basically in a state of mutual observation.

The more the attacker relinquishes his active advance, the less the defender feels threatened; the less he is narrowly confined to resistance by the urgent need for safety, the more the situation will balance out on both sides. The activity of each will be aimed at gaining an advantage from the other, while avoiding any disadvantage to himself.

This is a phase of true strategic maneuver and is certainly more or less characteristic of all campaigns where a major decision is precluded by external motives or the general state of internal affairs. Since strategists have frequently attributed false importance to this balanced play of forces, particularly in the context of defense, we feel obliged to discuss the subject here in some detail.

Wherever the whole is not in motion, a state of balance exists. We call it a balanced play of forces. And where there is no great purpose to impel it, the whole will not be in motion. That being the case, both sides, no matter how unequal, must be deemed to be in balance. Motives for minor actions are now able to emerge from the balanced state of the whole.

They can develop at this point, since they are no longer under the strain of a great decision or danger. Thus, whatever may be gained or lost has been converted into smaller tokens. And the conflict as a whole has splintered into minor actions.

Given these minor campaigns for more modest prizes, the two leaders now engage in a test of skill. But since chance, or luck, can never be kept completely out of conflict, this match will never cease to be a gamble.

Two further questions now arise in the course of these maneuvers: Will chance play a smaller part in shaping the decision than when everything is concentrated into one great act? And will intelligence play a greater role? The answer to this last question must be positive.

The more complex the whole is, the more time and space enter into consideration, and then the wider will be the field for calculation—and thus the greater the supremacy of the reasoning mind.

We should remember in this connection that a reasoning mind is not the leader's only mental asset. Courage, energy, determination, prudence, and so forth are attributes that will weigh more heavily where a single great decision is at stake.

They will count somewhat less in a balanced play of forces, for the primary importance of intelligent calculations increase at the expense of these qualities. At the hour of a great decision, on the other hand, these brilliant qualities can deprive chance of a great deal of its dominance, and, in a way, secure some things that the reasoning minds had been forced to release.

COMMENTARY

Clausewitz's reference to "intelligent calculations" is worth singling out for comment. Here, again, the ancient commentator on strategy, Sun Tzu, makes the following comparative statement:

> Now if the estimates made before hostilities indicate victory, it is because calculations show one's strength to be superior to that of his enemy; if they indicate defeat, it is because calculations show that one is inferior. With many calculations, one can win; with few one cannot. How much less chance of victory has one who makes none at all! By this means I examine the situation and the outcome will be clearly apparent.

Keeping in mind Sun Tzu's guidance and Clausewitz's reference to intelligent calculations, what exactly would you estimate? The following five all-encompassing categories provide a useable structure: internal and external relationships, leadership, seasonal forces, market selection, and policy.

First, look to the cross-functional relationships that exist among individuals within your business unit or product lines, as well as to those among external contacts. Relationships can vary from the extremes of cooperation and enthusiasm to the inflexible attitudes reflected in sluggish and bored individuals who are fearful of personal risk.

Second, observe the caliber of leadership in this calculation, which is often pivotal to the outcome of a competitive encounter. Determine the extent to which leaders positively influence personnel by providing purpose, direction, and motivation while confidently staying in charge of accomplishing the mission and improving the organization.

Third, consider seasonal forces. Comments about this calculation were made earlier in this chapter.

Fourth, focus on market selection. Seek data on the efficient movement of products and services throughout the supply chain to targeted markets. Also include calculations about the economic conditions and the intensity of competition in a given territory.

Fifth, look at policy. Reexamine the fundamental guidelines that control an organization. They form a tangible imprint of an organization's ethical and operating procedures. As such, policy gives an organization consistency and a distinctive personality. In turn, it holds a legitimate and powerful grasp on your business plans.

Obviously, a number of factors are in conflict here. And one cannot flatly say there is more room for chance in a great decision than in the final score of a balance of forces. Therefore, when we suggest that the play of forces is mainly a trial of skill, we mean skill in intelligent calculations.

This aspect of strategic maneuver has given it the exaggerated importance that we mentioned before. For one thing, skill in this area has been confused with the sum total of a leader's intellectual powers, which is a serious mistake.

We must repeat that, at times of decision, a leader's other psychological qualities may control the power of circumstances. Even if this control stems from an impulse prompted by strong emotions and from flashes of intuition, rather than being the product of a lengthy chain of reasoning, nonetheless, it pertains to the art of conflict.

After all, waging a confrontation is not merely an act of reason, nor is reasoning its foremost activity. Second, there has been a feeling that every unsuccessful action in a campaign was the result of skill on the part of one or even both of the leaders. Actually, its chief basis lay in the prevalent conditions created by conflict for this kind of gamble.

Since most conflicts have been more a matter of observing the rival than of defeating him, it follows that strategic maneuver is characteristic of most campaigns where no famous leader was engaged. Yet, when some great leader was there to catch the eye, or where indeed there was one on each side, their names alone were enough to give the final stamp of approval to the whole art of maneuver.

It is possible for one leader to show greater skill in this game than the other. If he matches him in strength, he may thereby win some advantages. If he is weaker, he may use his greater skill to hold the balance. But it would be a real contradiction to seek a leader's highest honor and glory in this area.

On the contrary, campaigns of that sort are the surest sign that neither leader has great gifts, or that the one who does is prevented by circumstances from taking the risk of seeking a decision.

The subject of this chapter has been the defense of an operational area when no great decision is in prospect. Now we come to another question: whether a set of all-encompassing principles, rules, and methods may be formulated for these various endeavors.

Our reply must be that history has certainly not guided us to any recurrent forms. Nevertheless, for a subject of such constantly changing nature one can hardly formulate a theoretical law that is not based on experience.

A confrontation in which decisions are involved is not only simpler but also less inconsistent, more in concert with its own nature, more objective, and more obedient to the law of necessity. In such a case, reason can make rules and laws, but in the type of conflict we have been describing this seems far more difficult.

Yet this is where, as purely formal principles, they should be at their most effective. The more operations expand in time and space, the more rules tend to increase in effectiveness and dominate all other factors in the result. Nevertheless, they turn out to be merely special aspects of the subject—certainly anything but decisive advantages. It is plain that circumstances exert an influence that cuts across all general principles.

We admit, in short, that in this chapter we cannot formulate any principles, rules, or methods. History does not provide a basis for them. On the contrary, at almost every turn one finds peculiar features that are often incomprehensible, and sometimes astonishingly odd. Nevertheless, it is useful to study history in connection with this subject, as with others.

While there may be no system and no mechanical way of recognizing the truth, truth does exist. To recognize it, one generally needs seasoned judgment and an instinct born of long experience. While history may yield no formula, it does provide an exercise for judgment here as it does everywhere else.

We have but a single comprehensive principle to offer. Or, rather, we shall express the natural assumption underlying all we have said in the form of an independent principle, so as to increase its impact on the reader's mind. All means described previously have only a relative value; all are inhibited by certain limitations on both sides.

Beyond this sphere, a different set of rules applies, in a totally different universe of phenomena. A leader must never forget this. He must never expect to move on the narrow ground of imagined security as if it were absolute. He must never permit himself to feel that the means he is using are absolutely necessary and the only ones possible, and persist in using them even though he may shudder at the thought of their possible inadequacy.

Once again, we must remind the reader that, in order to lend clarity, distinction, and emphasis to our ideas, only perfect contrasts have been included in our observations. As an actual occurrence, confrontation generally falls somewhere in between and is influenced by these extremes only to the extent to which it approaches them.

Broadly speaking, then, it is crucial that the leader decide from the start whether his opponent is both willing and able to outdo him by using stronger, more decisive measures. If this is what he suspects, he must abandon the minor measures he had employed in order to escape minor disadvantages.

Then he may avail himself of the means of achieving a better position, and will thus be able to cope with a weightier decision. In other words, the first requirement is that the leader applies the right standard of measurement in his plan of operations.

Chapter 10

The Nature of Strategic Attack

Clausewitz makes these key points about the strategic attack:

- Just as defense is permeated with pronounced elements of the offensive, attack is perpetually combined with defense.
- As soon as the objective has been attained, the attack ends and the defense takes over.
- The diminishing force of the attack is one of the strategist's main concerns.
- What matters is to detect the culminating point of actions with discriminative judgment.
- The aim of maneuver is to bring about favorable conditions for success, rather than to use them to gain an advantage over the opponent.
- If an attack lacks material superiority, it must have moral superiority to make up for its inherent weakness.
- Prudence is the true spirit of defense; courage and confidence are the true spirit of attack.
- Every attacker has to ask himself how he will exploit his victory after the encounter.
- Victory normally results from the superiority of one side, from an aggregate of physical and psychological strength.
- The most important factor besides the spirit of the personnel is the spirit at the highest levels of the organization.
- The natural goal of all campaign plans is the turning point at which attack becomes defense. If one were to go beyond that point, it would merely be a useless effort.
- Only the leader who can achieve great results with limited means has really hit the mark.

Clausewitz talks more extensively about these points of attack:

As we have seen, defense in general (including strategic defense) is not an absolute state of waiting and repulse. It is not total, but only relatively passive endurance. Consequently, it is permeated with more or less pronounced elements of the offensive. In the same way, the attack is not a homogeneous whole: It is perpetually combined with defense.

The difference between the two is that one cannot think of the defense without that necessary component: the counterattack. This does not apply to the attack. The offensive thrust or action is complete in itself. It does not have to be complemented by defense. But dominating considerations of time and space do introduce defense as a necessary evil.

In the first place, an attack cannot be completed in a single steady movement. Periods of rest are needed, during which the attack is neutralized, and defense takes over automatically. Second, the area left in rear of the advancing forces, an area vital to their existence, is not necessarily covered by the attack and needs special protection.

The act of attack, particularly in strategy, is thus a constant interchange and combination of attack and defense. The latter, however, should not be regarded as a useful preliminary to the attack and thereby an active principle. Rather, it is simply a necessary evil, an impeding burden created by the sheer weight of the mass.

COMMENTARY

Clausewitz makes it quite clear that an active campaign, such as an attack, is not sustainable. In fact, the attack eventually weakens as it progresses. Any number of factors can contribute to the situation, such as management shifts attention to exploit new opportunities, or it defends a loss elsewhere; budgets are depleted and no new funds are available; or personnel are transferred to new areas and no replacements are forthcoming.

Then, there is the issue of exhaustion when the attack is dragged out over an extended period of time, with the consequences that morale declines and inertia takes over, which places the entire campaign in jeopardy and, in turn, swings the advantage to the competitor.

Thus, deliberate attention should be given to developing a flexible strategy that changes the attack to a defense. As Clausewitz points out, "The act of attack ... is a constant interchange and combination of attack and defense."

We call defense an impeding burden, unless it contributes to the attack, and then it will tend to diminish its effect because of the loss of time involved. Is it possible for this defensive component, which is part of every offensive, to be actually disadvantageous? When we assume attack to be the weaker and defense the stronger form of conflict, it seems to follow that the latter cannot be detrimental to the former.

If there are enough forces to serve the weaker form, they must surely suffice for the stronger. That is generally so. We shall examine the subject more closely in the section on the culminating point of victory. However, we must not forget that the superiority of strategic defense arises partly from the fact that the attack itself cannot exist without some measure of defense—even of a much less effective kind.

What was true of defense as a whole no longer holds true for these parts, and it thus becomes clear how these features of defense may positively weaken the attack. It is these very moments of weak defense during an offensive that the positive activity of the offensive principle in defense seeks to exploit.

Consider the difference of the situations during the rest period that usually follows an action. The defender holds a well-chosen position, which he knows and has prepared with care. The attacker stumbles into his area like a blind man. A longer halt will find the defender close to his fortresses and awaiting reinforcements, while the attacker is like a bird perched on a limb.

COMMENTARY

The fortress, referred to in Chapter 9, can be likened to such stronghold positions as proprietary technology that is not likely to be duplicated or surpassed over the period covered by the strategic plan, a strong market position anchored to excellent customer service and reputation, solid contractual arrangements with organizations along the supply chain, and suppliers secured by long-term contracts.

As for an example of the latter point, this impacts some of the other stronghold positions: China actively seeks sources of energy and other commodities worldwide through outright purchase or long-term contracts. The "fortress" strategy has a two-pronged purpose: First, secure vital sources of supply and suppliers to match its strategic needs; second, deny those sources to competitors.

Every attack will end in a defense whose nature will be decided by the circumstances. These may be very favorable when the adversary has been neutralized. But where this is not the case things may be very difficult. Even though this type of defense is no longer part of the offensive, it must affect it and help determine its effectiveness.

It follows that every attack has to take into account the defense that is necessarily inherent in it, in order to understand clearly its disadvantages and to anticipate them. But in other respects, attack remains consistent and unchanged, while defense has its stages, insofar as the principle of waiting is exploited. From these, essentially different forms of action will result, as has been previously discussed.*

---

* See Chapters 8 and 9 on kinds of resistance.

Since attack has but one single active principle, one will find no such differentiations. Admittedly, there are tremendous differences in terms of vigor, speed, and striking power, but these are differences of degree, not of kind.

It even might be conceivable for the attacker to choose the defensive form to further his aims. He might, for instance, occupy a strong position in the hope that the defender would attack him there. But such cases are so rare that in the light of actual practice they do not require consideration in our listing of concepts and principles. To sum up, there is no growth of intensity in an attack comparable to those of the various types of defense.

Finally, the means of attack available are usually limited to the fighting forces, which may have a substantial influence on the attack. But this influence will weaken as the advance proceeds. Clearly, the attacker's fortresses can never play so prominent a part as the defender's, which often becomes a main feature.

Popular support of the attack is conceivable where the inhabitants are more favorably inclined toward the attacker than toward their own forces. Finally, the attacker may have allies, but only as a result of special or fortuitous circumstances. Their support is not inherent in the nature of the attack.

Thus, while we have included fortresses and allies among the possible means of defense, we cannot include them among the means of attack. In the first they are intrinsic; in the second they are rare and then usually accidental.

THE OBJECT OF STRATEGIC ATTACK

In conflict, the overthrow of the rival is the end, and the neutralization of his capabilities is the means. That applies to attack and defense alike. By means of the neutralization of the opponent's forces, defense leads to attack, which in turn leads to the takeover of the territory. That, then, is the objective, but it need not be the whole territory; it may be limited to a smaller area.

The object of strategic attack, therefore, may be thought of in numerous gradations, from the conquest of a whole territory to that of an insignificant section. As soon as the objective has been attained, the attack ends and the defense takes over. One might therefore think of a strategic attack as an entity with well-defined limits. But in practice, seeing things in the light of actual events does not bear this out.

In practice, the stages of the offensive often turn into defensive action as defensive plans grow into the offensive. It is rare, or at any rate uncommon, for a leader to set out with a firm objective in mind. Rather, he will make it dependent on the course of events.

Frequently, his attack may lead him further than expected. After a more or less brief period of rest, he often acquires new strength. But this should not be considered as a second, wholly separate action. At other times he may be stopped earlier than he had anticipated, but without abandoning his plan and moving over to a genuine defensive.

Thus, it becomes clear that if a successful defense can imperceptibly turn into attack, the same can happen in reverse. These gradations must be kept in mind if we wish to avoid a misapplication of our general statements on the subject of attack.

COMMENTARY

Clausewitz's comment that "if a successful defense can imperceptibly turn into attack, the same can happen in reverse" applies directly to the need for building contingency what-if scenarios into your plan. That is, within the objectives section of the plan, state the desired outcome of the intended campaign, along with alternate objectives in the event that "other times he may be stopped earlier than anticipated," whereby the attack could diminish in strength and revert to the defensive.

Building such flexibility into your plan also translates into introducing the appropriate analytics for determining when to use reserves where the "attack ... leads him further than expected." What prudently follows is to make certain that channels of communications are open from the field back to the home office, where decisions can be made to strengthen or weaken a position or to alter directions from attack to defense. In situations where first-line managers are suitably trained, those decisions can be made on the spot, especially where timing is critical.

Clausewitz now continues by listing the reasons for the diminishing force of the attack:

THE DIMINISHING FORCE OF THE ATTACK

The diminishing force of the attack is one of the strategist's main concerns. His awareness of it will determine the accuracy of his estimate and the options open to him.

Overall strength is depleted:

1. If the object of the attack is to occupy the rival's territory
2. If the attacking forces need to occupy the area to secure lines of communication and take advantage of its resources
3. By losses incurred in action
4. By distance from the source of replacements
5. By barriers
6. By a relaxation of effort
7. By the defection of allies

But these difficulties may be balanced by other factors that tend to strengthen the attack. Yet it is clear that the overall result will be determined only after these various quantities have been evaluated. For instance, a weakening of the attack may be partially or completely cancelled out or outweighed by a weakening of the defense. This is unusual. In any case, one should never compare all the forces in the field, but only those facing each other at the front or at decisive points.

THE CULMINATING POINT OF THE ATTACK

Success in attack results from the availability of superior strength. And if the superior strength of the attack—which diminishes day by day—leads to a peaceful outcome, the object will have been attained.

There are strategic attacks that have led directly to peace, but these are in the minority. Most of them only lead up to the point where their remaining strength is just enough to maintain a defense and wait for peace. Beyond that point, the scale turns and the reaction follows with a force that is usually much stronger than that of the original attack.

This is what we mean by the culminating point of the attack. Since the object of the attack is the possession of the opponent's territory, it follows that the advance will continue until the attacker's superiority is exhausted. It is this that drives the offensive on toward its goal and can easily drive it further.

If we remember how many factors contribute to an equation of forces, we will understand how difficult it is in some cases to determine which side has the upper hand. Often it is entirely a matter of the imagination. What matters, therefore, is to detect the culminating point with discriminative judgment.

COMMENTARY

The culminating point should be of vital interest to most senior executives and line managers. This is especially so among those with decision-making responsibilities for shaping strategies and committing their organizations' resources in campaigns that involve entering new markets against entrenched competitors. Clausewitz indicates that "the object of the attack is the possession of the opponent's territory," and that "the advance will continue until the attacker's superiority is exhausted." If "territory" can be assumed to mean the market segment defended by a dominant competitor, then the level of market share becomes the dominant and measurable objective.

Therefore, the leader's task is to determine what would represent the culminating point in a campaign where gaining an extra 2, 3, or 4 percent of market share would be worth the expenditures. Stated another way: Would continuing the attack and expending more resources place the entire campaign in doubt and result in exhausting financial, material, and personnel resources?

> The culminating point can be determined by quantitative calculations, compiling a list of nonquantitative criteria, or assessing various opportunities highlighted in the strategic business plan. In the end, however, an answer may come to you intuitively and be "entirely a matter of the imagination."*
>
> ---
> * The Appendix provides useful assessment tools to assist in determining a culminating point.

Clausewitz refers again to the culminating point later in this chapter.

NEUTRALIZATION OF THE OPPONENT'S FORCES

Neutralization of the rival's forces is the means to the end. What does this mean?

Different points of view are possible:

1. To neutralize only what is needed to achieve the object of the attack
2. To suppress as much as possible
3. To preserve one's own forces as the dominant consideration

The engagement is the only means of neutralizing the rival's forces. But it may act in two different ways, either directly or indirectly, or by a combination of campaigns. Thus, while a campaign is the principal means, it is not the only one. The occupation of a strip of territory* also amounts to a suppression of the opponent's forces. It may lead to further elimination of his capabilities and thereby become an indirect means as well.

Thus the occupation of an undefended strip of territory may, aside from its direct value in achieving an aim, also have value in terms of neutralizing rival forces. Maneuvering the opponent out of an area he has occupied is not very different from this and should be considered in the same light, rather than as a true success of a confrontation.

These means are generally overrated. They seldom achieve so much as a campaign and involve the risk of drawbacks that may have been overlooked. They are tempting because they cost so little.

They should always be looked upon as minor investments that can only yield minor dividends, appropriate to limited circumstances and weaker motives. But they are obviously preferable to pointless confrontations—victories that cannot be fully exploited.

---
* To gain practical meaning from Clausewitz's reference, transpose "strip of territory" to a market segment, or the combination of several niches that comprise the segment. You can further characterize the segment or niche as emerging, neglected, or poorly served.

THE OFFENSIVE BATTLE

What we have said about the defensive campaign will have already cast considerable light on the offensive campaign. We were thinking of the kind of encounter in which the defensive is most prominent, in order to clarify the nature of the defensive. But very few campaigns are of that type. Most of them are in part encounters in which the defensive element tends to be lost.

This is not so with the offensive campaign, which retains its character under all circumstances—and can assert it all the more since the defender is not in his proper element. Therefore, a certain difference in the character of the confrontation—the way in which it is conducted by one side or the other—remains between those campaigns that are not really defensive and those that are true encounters. The main feature of an offensive battle is the bypassing of the defender that is taking the initiative.

Enveloping actions obviously possess great advantages. The attacker should not forgo these advantages simply because the defender has a means of countering them. It is a means the attacker cannot use, for it is too much bound up with the rest of the defender's situation. A defender, in order to outflank an opponent who is attempting to outflank him, must operate from a well-chosen, well-prepared position.

Even more important is that the defender cannot actually use the full potential offered by his situation. In most cases, defense is a sorry, makeshift affair. The defender is usually in a tight and precarious spot in which, because he expects the worst, he meets the attack halfway. Consequently, campaigns that make use of enveloping approaches, which ought to be the result of advantageous lines of communication, tend in reality to be the result of moral and physical superiority.

Just as the leader's aim in a defensive campaign is to postpone the decision as long as possible, the aim of the leader in an offensive battle is to expedite the decision. Too much haste, on the other hand, leads to the risk of wasting one's forces. A peculiarity in most offensive campaigns is doubt about the rival's position.

They are characterized by groping in the dark. The more this is so, the more it becomes necessary to concentrate one's forces and to outflank rather than to envelop the opponent. We have already demonstrated that the real fruits of victory are won only in pursuit. By its very nature, pursuit tends to be a more integral part of the action in an offensive campaign than in a defensive one.

ATTACK ON DEFENSIVE POSITIONS

In the previous two chapters on defense, there is a detailed discussion on the extent to which defensive positions compel an adversary either to attack or to abandon his advance. Only those that achieve these aims are appropriate: (1) wearing down the opponent's forces, whether totally or partially, or (2) neutralizing them. The attack cannot prevail against them. It has no means at its disposal to counteract their advantage.

COMMENTARY

Both of the aims Clausewitz talks about—"wearing down the opponent's forces" and "neutralizing them"—have competitor intelligence as a common platform. For instance, consider what precise actions would wear down your rival. How would you know when that level was met? Does wearing down refer to the morale of the competitor's personnel, or access to material and financial resources to sustain an aggressive campaign? And what factors—product, technology, logistics, and others—would represent the competitive advantage that needs to be neutralized?

The ancient Chinese strategist, Sun Tzu, makes these pertinent comments:

"Know the enemy* and know yourself; in a hundred battles you will never be in peril.
"When you are ignorant of the enemy, but know yourself, your chances of winning or losing are equal.
"If ignorant both of your enemy and of yourself, you are certain in every battle to be in peril."

Consequently, given the scope of information required to achieve Clausewitz's aims, it is up to you to look at a competitor with a 360-degree view. That is, use a circular approach to open your eyes to a changing marketplace of evolving technologies, environmental trends, and shifting buying patterns among your customers.

In this panoramic scene, seek information and insight that can impact your decisions about selecting markets, launching new products, and devising competitive advantages. You will improve your chances for establishing a formidable defense in those segments that represent your core business.

In all, reliable intelligence helps you to wear down and neutralize your competitor before he can react to your movements.

---

* As in previous references, substitute *enemy* with its business equivalent, *opponent* or *rival*.

If the attacker sees that he can get his way against a defensive position, it would be senseless for him to attempt it. If he cannot, the question is whether he can maneuver the defender out by threatening his flank (by an indirect attack.)

He will decide to attack a good position only where these means are ineffective. In that case, a flank attack will always pose somewhat fewer problems. The choice between the two flanks will then be determined by the location and direction of each side's lines of communication.

In other words, the threat to the opponent's retreat and the security of one's own are two factors that may easily clash. In this case, threatening the rival's line should receive preference. Its nature is offensive and therefore of the same type as the attack, whereas the nature of the other is defensive.

One thing, however, is sure and fundamental to the issue: It is a risky business to move against an able opponent in a good position. On the whole, however, the number is small and insignificant when compared with the immense number of cases in which the most resolute of leaders did not attack such positions.

But our topic should not be confused with ordinary campaigns. Most confrontations are true clashes in which one side is admittedly on the defensive but not in entrenched positions.

MANEUVER

The subject of maneuver has already been touched on. While the device is common to attacker and defender, its nature is more closely related to attack than to defense, and we shall now therefore define it more closely.

Maneuver must be distinguished, not only from aggressive conduct of the attack by means of major engagements, but also from every operation that arises immediately out of such an attack: whether it be a diversion or pressure on the opponent's lines of communication or on his retreat.

In its ordinary meaning the term *maneuver* carries the idea of an effect created out of nothing—that is, out of a state of equilibrium by using the mistakes into which the rival can be lured. It can be compared to the opening gambits in a game of chess. In fact, it is a play of balanced forces whose aim is to bring about favorable conditions for success, rather than to use them to gain an advantage over the opponent.

Considerations to be borne in mind, partly as goals and partly as a frame of reference for our actions, are the following:

1. The opponent's resources, which one aims to cut off or reduce
2. A combination with other units
3. A threat to other communications within the territory
4. A threat to the retreat
5. An attack on individual points with superior forces

These five factors can be found in the smallest detail of a particular situation, which then becomes the object around which everything revolves. Yet, in every case, it would be easy to show that its importance is derived entirely from its relation to one of the factors named previously.

For the attacker or, rather, for the active party (who admittedly may be the defender), the outcome of a successful maneuver will consist of a strip of territory or the like.

The weaker side must remain more closely concentrated and make up for the resulting disadvantages by mobility. This greater mobility assumes a greater degree of competence. The weaker side, therefore, must exert itself more, both physically and morally. That is the inevitable conclusion, if our argument has been consistent.

We are therefore certain that no rules of any kind exist for maneuver and no method or general principle can determine the value of the action. Rather, superior application, precision, order, discipline, and fear will find the means to achieve tangible advantage in the minutest circumstances. It is on these qualities that victory in this type of contest largely depends.

COMMENTARY

Clausewitz talks about achieving tangible advantage through "superior application, precision, order, discipline, and fear." There is still an additional factor vital to maneuver: speed. Maneuvering with speed is an integral part of implementing the campaign plan and realizing an advantage.

"Without exception, all of my biggest mistakes occurred because I moved too slowly," declared John Chambers, CEO of Cisco Systems. Expanding on Chambers's comment, extended deliberations, procrastination, cumbersome committees, and indecisiveness are all potential detriments to the attacker. Drawn out efforts often divert interest, diminish enthusiasm, and damage morale. Consequently, exhaustion through the excessive draining of resources has killed more companies than almost any other factor.

Additionally, employees become bored and their skills lose sharpness. As damaging, the gaps created through lack of action give defending competitors extra time (the waiting period) to create barriers that can blunt your efforts. Therefore, it is in your best interest to evaluate, maneuver, and concentrate your forces in the shortest span of time.

As to how the positive aspect of speed relates to employees: Beyond the quantitative measures of success, such as sales, profits, and market share, they can see with satisfaction, and perhaps some feeling of pride, that stalled projects move forward, products are launched on time, or market coverage is expanded.

Speed, then, does have an impact on employees; it acts as a unifying element that gives wholeness to managing people and resources. Yet even with the most convincing evidence and far-reaching experiences from such diverse fields as politics, military, and sports, speed is still largely ignored by many managers.

Finally, there is Clausewitz's earlier reference to the culminating point where he states, "The advance will continue until the attacker's superiority is exhausted." Again, by extrapolating the significance of exhaustion, speed thereby becomes an essential ingredient in the strategy of maneuver.

ATTACK ON AN AREA OF CONFLICT: SEEKING A DECISION

Most aspects of this question have already been touched upon in defense, which will have reflected sufficient light on the subject of attack. The concept of a self-contained area of operations is in any case more closely associated with defense than with attack.

A number of salient points, such as the object of the attack and the sphere of effectiveness of the victory, have already been dealt with and the really basic and essential features of attack can be expounded only in connection with the subject of plans. Still, enough remains to be set forth here:

1. The immediate object of an attack is victory.
   Only by means of his superior strength can the attacker make up for all the advantages that accrue to the defender by virtue of his position, and possibly by the modest advantage that his organization derives from the knowledge that it is on the advancing side.
   Naturally we assume that the defender will act as sensibly and correctly as the attacker. We say this in order to exclude certain vague notions about sudden assaults and surprise attacks, which are commonly thought of as bountiful sources of victory. They will only be that under exceptional circumstances.
   We have already discussed elsewhere the nature of a genuine strategic surprise. If an attack lacks material superiority, it must have moral superiority to make up for its inherent weakness. Where even moral superiority is lacking, there is no point in attacking at all, for one cannot expect to succeed.
2. Prudence is the true spirit of defense, and courage and confidence the true spirit of attack.
   Not that either form can do without both qualities, but each has a stronger affinity with one of them. After all, these qualities are necessary only because action is no mathematical construction, but has to operate in the dark or, at best, in twilight.
   Trust must be placed in the guide whose qualifications are best suited to our purposes. The lower the defender's morale is, the more daring the attacker should be.
3. Victory presupposes a clash of the two main forces.
   This presents less uncertainty to the attacker. His role is to confront the defender, whose positions are usually already known. In our discussion of the defense, on the other hand, we argued that if the defender has chosen a poor position, the attacker should not seek him out because the defender would have in that case to seek him out instead, and he would then have the advantage of catching the defender unprepared.
4. Objectives of an attack lie within the area of conflict that we intend to attack and within the probable sphere of victory.

One should not forget that the object of the attack usually gains significance only with victory. Victory must always be conceived in conjunction with it.

Thus, the attacker is not interested simply in reaching the objective. He must get there as victor. Consequently, his movement must be aimed not just at the objective but also at the road that the opponent will have to take to reach it. The road then becomes the first objective.

Every attacker, therefore, has to ask himself how he will exploit his victory after the encounter. The next objective to be won will then indicate the natural direction of his movement.

If the defender has taken up his new position in that area, he has made the correct choice and the attacker has got to seek him out there. If that position is too strong, the attacker must try to bypass it, making a virtue of necessity.

5. An attacker bent on a major decision has no reason whatever to divide his forces.

If in fact he does so, it may usually be ascribed to a state of confusion. If, however, the rival's force is divided, so much the better; in that case, minor diversions are in order. Should the attacker choose to divide his forces for that purpose, he would be quite justified in doing so.

The division of the forces, which in any case is indispensable, must be the basis for envelopment, for envelopment is the most natural form of attack and should not be disregarded without good cause. It can only be justified if the attacker is strong enough not to have any doubts about the outcome.

6. Attack also requires caution.

The attacker himself has a rear and communications to protect. This protection should, if possible, consist in the direction of advance.

If forces have to be detached for this purpose, thus causing a diversion of strength, it can only lessen the impact of the blow. Dangers of this sort to which the attacker is exposed can be gauged chiefly by the opponent's character and situation.

If everything is subordinated to the pressure of an imminent major decision, the defender will have little scope for auxiliary operations, and the attacker, therefore, will not ordinarily be in great danger. But once the advance is over and the attacker gradually goes over to a state of defense, the protection of the rear assumes increasing urgency and importance.

The attacker's rear is inherently more vulnerable than the defender's. Thus the latter may have started operations against the attacker's lines of communication long before he goes over to an actual offensive, and even while he is still on the retreat.

DIVERSIONS

The term "diversion" in ordinary usage means an attack on a rival's territory that draws off its forces from the main objective. Only where this is the chief intention is a diversion a distinct operation. Otherwise, it remains an ordinary attack.

In such a diversion there must, of course, be an objective to attack. Only the value of this objective can induce the opponent to dispatch personnel for its protection. Besides, if the operation fails as a diversion, the objective will serve as a compensation for the effort expended.

These objectives may be important and wealthy areas. Diversions can obviously be useful, but this is not by any means invariably the fact. Sometimes they can actually do harm. The main requirement is that the opponent should withdraw more personnel from the main scene of operations than are used for the diversion.

If the numbers are even, the effectiveness of the diversion as such ceases, and the operation becomes merely a subordinate engagement. Even where a subordinate attack is called for because a major objective might be achieved by a very small expenditure of strength, one should not call it a diversion.

If small forces are to draw off larger ones, there must obviously be special circumstances at the root of it. For a diversion to be effective, it is not enough arbitrarily to dispatch personnel to a previously unoccupied place. Thus, the value of large-scale diversion is very doubtful. And the larger it is, the more the remaining circumstances must favor the diversion if it is to be successful at all.

The following factors may be favorable:

1. Forces that the attacker can make available for the diversion without detracting from his main offensive
2. Vulnerable objectives of great importance to the opponent
3. Disaffected opponents
4. An area rich enough to yield substantial benefits

Diversions are attempted only if they promise success after having passed these various tests. However, we find that favorable opportunities do not arise very often. Another important point remains to be considered: Diversions always bring the conflict into an area that would otherwise have been left untouched. It is quite natural, and experience has frequently illustrated that when an area is suddenly threatened and no preparations have been made to defend it, new means of resistance are created.

COMMENTARY

Clausewitz asserts that "in a diversion there must, of course, be an objective to attack." The inference is that the objective must be part of the overall business plan and a key component of the strategies and tactics section of the plan.

Yet, it is not uncommon to find that diversions often mean running after some Monday-morning headline that intrigues an executive, rather than serving some strategic purpose. During such spur of the moment diversions, there often is insufficient time to develop a follow-through plan of what resources it takes to make the initial penetration, how to follow through, when to culminate the attack, and when to proceed to the defense. In the end, the expedition can end up as just a whim that results in splitting forces, resources, and shifting management's attention from the primary objectives of the plan.

EXECUTION

The more remote the likelihood of a great decision in a conflict is, the more legitimate it is to make diversions. Of course, the smaller are the gains one can expect. Such diversions are simply a means of stirring up a situation.

A diversion may include a real attack. In that event its execution calls for no special characteristics apart from speed and daring. It may, however, be calculated to look more important than it is, thus being at the same time a feint. The exact means that should be used to achieve this can only be determined by an acute mind, with close knowledge of the circumstances and forces involved.

It will inevitably involve considerable dispersal of forces. However, if the forces involved are not inconsiderable and the retreat is restricted to certain points, it is essential to maintain a reserve on which the rest can fall back.

THE CULMINATING POINT OF VICTORY

It is not possible in every conflict for the victor to overthrow his adversary completely. Often even victory has a culminating point. This has been demonstrated by experience. Because the matter is particularly important in the theory of conflict and forms the keystone for most campaign plans, and because its surface is distorted by apparent contradictions, we shall examine it more closely and seek out its inner logic.

Victory normally results from the superiority of one side from an aggregate of physical and psychological strengths. This superiority is certainly augmented by the victory. Otherwise, it would not be so coveted or command so high a price. That is an automatic consequence of victory itself.

Its effects exert a similar influence, but only up to a point. That point may be reached quickly—at times so quickly that the total consequences of a victorious campaign may be limited to an increase in psychological superiority alone. We only propose to examine how that comes about.

As a conflict unfolds, organizations are constantly faced with some factors that increase their strength and with others that reduce it. The question, therefore, is one of superiority. Every reduction in strength on one side can be considered as an increase on the other. It follows that this two-way process is to be found in attack as well as in defense. What we have to do is examine the principal cause of this change in one of these instances and thus, at the same time, determine the other.

In an advance, the principal causes of additional strength are:

1. The losses suffered by the defending forces are usually heavier than those of the attacker.
2. The defender's loss of fixed assets is not experienced by the attacker.
3. The defender loses ground, and therefore resources, from the time we enter his territory.
4. The attacker benefits from the use of some of these resources. In other words, he can live at the opponent's expense.
5. The opponent loses his inner cohesion and the smooth functioning of all components of his force.
6. Some allies are lost to the defender; others turn to the attacker.
7. The defender is discouraged and thus, to some extent, disarmed.

The causes of loss in strength for an attacker are:

1. The attacker has to challenge or observe the rival's strong areas. The defender, if he has previously been doing the same, will now add the resources to his main force.
2. The moment an attacker enters the opponent's territory, the nature of the operational area changes. It becomes hostile. It must be controlled if only to the extent that the attacker has done so. But this creates difficulties, which will inevitably weaken its effectiveness.
3. The attacker moves away from his sources of supply, while the defender moves closer to his own. This causes delay in the replacement of the attacker's forces.
4. The danger threatening the defender will bring allies to his aid.
5. The defender, being in real danger, makes the greater effort, whereas the efforts of the victor slacken off.

All these advantages and disadvantages may coexist. They can meet and pursue their ways in opposite directions. That alone is enough to show the infinite range of effects a victory can have, depending on whether they stun the loser or rouse him to greater efforts.

We shall try to qualify each of the preceding points in a few brief comments:

Initially, the opponent's losses may be at their maximum directly after his defeat and then diminish daily until the point is reached where his strength equals ours. On the other hand, his losses may grow progressively day by day. All depends on differences in the overall situation and circumstances. Generally speaking, one can only say that the former is more likely to occur with a good group and the latter with a bad one.

Second, the most important factor besides the spirit of the personnel is the spirit at the highest levels of the organization. It is vital to distinguish between the two, or one may stop at the very point where one should really start. The rival's loss of fixed assets may decrease or increase in the same way, depending on the location and nature of his supply.

The third advantage cannot fail to grow with the progress of the advance. Indeed, one can say that it only begins to count when the attack has penetrated deeply into the opponent's territory. A further factor is an area's intrinsic value in relation to the total effort.

The fourth advantage is also bound to increase as the advance proceeds. In connection with these two last points, it should be noted that they seldom have an immediate effect on personnel in action. Their work is slow and indirect. Therefore, one should not on their account make too great an effort and thus place oneself in too dangerous a situation.

Now let us turn to the causes for loss in strength.

In most cases as an advance proceeds, there will be more obstacles. These may be so debilitating as easily to cancel out all other advantages, and the further the advance goes, the risks they represent will progressively increase. Not only are they hard to cover, but the very length of unprotected lines of communication tends to challenge the opponent's spirit of enterprise; the consequences their loss can have in the event of a retreat are very grave indeed.

All this contributes to place a new burden on an advancing group with every step it takes. Therefore, unless it started with exceptional superiority, it will find its freedom of action dwindling and its offensive power progressively reduced. In the end, it will feel unsure of itself and nervous about its situation.

Although the wealth of the overcome areas may mitigate this problem, it can never eliminate it altogether. There are always things that must be supplied.

Further, if a leader does not command his personnel in person—if he is no longer easily available, a new and very serious handicap arises from the loss of time involved in the transmission of messages. Even the widest powers conferred on a leader will not suffice to meet every contingency that may arise in his sphere of action.

Then, there is the change in organizational alignments. If these changes, resulting from his victories, are likely to be to the disadvantage of the victor, they will probably be so in direct proportion to his advance. All depends on the existing affiliations, interests, traditions, lines of policy, and various personalities.

The last two points alone can make an infinite difference to the plans that one can and must make in a conflict to take account of either possibility. While one man may lose his best chance through timidity and following so-called orthodox procedures, another will plunge in headfirst and end up looking as dazed and surprised as if he had just been fished out of the water.

Also, one should be conscious of the slackening of effort that not infrequently occurs on the part of the victor after the danger has been overcome and when fresh efforts are called for to follow up the victory. If we take an overall view of these differing and opposing principles, we will doubtless conclude that the utilization of the victory and a continued advance in an offensive campaign will usually swallow up the superiority with which one began or that was gained by the victory.

At this point we are bound to ask: If all this is true, why does the winner persist in pursuing his victorious course, in advancing his offensive? Can one really still call this a "utilization of victory?" Would he not do better to stop before he begins to lose the upper hand?

The obvious answer is that superior strength is not the end but only the means. The end is either to neutralize the opponent or at least to deprive him of some of his territory. The point in that case is not to improve the current position, but rather to improve one's general prospects in the conflict.

Even if one tries to destabilize the opponent completely, one must accept the fact that every step gained may weaken one's superiority. One may do so at an earlier point, and if this can be accomplished with one's last ounce of superiority, it would be a mistake not to use it.

Thus, the superiority one has or gains in a conflict is only the means and not the end. It must be risked for the sake of the end. But one must know the point to which it can be carried in order not to overshoot the target. Otherwise, instead of gaining new advantages, one will disgrace oneself.

This culminating point in victory is bound to recur in every conflict in which the neutralization of the opponent cannot be the aim, and this will presumably be true of most conflicts. The natural goal of all campaign plans, therefore, is the turning point at which attack becomes defense.

If one were to go beyond that point, it would not merely be a useless effort that could not add to success. It would in fact be a damaging one, which would lead to a reaction. And experience goes to show that such reactions usually have completely disproportionate effects. This is such a universal experience and appears so natural and easy to understand, that there is no need for a laborious investigation of its causes.

COMMENTARY

Clausewitz referred to the culminating point earlier in this chapter. Here, he again talks about the concept and positions it as part of "universal experience." Then, he adds his often mentioned comment that the "natural goal of plans is the turning point at which attack becomes defense."

Next, in unusually strong terms, Clausewitz states that the mere notion to "overshoot the target ... one can disgrace oneself." In equally strong terms, the clear implication of his dramatic statement is that the executive's obligation and the line manager's essential responsibility are to stay as close as possible to an evolving campaign and determine the critical culminating point when an attack turns into a defense.

It appears that many of Clausewitz's primary concepts regarding conflict, attack versus defense, waiting and acting, and neutralizing the opponent all converge in the culminating point.

At this point we must eliminate an apparent inconsistency. This rests on the assumption that so long as an attack progresses, there must still be some superiority on its side. Further, that since defense must start when the advance ends, one may not really be in much danger of imperceptibly becoming the weaker side.

Yet that is what happens; history forces us to admit that the risk of a setback often does not reach its peak until the moment when the attack has lost its impetus and is turning into defense. We must look for the reason.

The superiority that I have attributed to the defensive position rests on the following:

1. The utilization of terrain
2. The possession of an organized area of operations
3. The support of the population
4. The advantage of being on the waiting side

It is obvious that these factors will not be found everywhere in equal strength or always be equally effective. Therefore, one defense is not exactly like another, nor will defense always enjoy the same degree of superiority over attack. In particular, this will be the case in a defense that follows directly the exhaustion of an offensive.

Only the first of the four factors listed before—the utilization of terrain—will remain unchanged in such a defense; the second is usually eliminated, the third works in reverse; and the fourth is much reduced in strength. A word or two in explanation of this last point may be useful.

In an imaginary equilibrium, whole campaigns might often end without result because the side that should take the initiative lacks determination. That, in our view, is exactly why it is an advantage to be able to await the opponent.

But if an offensive act upsets this equilibrium, damages the opponent's interests, and impels him into action, he is far less likely to remain inactive and irresolute. A defense is far more provocative in character when it is undertaken on occupied territory than it is on one's own.

It is, so to speak, infected with the virus of attack, and this weakens its basic character. It is clear, therefore, that a defense that is undertaken in the framework of an offensive is weakened in all its key elements. It will thus no longer possess the superiority that basically belongs to it.

Just as no defensive campaign consists simply of defensive elements, so, too, no offensive campaign consists purely of offensive ones. Apart from the short intervals in every campaign during which both sides are on the defensive, every attack that does not lead to peace must necessarily end up as a defense.

Thus, it is defense itself that weakens the attack. Far from this being idle subtlety, we consider it to be the greatest disadvantage of the attack that one is eventually left in a most awkward defensive position.

This will explain why there is a gradual reduction in the difference between the original effectiveness of attack and defense as forms of conflict. We now propose to show how this difference can for a time vanish altogether and reverse itself completely.

Once our train of thought is set in a certain direction, many reasons that would otherwise be basically adequate will not be able to deflect or arrest it. Time and rest are needed to have a sustained impact on one's consciousness.

It is the same in conflict. Once the mind is set on a certain course toward its goal, or once it has turned back toward a refuge, it may easily happen that arguments that would compel one man to stop, but justify another in acting, will not easily be fully appreciated.

Meanwhile the action continues, and in the sweep of motion one crosses the threshold of equilibrium—the line of culmination—without knowing it. It is even possible that the attacker, reinforced by the psychological forces peculiar to attack, will in spite of his exhaustion find it less difficult to go on than to stop.

We believe that this demonstrates without inconsistency how an attacker can overshoot the point at which, if he stopped and assumed the defensive, there would still be a chance of success—that is, of equilibrium. It is therefore important to calculate this point correctly when planning the campaign. An attacker may otherwise take on more than he can manage and, as it were, get into debt. A defender must be able to recognize this error if the opponent commits it and exploit it to the full.

In reviewing the whole array of factors a leader must weigh before making his decision, we must remember that he can gauge the direction and value of the most important ones only by considering numerous other possibilities—some immediate, some remote. He must guess whether the first shock of a confrontation will steel the rival's resolve and stiffen his resistance, or whether they will shatter as soon as the surface is scratched.

When we realize that he must hit upon these and much more by means of his discreet judgment, we must admit that such an accomplishment of the human mind is no small achievement. Thousands of wrong turns running in all directions tempt his perception. And if the range, confusion, and complexity of the issues are not enough to overwhelm him, the dangers and responsibilities may.

This is why the great majority of leaders will prefer to stop well short of their objective rather than risk approaching it too closely—and why those with high courage and an enterprising spirit will often overshoot it and thus fail to attain their purpose. Only the leader who can achieve great results with limited means has really hit the mark.

Chapter 11

Plans

Clausewitz makes these key points about plans:

- Plans cover every aspect of a conflict and weave them into a single operation that must have a single objective.
- No one starts a conflict—or, rather, no one in his senses ought to do so—without first being clear in his mind what he intends to achieve by that conflict and how he intends to conduct it.
- Conflict is dependent on the interplay of possibilities and probabilities and of good and bad luck—conditions in which logical reasoning often plays no part at all.
- To discover how many of our resources must be mobilized for conflict, we must first examine our own aim and that of the rival. We must gauge the character and abilities of competing leaders and personnel and do the same with our own.
- If conflict is part of policy, then policy will determine its character. As policy becomes more ambitious and vigorous, so will conflict.
- It is policy that creates conflict. Policy is the guiding intelligence and conflict is only the instrument, not vice versa. No other possibility exists.
- Two basic principles underlie all strategic planning: First, act with the utmost concentration; second, act with the utmost speed.
- The first task in planning for an encounter is to identify the opponent's center of gravity. The second task is to ensure that the forces to be used against that point are concentrated.
- The grand objective of all action is to overthrow the opponent, which means neutralizing his forces.
- Even the weakest party must possess some way of making the opponent conscious of its presence—some means of threatening him.

- Once a major victory is achieved there must be no talk of rest, of a breathing space, of reviewing the position, or consolidating, but only of the pursuit. Every pause between one success and the next gives the opponent new opportunities.

Clausewitz talks more extensively about the preceding points:

In the chapter on the nature and purpose of conflict, we roughly sketched the general concept of conflict and alluded to the connections between conflict and other physical and social phenomena, in order to give our discussion a sound theoretical starting point. We indicated what a variety of intellectual obstacles besets the subject, while reserving detailed study of them until later.

We ended up with the conclusion that the grand objective of all action is to overthrow the opponent, which means neutralizing his forces. It was therefore possible to show that the campaign is the one and only means that a confrontation can employ. With that, we hoped, a sound working hypothesis had been established.

Then we examined, one by one, the salient patterns and situations that occur in a confrontation, trying to gauge the value of each with greater precision, both according to its inherent characteristics and in the light of actual experience. We also sought to strip away the vague, ambiguous notions commonly attached to them and tried to make it absolutely clear that the neutralization of the opponent is what always matters most.

We now revert to conflict as a whole, to the discussion of the planning for a conflict and of a campaign. This chapter will deal with the problem of conflict as a whole. It covers its dominant and most important aspect: pure strategy. Not without some hesitancy do we enter this crucial area—the central point on which all other threads converge. Indeed, this reserve is amply justified.

On the one hand, operations appear extremely simple. The greatest leaders discuss them in the plainest and most forthright language. And to hear them tell how they control and manage that enormous, complex apparatus one would think the only thing that mattered was a contest between individuals, a sort of duel.

A few uncomplicated thoughts seem to account for their decisions; either that, or the explanation lies in various emotional states and one is left with the impression that great leaders manage matters in an easy, confident, and one would almost think, off-hand sort of way. At the same time we can see how many factors are involved and have to be weighed against each other. The function of theory, therefore, is to put all this in systematic order, clearly and comprehensively, and to trace each action to an adequate, compelling cause.

When we contemplate all this, we are overcome by the fear that we shall be irresistibly dragged down to a state of dreary unimaginativeness, and grub around in the underworld of ponderous concepts where no great leader, with his effortless *coup d'oeil,* his ability to see things simply, was ever seen. If that were the best that theoretical studies could produce, it would be better never to have attempted them in the first place.

Men of genuine talent would despise them and they would quickly be forgotten. When all is said and done, it really is the leader's *coup d'oeil* to identify the whole business of conflict completely with him. That is the essence of good leadership. Only if the mind works in this comprehensive fashion can it achieve the freedom it needs to dominate events and not be dominated by them.

We resume our task then, with humility, and we shall fail unless we keep to the path we set ourselves at the beginning. Theory should cast a steady light on all phenomena so that we can more easily recognize and eliminate the weeds that always spring from ignorance.

It should show how one thing is related to another and keep the important and the unimportant separate. If concepts combine of their own accord to form that nucleus of truth we call a principle and if they spontaneously compose a pattern that becomes a rule, it is the task of the theorist to make this clear.

Any insights gained and garnered by the mind in its wanderings among basic concepts are the benefits that theory can provide. Theory cannot equip the mind with formulas for solving problems, nor can it mark the narrow path on which the sole solution is supposed to lie by planting a hedge of principles on either side. But it can give the mind insight into the great mass of phenomena and of their relationships and then leave it free to rise into the higher realms of action.

There the mind can use its innate talents to combine them all, to seize on what is right and true, as though this were a single idea formed by their concentrated pressure—as though it were a response to the immediate challenge rather than a product of thought.

ABSOLUTE CONFLICT AND REAL CONFLICT

Plans cover every aspect of a conflict and weave them all into a single operation that must have a single, ultimate objective in which all particular aims are reconciled. No one starts a conflict—or rather, no one in his senses ought to do so—without first being clear in his mind what he intends to achieve by that conflict and how he intends to conduct it. The former is its political purpose; the latter is its operational objective.

This is the governing principle that will set its course, prescribe the scale of means and effort required, and make its influence felt throughout, down to the smallest operational detail.

COMMENTARY

Clausewitz's reference to "political purpose" is best transposed to mean the policies of the organization. They typically cover those foundation operational guidelines that control an organization. Policies form a tangible imprint of your company's culture and its functional procedures and practices, which give your organization consistency and a distinctive personality.

While policy making may be outside your area of input, it does influence heavily your ability to:

- Select the types of strategies to grow your business.
- Determine the parameters by which you are able to innovate and compete for market advantage.
- Attract new talent and assign existing personnel to new levels of authority and responsibility.
- Secure your position on the supply chain, with particular attention to solidifying relationships and blocking competitive threats.
- Deploy your financial and human resources to exploit market opportunities.

Policy, therefore, should hold a legitimate and powerful influence on your business plans. It impacts your vision to cultivate the growth of your markets. And it controls the strategy options you can use to avoid major conflicts and local confrontations, especially against competitors with little interest in nurturing the long-term prosperity of the marketplace.

Clausewitz continues:

We said that the natural aim of operations is the opponent's neutralization, and that strict adherence to the logic of the concept can, in the last analysis, admit of no other. Since both adversaries must hold that view, it would follow that operations could not be suspended, that confrontations could not end, until one or the other side was finally overwhelmed.

We must allow for natural inertia, for all the friction of its parts, for all the inconsistency, imprecision, and timidity of man. And we must face the fact that conflict and its forms result from ideas, emotions, and conditions prevailing at the time.

If this is the case, if we must admit that the origin and the form taken by a conflict are not the result of the vast array of unresolved circumstances, but only of those features that happen to be dominant, it follows that conflict is dependent on the interplay of possibilities and probabilities, of good and bad luck. These are the conditions in which strictly logical reasoning often plays no part at all and is always apt to be a most unsuitable and awkward intellectual tool. It follows, too, that conflict can be a matter of degree.

Theory must concede all this. But it has the duty to give priority to the absolute form of conflict and to make that form a general point of reference so that he who wants to learn from theory becomes accustomed to keeping that point in view constantly, to measuring all his hopes and fears by it, and to approximating it when he can or when he must.

A principle that underlies our thoughts and actions will undoubtedly lend them a certain tone and character, though the immediate causes of our action may have different origins, just as the tone a painter gives to his canvas is determined by the color of the underpainting.

INTERDEPENDENCE OF THE ELEMENTS OF CONFLICT

Since conflict can be thought of in two different ways—its absolute form or one of the variant forms that it actually takes—two different concepts of success arise. In the absolute form of conflict, where everything results from necessary causes and one action rapidly affects another, there is no intervening neutral void.

Since conflict contains a host of interactions, since the whole series of engagements is linked together, and since in every victory there is a culminating point beyond which lies the realm of losses and defeats, we say there is only one result that counts: final victory.

Until then, nothing is decided, nothing won, and nothing lost. In this form of conflict, we must always keep in mind that it is the end that crowns the work. Within the concept of absolute conflict, then, conflict is indivisible. Its component parts—the individual victories—are of value only in their relation to the whole.

Contrasting with this extreme view of the connection between successes in conflict is another view, which holds that conflict consists of separate successes, each unrelated to the next, as in a match consisting of several games. The earlier games have no effect upon the later ones. All that counts is the total score, and each separate result makes its contribution toward this total.

The first of these two views of conflict derives its validity from the nature of the subject and the second from its actual history. Countless cases have occurred where a small advantage could be gained without a burdensome condition being attached to it.

The more the element of force is moderated, the commoner these cases will be. Yet just as absolute conflict has never been achieved, so we will never find a conflict in which the second concept is so prevalent that the first can be disregarded altogether.

If we hypothesize the first of the two concepts, it necessarily follows from the start that every conflict must be conceived of as a single whole. And with his first move the leader must already have a clear idea of the goal on which all lines are to converge.

If we conjecture about the second concept, we will find it legitimate to pursue minor advantages for their own sake and leave the future to itself. Since both these concepts lead to results, theory cannot dispense with either.

Theory makes this distinction in the application of the two concepts: All action must be based on the former, since it is the fundamental concept. The latter can be used only as a modification justified by circumstances.

SCALE OF THE OBJECTIVE AND
OF THE EFFORT TO BE MADE

The degree of force that must be used against the rival depends on the scale of demands on either side. These demands, so far as they are known, would show what efforts each must make. Yet, they seldom are fully known, which may be one reason why both sides do not exert themselves to the same degree. Nor are the situations and conditions of the adversaries alike.

This can be a second factor. Just as unequal are the organizations' strength of will, their character, and abilities. These considerations introduce uncertainties that make it difficult to gauge the amount of resistance to be faced—as well as the means required and the objectives to be set. Since in conflict too small an effort can result not just in failure but in positive harm, each side is driven to outdo the other, which sets up an interaction.

Such an interaction could lead to a maximum effort, if such a maximum could be defined. But in that case all proportion between action and demands would be lost. Means would cease to be commensurate with ends, and in most cases a policy of maximum exertion would fail on account of the domestic problems it would raise.

In this way the aggressor is again driven to adopt a middle course. He would act on the principle of using no greater force, and setting himself no greater planning aim, than would be sufficient for the achievement of his purpose. To turn this principle into practice he must renounce the need for absolute success in each given case, and he must dismiss remoter possibilities from his calculations. At this point, then, intellectual activity leaves the field of the exact sciences of logic and mathematics.

It then becomes an art in the broadest meaning of the term—the faculty of using judgment to detect the most important and decisive elements in the vast array of facts and situations. Undoubtedly, this power of judgment consists to a greater or lesser degree in the intuitive comparison of all the factors and circumstances.

What is remote and secondary is at once dismissed while the most pressing and important points are identified with greater speed than could be done by strictly logical deduction. To discover how many of our resources must be mobilized for conflict, we must first examine our own aim and that of the rival. We must gauge the strength and situation of the opposition.

We must gauge the character and abilities of its leaders and personnel and do the same in regard to our own. Finally, we must evaluate the political sympathies of other groups and the effect the conflict may have on them. To assess these things in all their ramifications and diversity is plainly a colossal task.

Rapid and correct appraisal of them clearly calls for the intuition of a genius. To master all this complex mass by sheer methodical examination is obviously impossible. Newton himself would quail before the algebraic problems it could pose.

The size and variety of factors to be weighed and the uncertainty about the proper scale to use are bound to make it far more difficult to reach the right conclusion. We should also bear in mind that the vast, unique importance of conflict, while not increasing the complexity and difficulty of the problem, does increase the value of the correct solution.

Responsibility and danger do not tend to free or stimulate the average person's mind—rather, the contrary. Wherever they do liberate an individual's judgment and confidence, we can be sure that we are in the presence of exceptional ability.

At the outset, then, we must admit that an imminent conflict, its possible aims, and the resources it will require are matters that can only be assessed when every circumstance has been examined in the context of the whole, which of course includes the most transient factors as well.

We must also recognize that the conclusion reached can be no more wholly objective than any other in conflict, but will be shaped by the qualities of mind and character of the men making the decision—of the leaders, whether these roles are united in a single individual or not.

COMMENTARY

Clausewitz's comments about "the complex mass ... and variety of factors to be weighed," can be modified somewhat for today's practices when considering the vast array of computer programs that sort, calculate, and interpret huge amounts of data. Yet, there is still the judgmental factor of what to do with the analysis. As important is the pressure to make insightful judgments about what the competing manager will do with his or her analysis.

As Clausewitz says: "The conclusion reached ... will be shaped by the qualities of mind and character of the men making the decision."

DEFINITION OF THE OBJECTIVE CONTINUED: LIMITED AIMS

The conditions for defeating an opponent presuppose great physical or moral superiority or else an extremely enterprising spirit—that is, an inclination for serious risks. When neither of these is present, the object of activity can only be one of two kinds: seizing a small piece of the rival's territory or holding one's own until things take a better turn. This latter is normally the aim of a defensive conflict.

In considering which the right course is, it is well to remember the phrase used about the latter, waiting until things take a better turn, which assumes that there is ground for expecting this to happen. That prospect always underlies a "waiting" conflict—that is, a defensive conflict.

The offensive—exploiting the advantages of the moment—is advisable whenever the future affords better prospects to the opponent than it does to us. Another possibility, perhaps the most usual, arises when the future seems to promise nothing definite to either side and hence affords no grounds for a decision.

Obviously, in that case, the offensive should be taken by the side that possesses the initiative. That is, the side that has an active purpose, the aim for which it went into a conflict. If any time is lost without good reason, the initiator bears the loss.

The grounds we have just defined for choosing offensive or defensive conflict have nothing to do with the relative strength of the two sides, although one might suppose that to be the main consideration. But we believe that if it were, the wrong decision would result. No one can say the logic of our simple argument is weak. But does it in practice lead to absurd conclusions?

Suppose that a minor group is in conflict with a much more powerful one and expects its position to grow weaker every year. If conflict is unavoidable, should it not make the most of its opportunities before its position gets still worse?

In short, it should attack. Not because attack in itself is advantageous, but because the smaller party's interest is either to settle the quarrel before conditions deteriorate, or at least to acquire some advantages so as to keep its efforts going. No one could consider this a ludicrous argument.

But if the smaller group is quite certain its rival will attack, it can and should stand on the defensive, so as to win the first advantage. By doing so, it will not be placed at any disadvantage because of the passage of time.

Again, suppose a small group is in a confrontation with a greater one and that the future promises nothing that will influence either side's decisions. If the initiative lies with the smaller group, it should take the offensive.

Having had the nerve to assume an active role against a stronger adversary, it must do something definite. In other words, attack the opponent unless he obliges by attacking first.

Waiting would be absurd, unless the smaller group had changed its decision at the moment of executing its policy. That is what often happens, and partly explains why the indeterminate character of some confrontations leaves a student very much perplexed.

Our discussion of the limited aim suggests that two kinds of limited conflict are possible: offensive conflict with a limited aim and defensive conflict. But first there is a further point to consider. The nature of the political aim, the scale of demands put forward by either side, or the total political situation of one's own side are all factors that in practice must decisively influence the conduct of a confrontation.

CONFLICT IS AN INSTRUMENT OF POLICY

Up to now we have considered the difference that distinguishes conflict from every other human interest, individual or social—a difference that derives from human nature and therefore that no philosophy can resolve. We have examined this incompatibility from various angles so that none of its conflicting elements should be missed.

Now we must seek out the unity into which these contradictory elements combine in real life, which they do by partly neutralizing one another. This unity lies in the concept that conflict is only a branch of political activity—that it is in no sense autonomous.

It is, of course, well known that the only source of conflict is politics—the intercourse of governments and peoples. But it is apt to be assumed that conflict suspends that intercourse and replaces it by a wholly different condition, ruled by no law but its own.

We maintain, on the contrary, that conflict is simply a continuation of political intercourse, with the addition of other means. We deliberately use the phrase "with the addition of other means" because we also want to make it clear that conflict in itself does not suspend political intercourse or change it into something entirely different.

It is essential that intercourse continues, irrespective of the means it employs. The main lines along which events progress and to which they are restricted are political lines that continue throughout the conflict into the subsequent peace.

COMMENTARY

"Conflict is an instrument of policy" is one of Clausewitz's most famous and often repeated statements. Other translators have expressed it as "war is an extension of policy by other means."

In the context of this chapter, one central interpretation is that operational plans must be an extension of the strategic plan, which should incorporate the strategic direction of the organization (also known as the vision or mission statement); its corporate values, which reflect the intrinsic culture of the company; and its operating policies.

The strategic plan also addresses the economic, environmental, technological, and other relevant factors that face the organization. And within the framework of conflict, the plan must take into consideration the competitive issues that relate to the inevitable encounters with rivals.

Consequently, the mere thought of developing a business or campaign plan to enter a new market and to face a competitive threat without taking into account the political meaning of the company's strategic direction is a violation of Clausewitz's salient points regarding "conflict is an instrument of policy."

Do political relations between people and between their leadership stop when diplomatic notes are no longer exchanged? Is conflict not just another expression of their thoughts, another form of speech or writing? Its grammar, indeed, may be its own—but not its logic.

If that is so, then conflict cannot be divorced from political life. And whenever this occurs in our thinking about conflict, the many links that connect the two elements are destroyed and we are left with something pointless and devoid of sense.

This conception would be unavoidable even if conflict were total conflict, the pure element of hostility unleashed. All the factors that go to make up conflict and determine its significant features—the strength and allies of each adversary, the character of the people and their leaderships, and so forth—are these not so closely connected with political activity that it is impossible to separate the two?

But it is yet more vital to bear all this in mind when studying actual practice. We will then find that conflict does not advance relentlessly toward the absolute, as theory would demand. Being incomplete and self-contradictory, it cannot follow its own laws, but has to be treated as a part of some other whole, the name of which is policy.

In making use of conflict, policy evades all rigorous conclusions proceeding from the nature of a confrontation, bothers little about ultimate possibilities, and concerns itself only with immediate probabilities. Although this introduces a high degree of uncertainty into the whole business, turning it into a kind of game, each leadership is confident that it can outdo its opponent in skill and acumen.

Therefore, the contradictions in which conflict involves that naturally timid creature, man, are resolved, if this is the solution we choose to accept. If conflict is part of policy, policy will determine its character.

As policy becomes more ambitious and vigorous, so will conflict. And this may reach the point where conflict attains its absolute form. If we look at conflict in this light, we do not need to lose sight of this absolute. On the contrary, we must constantly bear it in mind.

Only if conflict is looked at in this way does its unity reappear. Only then can we see that all conflicts are things of the same nature. And this alone will provide the right criteria for conceiving and judging great designs.

Political considerations do not determine the employment of small groups. But they are the more influential in the planning of conflict and of the campaign. That is why we felt no urge to introduce this point of view at the start. At the stage of detailed study, it would not have been much help and might have been distracting.

However, when plans for a conflict or a campaign are under study, this point of view is indispensable. Nothing is more important in life than finding the right standpoint for seeing and judging events and then adhering to it. One point only yields an integrated view of all phenomena. By holding to that point of view one can avoid inconsistency.

It can be agreed that the aim of policy is to unify and reconcile all aspects of internal administration as well as of spiritual values and whatever else the moral philosopher may care to add. Policy, of course, is nothing in itself; it is simply the trustee for all these interests against the outside world.

That it can err and serve the ambitions, private interests, and vanity of those in power is neither here nor there. In no sense can the art of conflict ever be as the instructor of policy. We can only treat policy as representative of all interests of the community.

That the political view should wholly cease to count on the outbreak of conflict is hardly conceivable. In fact, as we have said, it is nothing but an expression of policy itself. Subordinating the political point of view to the combative forces would be absurd.

It is policy that creates conflict. Policy is the guiding intelligence and conflict only the instrument, not vice versa. No other possibility exists.

It is from this point of view, then, that plans are cast. Judgment and understanding are easier and more natural; convictions gain in strength, motives in conviction, and history in sense. From this point of view again, no conflict need arise any longer between political and other interests. And should it arise, it will show no more than lack of understanding.

It might be thought that policy could make demands on conflict that a confrontation could not fulfill. That hypothesis would challenge the natural and unavoidable assumption that policy knows the instrument it means to use. If policy reads the course of campaign events, it is wholly and exclusively entitled to decide which events and trends are best for the objectives of the conflict.

This is as it should be. No major proposal required for a conflict can be worked out in ignorance of political factors. And when people talk about harmful political influence on the management of a conflict, they are not really saying what they mean.

Their quarrel should be with the policy itself, not with its influence. If the policy is right—that is, successful—any intentional effect it has on the conduct of the conflict can only be to the good. If it has the opposite effect, the policy itself is wrong.

Once again, conflict is an instrument of policy. It must necessarily bear the character of policy and measure by its standards. The conduct of a confrontation, in its great outlines, is therefore policy itself, which takes up the sword in place of the pen, but does not on that account cease to think according to its own laws.

THE LIMITED AIM: OFFENSIVE WAR

Even when we cannot hope to neutralize the rival totally, a direct and positive aim still is possible: the occupation of part of his territory. The point of such a takeover is to reduce his resources. We thus reduce his capability and increase our own. As a result, we fight partly at his expense.

This is a very natural view to take of acquired territory. The only drawback is the necessity of defending that territory once we have occupied it, which might be a source of some anxiety.

In the previous chapter on the culminating point of victory, we dealt at some length with the way in which an offensive weakens the attacking force.

We showed how a situation might develop that could give rise to serious consequences.

Capturing rival territory will reduce the strength of our forces in varying degrees, which are determined by the location of the occupied territory. If it adjoins our own, the more directly it lies on the line of our main advance, the less our strength will suffer.

If, on the other hand, the territory taken is flanked by rival ground on either side, its occupation will become so plain a burden as to make an opponent's victory not just easier but perhaps superfluous.

The question of whether one should aim at such a conquest, then, is whether one can be sure of holding it or, if not, whether a temporary occupation will really be worth the cost of the operation and, especially, whether there is any risk of being strongly counterattacked and thrown off balance. In the chapter on the culminating point (Chapter 10), we emphasized how many factors need to be considered in each particular case.

Only one thing remains to be said. An offensive of this type is not always appropriate to make up for losses elsewhere. While we are busy occupying one area, the opponent may be doing the same somewhere else. If our project is not of overwhelming significance, it will not compel the rival to up his own conquest. Thorough consideration is therefore necessary to decide whether, on balance, we will gain or lose.

In general, one tends to lose more from occupation by the opponent than one gains from conquering his territory, even if the value of both areas should be identical. The reason is that a whole range of resources is denied to us.

However, since this is also the case with the opponent, it ought not to be a reason for thinking that retention is more important than conquest. Yet this is so. The retention of one's own territory is always a matter of more direct concern, and the damage that we suffer may be balanced.

It follows from all this that a strategic attack with a limited objective is burdened with the defense of other points, which the attack itself will not directly cover. It would be far more burdened than it would be if aimed at the heart of the opponent's power. The effect is to limit the scale on which forces can be concentrated, both in time and in space.

If this concentration is to be achieved, at least in terms of time, the offensive must be launched from every practicable point at once. Then, however, the attack loses the other advantage of being able to stay on the defensive here and there, and thus make do with a much smaller force.

The net result of having such a limited objective is that everything tends to cancel out. We cannot then put all our strength into a single massive blow, aimed in accordance with our major interest. Effort is increasingly dispersed; friction everywhere increases, and greater scope is left for chance.

That is how events tend to develop, dragging the leader down, frustrating him more and more. The more conscious he is of his own powers, the greater his self-confidence, and the larger the forces he commands, then the more he will seek to break loose from this tendency to give some single point importance.

THE LIMITED AIM: DEFENSIVE CONFLICT

The ultimate aim of a defensive conflict, as we have seen, can never be an absolute negation. Even the weakest party must possess some way of making the opponent conscious of its presence, some means of threatening him.

No doubt that end could be pursued by wearing the rival down. But the defender's loss is not incurred in vain. He has held his ground, which is all he meant to do. For the defender, then, it might be said that his positive aim is to hold what he has.

That might be sound if it were sure that a certain number of attacks would actually wear the opponent down and make him desist. But this is not necessarily so. If we consider the relative exhaustion of forces on both sides, the defender is at a disadvantage. The attack may weaken, but only in the sense that a turning point may occur.

Once that possibility is gone, the defender weakens more than the attacker, for two reasons. For one thing, he is weaker anyway, and if losses are the same on both sides, it is he who is harder hit. Second, the opponent will usually deprive him of part of his territory and resources.

In all this we can find no reason for the attacker to desist. We are left with the conclusion that if the attacker sustains his efforts while his opponent does nothing but ward them off, the latter can do nothing to neutralize the danger and sooner or later an offensive thrust will succeed.

Certainly the exhaustion or, to be accurate, the fatigue of the stronger has often brought about peace. The reason can be found in the half-hearted manner in which conflicts are usually waged. It cannot be taken in any scientific sense as the ultimate, universal objective of all defenses.

Only one hypothesis remains: that the aim of the defense must embody the idea of waiting, which is, after all, its leading feature. The idea implies, moreover, that the situation can develop in which if improvement cannot be effected from within by sheer resistance, it can only come from without. And an improvement from without implies a change in the political situation. Either additional allies come to the defender's help, or allies begin to desert his opponent.

Such, then, is the defender's aim if his lack of strength prohibits any serious counterattack. But according to the concept of the defense that we have formulated, this does not always apply. We have argued that the defensive is the more effective form of conflict, and because of this effectiveness it can also be employed to execute a counteroffensive on whatever scale.

These two categories must be kept distinct from the very start, for each has its effect on the conduct of the defense. The defender's purpose in the first category is to keep his territory intact and to hold it for as long as possible. That will gain him time, and gaining time is the only way he can achieve his aim.

The positive aim—the most he can achieve and the one that will get him what he wants—cannot yet be included in his plan of operations. He has to remain strategically passive, and the only success he can win consists in beating off attacks at given points.

These small advantages can then be used to strengthen other points, for pressure may be severe at all of them. If he has no chance of doing so, his only profit is the fact that the adversary will not trouble him again for a while.

That sort of defense can include minor offensive operations without their altering its nature or purpose. They should not aim at permanent acquisitions but at the temporary seizure of assets that can be returned at a later date. They can take the form of campaigns or diversions; but always on condition that sufficient forces can be spared from their defensive role.

The second category exists where the defense has already assumed a positive purpose. It then acquires an active character that comes to the fore as the scale of a feasible counterattack expands.

Of these, the boldest, if it works, is to retire into the interior. Such an expedient could hardly be more different from the first type of defensive. A major victory can only be obtained by positive measures aimed at a decision, never by simply waiting on events. In short, even in the defense, a major stake alone can bring a major gain.

THE PLAN OF A CONFLICT DESIGNED TO LEAD TO THE TOTAL NEUTRALIZATION OF THE OPPONENT

Having given a more detailed account of the various objects a conflict can serve, we shall now consider how the whole conflict should be planned with a view to the three distinguishable phases that can go with each particular aim. After everything we have said on the subject, we can identify two basic principles that underlie all strategic planning and serve to guide all other considerations.

The first principle is that the ultimate substance of the opponent's strength must be traced back to the fewest possible sources—ideally, to one alone. The attack on these sources must be compressed into the fewest possible actions—again, ideally, into one.

Finally, all minor actions must be subordinated as much as possible. In short, the first principle is to act with the utmost concentration.

The second principle is to act with the utmost speed. No halt or detour must be permitted without good cause.

COMMENTARY

Clausewitz's two planning principles are generally accepted in today's business practices. Unfortunately, they are not always followed. Thus, a few comments for reinforcement are in order.

As for the first principle, concentration: This classic principle is in sharp contrast to the overly common planning approach of spreading resources in several directions, covering numerous objectives, segments, and isolated actions. Whereas the thinking may be to play it safe and cover all contingencies, instead it has the potentially damaging effect of dramatically exposing weaknesses and revealing areas of vulnerability. The result is that the chances of failure multiply through the excessive thinning of resources.

What is behind this singular straightforward principle? In practice, it means concentrating your resources at a customer group, geographic segment, or a single competitor. It means finding the decisive point so that, as Clausewitz indicates, "The attack ... must be compressed into the fewest possible actions—ideally, into one."

The hardnosed evidence from history and current business methods leads unequivocally to adopting a strategy that aims at concentrating resources where you can gain superiority in as few areas as possible.

As for the second principle, speed: "There is no instance of a country having benefited from prolonged warfare," declared the ancient Chinese strategist Sun Tzu. In applicable terms, there are few cases of overlong, dragged-out campaigns that have been successful. Exhaustion—the draining of resources—has killed more companies than almost any other factor. "Without exception, all of my biggest mistakes occurred because I moved too slowly," declared John Chambers, CEO of Cisco Systems.

Thus, "no halt or detour must be permitted without good cause." Extended deliberation, procrastination, cumbersome committees, and indecisiveness are all detriments to success. Drawn-out efforts often divert interest, diminish enthusiasm, and damage morale.

Moreover, employees become bored and their skills lose sharpness. As damaging, the gaps created through lack of action give competitors extra time to develop strategies that can blunt your efforts. Therefore, it is in your best interest to evaluate, maneuver, and concentrate your forces in the shortest span of time.

The proverbs, opportunities are fleeting and the window of opportunity is open, have an intensified truth in today's markets. Speed, then, is essential for gaining the advantage and exploiting an opportunity.

Clausewitz continues with the same themes by talking about the opponent's center of gravity.

The task of reducing the sources of the rival's strength to a single center of gravity will depend on:

First, if the distribution of the opponent's power lies within the forces of a single organization, there will normally be no problem. If it is shared among allies, one of which is simply acting as an ally without a special interest of its own, the task is hardly any greater. But if it is shared among allies bound together by a common interest, the problem turns on the cordiality of the alliance.

Second, if all the opponent's forces are concentrated in one area, they in fact constitute a unity, and the question need not be pursued. But if the opponent in a single area consists of separate allied groups, their unity is less than absolute. Yet they will still be sufficiently integrated for a resolute attack on one to involve the rest.

From this it follows that the concept of separate and connected rival power runs through every level of operations. Only then can it be seen how far the rival's various centers of gravity can be reduced to one.

The principle of aiming everything at the opponent's center of gravity admits of only one exception: that is, when secondary operations look exceptionally rewarding. But we must repeat that only decisive superiority can justify diverting strength without risking too much in the principal area.

The first task, then, in planning for an encounter is to identify the opponent's centers of gravity and, if possible, trace them back to a single one. The second task is to ensure that the forces to be used against that point are concentrated for a main offensive.

A part of our first principle has still to be considered: namely, to keep each minor operation as subordinate as possible. If one seeks to concentrate all action on a single goal, and if a single massive operation is envisaged as the means of gaining it, the other points at which the opponents are in contact must lose part of their independence and become subordinate operations.

If absolutely everything could be concentrated into one action, those other contact points would be completely neutralized. But that is rarely possible, so the problem is to hold them strictly within bounds and make sure they do not draw off too much strength from the main operation.

We hold, moreover, that the plan of operations should have this tendency even when the rival's whole resistance cannot be reduced to a single center of gravity and when two almost wholly separate conflicts have to be fought simultaneously. Even then, one of them must be treated as the main operation, calling for the bulk of resources and of activities.

Seen in this light, it is advisable to operate offensively only in this main area and to stay on the defensive elsewhere. There an attack will only be justified if exceptional conditions should invite it. Moreover, the defensive at the minor points should be maintained with the minimum of strength.

This view applies with even greater force to any area of operations in which several opponent allied groups are engaged. In such a way they are all affected when the common center of gravity is struck.

Against the adversary who is the target of the main offensive there can therefore be no such thing as a defensive in subsidiary areas of operations. That offensive consists of the main attack and such subsidiary attacks as circumstances make necessary.

This removes all need to defend any point that the offensive does not itself directly cover. The main decision is what matters. It will compensate for any loss. If the forces are sufficient to make it reasonable to seek a major decision, then the possibility of failure can no longer be an excuse for trying to cover oneself everywhere, for this would make defeat in the decisive campaign that much more probable.

But while the main operation must enjoy priority over minor actions, the same priority must also be applied to all its parts. Which forces from each area shall advance toward the common center of gravity is usually decided on extraneous grounds.

All we are saying, therefore, is that there must be an effort to make sure the main operation has precedence. The more that precedence is realized, the simpler everything will be and the less will be left to chance.

The second principle is the rapid use of our forces. Every unnecessary expenditure of time and every unnecessary detour are a waste of strength and thus objectionable to strategic thought.

It is still more important to remember that almost the only advantage of the attack rests on its initial surprise. Speed and impetus are its strongest elements and are usually indispensable if we are to neutralize the opponent.

Thus, theory demands the shortest roads to the goal. Endless discussions about moving left or right, doing this or that, are futile. We believe no further elaboration is needed to show that this principle should be given the priority that we claim for it.

Now, what constitutes the main operation, which we have made central to all and for which we have demanded such rapid and straightforward execution? We already explained what we mean by the neutralization of the opponent, to the extent this can be done in general terms, and there is no need to repeat it.

Whatever the final act may turn to in any given case, the beginning is invariably the same—neutralization of the rival's forces, which implies a major victory. The earlier this victory can be sought, the easier it will be. The later the main campaign is fought, the more decisive its effect will be. Here, as everywhere, the ease of success and its magnitude are in balance.

In consequence, unless one is so much the stronger that victory is certain, the rival's main force must be sought out if possible. We say "if possible" because if it involves substantial detours, taking the wrong road and wasting time could easily prove a mistake.

If the opponent's main force is not on our line of advance, and if other reasons make it impossible for us to seek it out, we are bound to find it later, since it cannot fail eventually to oppose us. Then, as we have just argued, the campaign is fought under less favorable circumstances—a disadvantage we must accept. Nevertheless, if we win the campaign, our victory will be the more decisive.

We have been talking about a total victory—not simply a campaign won, but the complete neutralization of the opponent. It is essential, then, that any plan of operations should provide for this, both as regards the forces it requires and the direction to be given them. Once a major victory is achieved, there must be no talk of rest, of a breathing space, of reviewing the position or consolidating and so forth, but rather only of the pursuit, going for the opponent again if necessary.

Therefore, we demand that the main force should go on advancing rapidly and keeping up the pressure. We have already disposed of the idea that an advance toward the main objective should be made to wait upon success at minor points.

It is a problem, however. Might these tendencies not reach the stage at which further advance is brought to a halt? This is quite possible. Yet, we have argued that it would be a mistake to try from the very start to avoid a narrow area of operations and therefore rob the attack of its momentum. We continue to argue that so long as the leader has not yet neutralized the opponent and so long as he believes himself to be strong enough to gain his objectives, he must persevere.

He may do so with increasing danger, but his success will be all the greater. Should he reach a point beyond which he dare not go or should he feel he must expand to right and left in order to protect his rear, so be it. Very likely his attack has reached its culminating point. Its momentum is exhausted. And if the opponent is still unbroken, there is probably no future in it anyway.

Anything the leader can do to develop his offensive by overcoming fortresses and other obstacles still means slow progress. But the progress is relative, no longer absolute. The opponent's hasty retreat has stopped. He may be getting ready to renew his resistance.

And it is now possible that even though the attacker is still improving his position, the defender, by doing the same, is improving his chances every day. We repeat, in short, that once a pause has become necessary, as a rule there can be no recurrence of the advance.

All that theory requires is that so long as the aim is the opponent's neutralization, the attack must not be interrupted. If the leader relinquishes this aim because he considers the attendant risk too great, he will be right to break off and extend his front. Theory would blame him only if he does so in order to facilitate the neutralization of the opponent.

Every pause between one success and the next gives the opponent new opportunities. One success has little influence on the next and often none at all. The influence may well be adverse, for the rival either recovers and rouses himself to greater resistance or obtains help from somewhere else.

But when a single impetus obtains from start to finish, yesterday's victory makes certain of today's, and one fire starts another. Every case of an organization reduced to ruin by successive blows means that time, the defender's patron, has deserted to the other side. How many more are there in which time ruined the plans of the attacker!

So much for the main operation, the form it must assume, and the risks inseparable from it. As for secondary operations, we would emphasize that all have a common aim, but this aim must be such as not to paralyze the activities of the separate parts.

Thus, if groups do attack in different operational areas, each should be given a distinct objective. What matters is that the groups everywhere expend their full energies, not that all of them should make proportionate gains.

If one force finds its task too difficult because the opponent's defensive scheme is not what it expected, or if it runs into bad luck, the actions of the others must not be modified or a general success will be unlikely from the start. Only if most of them are unfortunate or if the principal operations fail is it right and necessary that the others should be affected. Then it is the plan itself that has gone wrong.

That rule should also be applied to forces originally given a defensive role but set free by their success to take the offensive—that is, unless one prefers to transfer their surplus resources to the main point of the offensive.

We do not think this point of view seems inconsistent to those who have spent much time and thought on the study of history, learned to distinguish between essentials and inessentials, and fully realized the influence of human weaknesses. As all experienced individuals will admit, it is difficult even from the tactical point of view to make a success of an attack in several separate pathways by smoothly coordinating every part.

How much more difficult or, rather, how impossible the same must be in strategy, where intervals are so much greater! If then the smooth coordination of all parts is a precondition of success, a strategic attack of that kind ought to be avoided altogether.

On the one hand, one is never wholly free to reject it since it may be imposed by circumstances that one cannot alter. On the other hand, the smooth coordination of every part of the action from start to finish is not even necessary in tactics, let alone strategy.

From the strategic point of view, then, there is all the more reason to ignore it. And it is all the more important to insist that every part be given an independent task.

CONCLUDING COMMENTARY

This concludes Clausewitz's monumental work, *On War*. In editing his book, every effort on my part was guided by the desire to clarify his concepts, preserve his "voice," and maintain the integrity of his extraordinary work.

Only where segments of Clausewitz's writings appeared somewhat obscure did I add commentary. The intent was to refine and interpret his meanings and thereby assist in internalizing the broader aspects associated with his concepts and applications of strategy. As for the tactical elements of running a day-to-day business campaign, those details were purposely left out of my commentary. Such specifics are adequately covered by a vast number of books that deal with those issues.

Also, where content was not pertinent to the business theme of this book, especially where Clausewitz discusses specific military campaigns, those sections were deleted entirely. The central aim was to maintain the flow of his salient principles and prevent them from getting submerged in some of his lengthy discourses.

As you have read through the previous chapters, you may have found concepts with which you were familiar—perhaps some that you have previously incorporated into your current management practices. Perhaps, too, you may have recognized principles and ideas that you learned through a variety of educational experiences, although expressed in different verbiage.

If so, it may be reassuring for you to discover that their historical roots existed in another discipline and were written by Clausewitz over 200 years ago. Also, it is fair to say that some of his concepts can be viewed as universal knowledge in that his writings can be systematically traced to antiquity through the writings of such masters of strategy as Sun Tzu, Thucydides, Pericles, and Antisthenes; and later through the works of Frederick the Great, Jomini, Machiavelli, Liddell Hart, and others.

As part of these concluding thoughts, I have included the following sampling of Clausewitz's more dynamic concepts from each of the previous chapters for your review and reinforcement:

- In conflict even the ultimate outcome is never to be regarded as final. The outcome is merely a transitory evil, for which a remedy may still be found in a variety of possible conditions at some later date.
- The opponent's capabilities must be neutralized; that is, they must be put in such a condition that they can no longer carry on the conflict.
- If we ask what sort of mind is likeliest to display the qualities of genius, it is the inquiring, rather than the creative mind, the comprehensive rather than the specialized approach, the calm rather than the excitable head to which we entrust the fate of our personnel, and the safety and honor of our organization.
- Action in conflict is like movement in a resistant element. Just as the simplest movement, walking, cannot easily be performed in water, so in conflict it is difficult for normal efforts to achieve even moderate results.
- Rather than comparing conflict to art we could more accurately compare it to commerce, which is also a conflict of human interests and activities.
- Just as a businessman cannot take the profit from a single transaction and put it into a separate account, so an isolated advantage gained in conflict cannot be assessed separately from the overall result.
- Conflicts consist of a large number of engagements, great and small, simultaneous or consecutive. Each of these has a specific purpose relating to the whole.
- We maintain unequivocally that the form of confrontation that we call defense offers greater probability of victory than attack.

- A leader must never expect to move on the narrow ground of imagined security and feel that the means he is using are the only ones possible—and persist in using them even at the thought of their possible inadequacy.
- What matters is to detect the culminating point of actions with discriminative judgment.
- Two basic principles underlie all strategic planning: First, act with the utmost concentration; second, act with the utmost speed.

Finally, the primary goal of *Clausewitz Talks Business* is to enhance your ability to think like a strategist, so that you can apply these time-honored concepts to developing your own unique plans and strategies and do so successfully as you face a turbulent competitive environment with its inevitable conflicts, confrontations, and contested campaigns. Good luck!

Appendix

In keeping with the themes developed in *Clausewitz Talks Business,* this section consists of the following two management tools to enhance your ability to think and act like a strategist[*]

1. *Strategy diagnostic system.* This tool helps assess your firm's internal capabilities and competitive strategies against those of your competitor. It functions as a reliable performance measure to look candidly inside your own organization or business group.
2. *Appraising internal and external conditions.* This 100-question checklist assists in analyzing key factors, such as your organization, markets, customers, and competitors, that could affect your ability to carry out your business plans. Further, in keeping with Clausewitz's advice—"What matters is to detect the culminating point of actions with discriminative judgment"—this tool assists you in making such astute assessments.

STRATEGY DIAGNOSTIC SYSTEM

The management tool is organized into nine strategy guidelines, along with key checkpoints to assist you in determining your organization's effectiveness or ineffectiveness within each guideline. Then, remedial solutions are offered for each.

Thus, each guideline consists of three parts:

- Part 1: indications that the guideline is functioning *effectively* in your organization
- Part 2: symptoms that the guideline is functioning *ineffectively* in your organization
- Part 3: remedial actions based on parts 1 and 2

---

[*] These tools can be used independently. Yet, to gain the perspectives of others who have a stake in developing and implementing strategies, you may wish to use a team approach to gain the benefits of, ideally, cross-functional perspectives.

To make the best use of this tool, either individually or as a group, rate each point in parts 1 and 2 of the following guidelines as *frequently, occasionally,* or *rarely.*[*]

Strategy Guideline 1: Shift to the Offensive

Standing still, stalled by lack of ideas and immobilized by fear, can fester into severe problems. If you are entangled in a tough competitive situation, rather than languish in indecision, it is in your best interest to develop a proactive approach and search for fresh market opportunities.

Part 1: Indications That Guideline 1 Functions Effectively

1. You and your staff display a proactive, shift-to-the-offensive mind-set when confronted with aggressive competitors.
    Frequently ___ Occasionally ___ Rarely ___

2. You encourage risk taking among your staff, with no serious repercussions for negative outcomes.
    Frequently ___ Occasionally ___ Rarely ___

3. You and other managers are adept at making timely maneuvers to block rivals from taking over your market position.
    Frequently ___ Occasionally ___ Rarely ___

4. You and your fellow managers act with boldness, which has a positive psychological impact on employee behavior and morale.
    Frequently ___ Occasionally ___ Rarely ___

5. Your firm is organized to support and facilitate communication among staff for rapid action on time-sensitive market opportunities.
    Frequently ___ Occasionally ___ Rarely ___

6. Recognizing the value of your employees' knowledge, skill, and prior experience, you actively encourage them to tap their expertise for reliable decisions.
    Frequently ___ Occasionally ___ Rarely ___

---

[*] For greater accuracy, you can weight each of the key points based on your company's actual situation, the extent of the competitive threat, and the appropriate culminating point for a campaign.

Part 2: Symptoms of Strategy Guideline 2 Functioning Ineffectively

1. You are stalled by a cloud of complacency and apprehension within your group, which results in a lack of fresh ideas and initiatives for defending against competitive attacks and growing the business.
   Frequently ___ Occasionally ___ Rarely ___

2. Your personnel are overly preoccupied with defending an existing market position. Negligible amounts of time and effort are spent searching for new market and product opportunities.
   Frequently ___ Occasionally ___ Rarely ___

3. Other managers and staff are caught up by fear of what competitors might do. Such negative behavior discourages any effort to mount a vigorous response strategy to counter competitors' efforts.
   Frequently ___ Occasionally ___ Rarely ___

4. You find yourself exhibiting undue caution, which permeates the group and prevents action on new market opportunities.
   Frequently ___ Occasionally ___ Rarely ___

5. The organization tends to lose momentum.
   Frequently ___ Occasionally ___ Rarely ___

Part 3: Remedial Actions Based on Parts 1 and 2

Parts 1 and 2 provide qualitative assessments of your ability to *shift to the offensive*. Based on your self- or team diagnosis, use the following remedies to apply corrective actions:

- Confront complacency: Develop ready-to-implement contingency plans that you can call upon to seize market opportunities or attack competitive threats.
- Prepare for new opportunities: Use market and competitor intelligence to support decisions and reduce the risks inherent in making bold moves.
- Instill confidence: Conduct specialized training related to enhancing employees' job skills using real-world competitive scenarios, improving discipline as well as elevating their self-assurance and morale.
- Regain momentum: Employ market segmentation to understand how and where to deploy resources at a decisive point, thereby increasing your chances of success against a numerically stronger competitor. You thereby reduce the risks of moving into heavily defended markets.
- Encourage an entrepreneurial mind-set: Require key personnel to submit detailed proposals that would take the company into new markets, products, and services.

- Support a market-driven orientation: Build a cross-functional strategy team that encourages creativity and visionary thinking.
- Prepare for unexpected events: Hold reserves to exploit a breakthrough or to pursue an opportunity that aligns with the strategic business plan.

Remedial action points: _____

Strategy Guideline 2: Maneuver by Indirect Strategy

An indirect strategy applies strength against a competitor's weakness. The aim is to resolve customer problems with offerings that outperform those of your competitors and achieve a psychological advantage by creating an unbalancing effect in the mind of your rival manager.

Part 1: Indications That Strategy Guideline 2 Functions Effectively

1. You intentionally integrate indirect strategies into your business plans, thereby increasing the success rate of your efforts. You also engage in open dialogues with colleagues and staff about new approaches to indirect strategies, along with their implementation.
    Frequently ___ Occasionally ___ Rarely ___

2. You act with the understanding that acquiring the skills to implement indirect strategies opens your mind to fresh ideas. You thereby reduce the risks of going after market leaders, even where limited resources are available.
    Frequently ___ Occasionally ___ Rarely ___

3. You deliberately employ indirect approaches that distract the competing manager into making false moves and costly mistakes.
    Frequently ___ Occasionally ___ Rarely ___

4. You intentionally avoid getting entangled in direct confrontations with competitors, which would result in the unnecessary draining of resources.
    Frequently ___ Occasionally ___ Rarely ___

Part 2: Symptoms of Strategy Guideline 2 Functioning Ineffectively

1. You fail to develop indirect strategies that outthink, outmaneuver, and outperform those of competitors.
    Frequently ___ Occasionally ___ Rarely ___

2. You neglect to probe for unserved market niches where there is minimal resistance from competitors—and where opportunities exist to establish a foothold and expand into a mainstream market.
   Frequently ___ Occasionally ___ Rarely ___

3. Personnel do not rely on competitor intelligence to formulate an indirect strategy.
   Frequently ___ Occasionally ___ Rarely ___

4. You lack a benchmarking system to evaluate strengths, weaknesses, or best practices periodically, which can then be used to develop indirect strategies.
   Frequently ___ Occasionally ___ Rarely ___

5. You do not employ an organized approach, such as through a cross-functional team, to tap the diverse backgrounds of individuals and develop indirect approaches to enter markets or defend against an aggressive competitor.
   Frequently ___ Occasionally ___ Rarely ___

Part 3: Remedial Actions Based on Parts 1 and 2

Parts 1 and 2 provide qualitative assessments of your ability to maneuver by indirect strategy. Based on your self- or team diagnosis, use the following remedies to apply corrective actions:

- Use a SWOT (strengths, weaknesses, opportunities, threats) examination or other comparative analysis tool to help you determine which indirect strategies to employ.
- Institute checkpoints to confirm that your indirect strategies are moving you from your current competitive situation toward the objectives you want to achieve. Make shifts quickly and assertively according to your findings.
- Use all available sources of intelligence to interpret your market position. Such input provides additional clues to the development of your indirect strategies and to determine a culminating point.
- Find an unattended, poorly served, or emerging market segment as a decisive target in which to implement an indirect strategy for market expansion.

Remedial action points: _____

_____

Strategy Guideline 3: Act with Speed

Nothing drains resources like an overlong campaign. There are few cases of prolonged operations that have been successful. Drawn out efforts often divert interest, diminish enthusiasm, and damage employee morale.

Part 1: Indications That Strategy Guideline 3 Functions Effectively

1. You realize that dragged-out campaigns have rarely been successful. You work to avoid them before they divert interest, depress morale, and deplete resources.
   Frequently ___ Occasionally ___ Rarely ___

2. You recognize that speed is an essential component to securing a competitive lead. This impacts market share, product positioning, and, ultimately, customer relationships.
   Frequently ___ Occasionally ___ Rarely ___

3. Your staff understands that even minor delays can result in a loss of momentum that could signal a vigilant competitor to fill the void.
   Frequently ___ Occasionally ___ Rarely ___

4. You and your staff know that a strategy that integrates speed with technology puts you in an excellent position to secure a competitive lead.
   Frequently ___ Occasionally ___ Rarely ___

5. You recognize that speed adds vitality to a company's operations and becomes a catalyst for growth.
   Frequently ___ Occasionally ___ Rarely ___

6. You understand that acting defensively to protect a market position is but a preliminary step to moving boldly and rapidly against a competitor.
   Frequently ___ Occasionally ___ Rarely ___

Part 2: Symptoms of Strategy Guideline 3 Functioning Ineffectively

1. You and your staff fail to understand that excessive delays in reacting to time-sensitive market opportunities can result in losing market share and acquiring a favorable competitive position.
   Frequently ___ Occasionally ___ Rarely ___

2. A general malaise exists in the organization, which results in missed opportunities.
   Frequently ___ Occasionally ___ Rarely ___

3. Overall, personnel lack initiative in implementing business plans with speed.
   Frequently ___ Occasionally ___ Rarely ___

4. You are slow in preventing a product from reaching a commodity status, a condition that often results in price wars.
   Frequently ___ Occasionally ___ Rarely ___

5. Inadequately trained or experienced staff has resulted in an absence of organizational vitality, thus hindering movement forward.
   Frequently ___ Occasionally ___ Rarely ___

6. Despite suitable market conditions, you are unable to act boldly and with speed.
   Frequently ___ Occasionally ___ Rarely ___

7. You have failed to secure a competitive lead due to sluggishness in integrating technology into the marketing mix or product portfolio.
   Frequently ___ Occasionally ___ Rarely ___

8. Organizational layers prolong deliberation and delay decisions, creating a trickle-down corporate culture of procrastination.
   Frequently ___ Occasionally ___ Rarely ___

9. There is a persistent lack of urgency in developing new products.
   Frequently ___ Occasionally ___ Rarely ___

Part 3: Remedial Action Based on Parts 1 and 2

Parts 1 and 2 provide qualitative assessments of your ability to *act with speed*. Based on your self- or team diagnosis, use the following remedies to apply corrective actions:

- Reduce organizational obstacles that prevent you and your staff from increasing speed of internal communication, as well as acquiring feedback from the field and integrating the intelligence into developing strategy plans.
- Require selected individuals on your staff to submit timely proposals with the prime objective of creating additional revenue streams through product innovations and new technology applications; and by identifying new, unserved, or poorly served market segments.
- Use a cross-functional strategy team to take maximum advantage of a diversity of backgrounds and perspectives as well as gain buy-in to business plans.
- Actively seek input from managers and field personnel in pinpointing competitors' weaknesses and areas of vulnerability.

- Conduct training to break down internal barriers and areas of friction that inhibit speed.

Remedial action points: _____
_____

Strategy Guideline 4: Grow by Concentration

Adopt strategies that concentrate resources at a decisive point where you can gain superiority in select territories. That includes targeting a competitor's specific weakness or a general area of vulnerability.

Part 1: Indications That Strategy Guideline 4 Functions Effectively

1. You recognize that concentration at a decisive point on a segment-by-segment approach is a prudent strategy when challenging larger competitors.
   Frequently ___ Occasionally ___ Rarely ___

2. You and your colleagues feel competent about concentrating your resources to gain a superior position in a selected market segment, even if it creates some exposure elsewhere.
   Frequently ___ Occasionally ___ Rarely ___

3. You use market intelligence to pinpoint a segment for initial market entry. You then use that position to expand toward additional growth segments.
   Frequently ___ Occasionally ___ Rarely ___

4. You and your staff are adept at reaching beyond traditional demographic and geographic segmentation approaches, employing more advanced behavioral classifications to identify new or underserved segments.
   Frequently ___ Occasionally ___ Rarely ___

5. You and others are flexible about pulling out of underperforming segments and concentrating on faster growing ones.
   Frequently ___ Occasionally ___ Rarely ___

6. You are capable of concentrating your resources against competitors' weaknesses by utilizing Clausewitz's concept of focusing on the decisive point.
   Frequently ___ Occasionally ___ Rarely ___

7. Marketing and sales personnel are skilled at pinpointing products and services to suit the specific needs of their customers.
   Frequently ___ Occasionally ___ Rarely ___

8. You understand that every market segment presents opportunities to fill market gaps, allocate resources efficiently, and exploit a rival's short-comings. And your organization has a practice of seeking out and uncovering them.
Frequently ___ Occasionally ___ Rarely ___

Part 2: Symptoms of Strategy Guideline 4 Functioning Ineffectively

1. You fail to select market segments that offer long-term growth.
Frequently ___ Occasionally ___ Rarely ___

2. You dissipate resources across too many segments.
Frequently ___ Occasionally ___ Rarely ___

3. In the absence of a strategy focused on segment needs, numerous product launches produce negative results.
Frequently ___ Occasionally ___ Rarely ___

4. Your people have not internalized the principle that achieving a competitive edge means employing a strategy of concentration.
Frequently ___ Occasionally ___ Rarely ___

Part 3: Remedial Actions Based on Parts 1 and 2

Parts 1 and 2 provide qualitative assessments of your ability to use a *strategy of concentration*. Based on your self- or team diagnosis, use the following remedies to apply corrective actions:

- Install an ongoing competitor intelligence system to identify a competitor's weaknesses.
- Concentrate on emerging markets or those that are poorly served in order to get a foothold into additional segments.
- Secure your position with dedicated services and customized products that would create barriers to competitors' entry.
- Within customer segments, tailor products and services built around product differentiation, value-added services, and business solutions that exceed those of competitors.
- Conduct internal strategy training sessions, especially for those individuals who do not understand the value of finding a decisive point and resist adopting a strategy of concentration.

Remedial action points: _____

_____

Strategy Guideline 5: Prioritize Competitor Intelligence

Worse than no information is wrong information. Commit to a practice of gathering and elevating competitor intelligence to the highest standard. Seek information that can impact your decisions about selecting markets, launching new products, and devising competitive advantages. Reliable intelligence helps you outthink, outmaneuver, and outperform your competitor.

Part 1: Indications That Strategy Guideline 5 Functions Effectively

1. A debriefing takes place after each major competitive encounter, and it includes (a) comparing competitors' performance against yours, (b) assessing strategies and tactics that worked or failed, and (c) identifying the most useful type of competitor intelligence.
   Frequently ___ Occasionally ___ Rarely ___

2. Your company provides adequate funding for competitor intelligence and makes it a key part in determining the culminating point of a campaign.
   Frequently ___ Occasionally ___ Rarely ___

3. You and others use competitor intelligence as an evaluation tool for assessing the levels of risk associated with strategy options.
   Frequently ___ Occasionally ___ Rarely ___

4. You use some type of comparative analysis to determine strong points and areas of vulnerability compared with those of competitors.
   Frequently ___ Occasionally ___ Rarely ___

5. You use competitor intelligence to increase accuracy in selecting markets, locating an optimum position, and determining how to defend against a competitor's intrusion.
   Frequently ___ Occasionally ___ Rarely ___

6. You and others recognize that competitor intelligence provides a way to anticipate rivals' moves and to devise strategies to outmaneuver them, enabling you to use your resources to maximum efficiency.
   Frequently ___ Occasionally ___ Rarely ___

Part 2: Symptoms of Strategy Guideline 5 Functioning Ineffectively

1. Competitors' actions frequently catch you by surprise, hampering your ability to respond with speed and effectiveness.
   Frequently ___ Occasionally ___ Rarely ___

2. Lack of real-time information about market events leads to indecisiveness, which filters down and affects the attitudes and morale of your staff.
   Frequently ___ Occasionally ___ Rarely ___

3. Personnel are inclined to misjudge, exaggerate, or underestimate a competitor's situation due to unreliable or insufficient backup intelligence.
   Frequently ___ Occasionally ___ Rarely ___

4. There is a tendency to develop product launch plans without documenting market conditions, competitors' strengths and weaknesses, and buyers' specific needs.
   Frequently ___ Occasionally ___ Rarely ___

5. Your organization lacks a flexible channel of two-way communication between the field and the home office, which would red-flag opportunities or threats.
   Frequently ___ Occasionally ___ Rarely ___

Part 3: Remedial Actions Based on Parts 1 and 2

Parts 1 and 2 provide qualitative assessments of your overall ability to *prioritize competitor intelligence*. Based on a self- or team-diagnosis of your company's situation, use the following remedies to implement corrective action:

- Integrate competitor intelligence into your business planning process. Use it as the centerpiece for developing offensive and defensive strategies.
- Train staffs from various functions—in particular, the sales force—to recognize the changing dynamics of consumer needs and competitive threats, as well as the urgency for them to gather reliable intelligence actively.
- Use a team approach, as well as agents, to track competitors' activities, with particular attention to decoding their strategies.
- Set up a procedure for competitive benchmarking to upgrade your firm's systems and processes.
- Use outside sources to expand the reach of your competitor intelligence activities.

Remedial action points: _____

_____

Strategy Guideline 6: Tune In to Your Corporate Culture

Corporate culture is the operating system and nerve center of your organization. It forms the backbone of your business strategy and shapes how your employees react in a variety of internal and external situations. It guides employee reaction in the face of a crisis. Understand it, tap into its strengths, and reenergize your company.

Part 1: Indications That Strategy Guideline 6 Functions Effectively

1. You actively tune in to your company's traditions, values, beliefs, and history. You acknowledge that corporate culture is at the heart of your operation and is at the core of what makes the organization tick.
Frequently ___ Occasionally ___ Rarely ___

2. You realize that your organization's culture shapes how employees think, act, and are likely to perform in a variety of competitive encounters.
Frequently ___ Occasionally ___ Rarely ___

3. You recognize corporate culture as the DNA that shapes all competitive strategies. It serves as a primary determinant in selecting strategies and tactics that will succeed.
Frequently ___ Occasionally ___ Rarely ___

4. You are aware that corporate culture influences your leadership style and consequently your ability to implement business plans.
Frequently ___ Occasionally ___ Rarely ___

5. You acknowledge that corporate culture, as one of the prime differentiators, gives your organization a unique identity among customers and competitors.
Frequently ___ Occasionally ___ Rarely ___

6. You attempt to study your competitors' corporate cultures to reveal their inner workings. Thus, you can predict with some accuracy how rivals will react under a variety of market conditions.
Frequently ___ Occasionally ___ Rarely ___

Part 2: Symptoms of Strategy Guideline 6 Functioning Ineffectively

1. Personnel operate within a closed-in (and consequently uninspiring) culture that prevents them from recognizing the hard-nosed realities of global competition.
Frequently ___ Occasionally ___ Rarely ___

2. The existing culture is passive with a staff that fails to internalize the consequences of falling behind in new technology. As such, they do not recognize its potential for exploiting fresh opportunities, as well as sustaining a strong defense of its existing markets.

Frequently ___ Occasionally ___ Rarely ___

3. The corporate culture is incompatible with the changing dynamics of the marketplace. And personnel are unresponsive to the subtle shifts in customers' buying behavior.

Frequently ___ Occasionally ___ Rarely ___

4. Competitive strategies are not aligned with the corporate culture, thereby jeopardizing the outcome of the overall business plan.

Frequently ___ Occasionally ___ Rarely ___

5. At times you go against the core values, beliefs, and historical traditions that represent the organization's deeply rooted culture.

Frequently ___ Occasionally ___ Rarely ___

Part 3: Remedial Actions Based on Parts 1 and 2

Parts 1 and 2 provide qualitative assessments of your overall ability to tune in to your *corporate culture*. Based on a self- or team diagnosis of your company's situation, use the following remedies to implement corrective action:

- Determine if the existing culture is compatible with the long-term vision and objectives of the organization.
- Create change—either rapidly forced or gradually nurtured. In so doing, use your organization's symbols, signs, and rituals to shift and reinterpret your culture without abandoning your core values.
- Determine which intrinsic qualities of your organization's culture are unique and could form a distinctive identity for use as a differentiation strategy.
- Through a cross-functional team committed to a total customer orientation and open communication, utilize the diverse talents of your employees to shape a vigorous corporate culture that is in tune with the global competitive environment.
- Consciously align your business plan with your corporate culture.

Remedial action points: _____

_____

Strategy Guideline 7: Develop Leadership Skills

The primary pillars of leadership are insightfulness, straightforwardness, compassion, strictness, and boldness. Develop your own personal style of leadership that fits your character and personality, suits the job requirements, and harmonizes with the organization's culture.

Part 1: Indications That Strategy Guideline 7 Functions Effectively

1. You display superior leadership skills by openly communicating to your personnel a clear vision, purpose, and direction for the business unit or company.
    Frequently ___ Occasionally ___ Rarely ___

2. You understand that leadership means inspiring your people, developing strategies, organizing actions, and responding to market and competitive issues rapidly and effectively.
    Frequently ___ Occasionally ___ Rarely ___

3. You score high in interpersonal skills, as well as in the ability to recognize the inherent dignity and worth of those you manage.
    Frequently ___ Occasionally ___ Rarely ___

4. As a leader, you demonstrate to your staff's satisfaction that you possess the ability and the expertise to develop competent offensive and defensive strategies.
    Frequently ___ Occasionally ___ Rarely ___

5. You reveal leadership competency in motivating your employees to win. This means winning customers and sustaining a long-term profitable position in the marketplace.
    Frequently ___ Occasionally ___ Rarely ___

6. You show superior leadership by helping subordinates to grow and succeed through ongoing training and coaching.
    Frequently ___ Occasionally ___ Rarely ___

7. You recognize that there is no single leadership style. You foster a competitive environment with a personalized and flexible managerial style.
    Frequently ___ Occasionally ___ Rarely ___

Part 2: Symptoms of Strategy Guideline 7 Functioning Ineffectively

1. Personnel display a hint of mistrust in your ability to assess market and competitive conditions and thereby in your ability to make timely and accurate strategy decisions.
    Frequently ___ Occasionally ___ Rarely ___

2. Employees exhibit negative behavior, confusion, and an unwillingness to take the initiative.
    Frequently ___ Occasionally ___ Rarely ___

3. The organization or business unit is enveloped by a malaise that creates stress and anxiety.
    Frequently ___ Occasionally ___ Rarely ___

4. You do not have an effective system of recognition and rewards.
    Frequently ___ Occasionally ___ Rarely ___

5. Employees show fear of loss: loss of pride in the organization, loss of status, loss of the respect of their peers, or possibly loss of employment.
    Frequently ___ Occasionally ___ Rarely ___

6. Subordinates are rarely asked for input, and feedback is seldom offered.
    Frequently ___ Occasionally ___ Rarely ___

7. Your overall leadership style tends to be inconsistent with the company's core values.
    Frequently ___ Occasionally ___ Rarely ___

Part 3: Remedial Actions Based on Parts 1 and 2

Parts 1 and 2 provide qualitative assessments of your overall ability to use *leadership skills.* Based on a self- or team diagnosis of your company's situation, use the following remedies to implement corrective action:

- Communicate to staff a vision for the firm (or business unit) so that they can picture their individual roles as relevant to the organization's long-term outlook.
- Permit individuals to act on their own initiative. Create and enforce a feedback-loop that serves the organization and the individuals who participate.
- Motivate employees to improve their skills via ongoing training and individual coaching.
- Create unity of effort through discipline and the fostering of a team effort.

- Develop a leadership style that harmonizes with the culture of the organization and its objectives and strategies.

Remedial action points: _____

_____

Strategy Guideline 8: Create a Morale Advantage

An organization is only as strong as its people. Morale tends to energize individuals with the resolve to act decisively under competitive pressures. As a dominant form of behavioral expression, focus on employee morale, discipline, and trust to strengthen your chances of winning in competitive strategy.

Part 1: Indications That Strategy Guideline 8 Functions Effectively

1. You actively seek to heighten morale and use it to energize staff, tap their inner strengths, and inspire them to act decisively under competitive pressures.
     Frequently ___ Occasionally ___ Rarely ___

2. You recognize that high morale holds a team together, affects day-to-day performance, and ultimately contributes to how well a business plan is implemented.
     Frequently ___ Occasionally ___ Rarely ___

3. You understand that even with cutting-edge technology and outstanding business strategies, your efforts will languish if employees are not roused with the driving will to succeed.
     Frequently ___ Occasionally ___ Rarely ___

4. You recognize that to be successful as a manager you need to boost morale via the following: (a) emphasize ethical standards of behavior, (b) encourage constructive communication, (c) reward individuals for meaningful performance, and (d) use cross-functional teams to encourage innovation.
     Frequently ___ Occasionally ___ Rarely ___

5. With morale affecting day-to-day employee performance, you try to create a work environment that fosters creative thinking and encourages employees to offer opinions and ideas—with the assurance they will be given serious attention.
     Frequently ___ Occasionally ___ Rarely ___

6. You move rapidly to overturn employee skepticism about the organization's commitment to meaningful change; and you do so before it festers into a morale problem.
   Frequently ___ Occasionally ___ Rarely ___

Part 2: Symptoms of Strategy Guideline 8 Functioning Ineffectively

1. Employees visibly display a lack of respect toward leadership.
   Frequently ___ Occasionally ___ Rarely ___

2. Employees seem to feel insecure about their jobs and have doubts about management's concern for their well-being.
   Frequently ___ Occasionally ___ Rarely ___

3. Some key managers do not appear to be concerned about morale and their employees are seemingly left to fend for themselves.
   Frequently ___ Occasionally ___ Rarely ___

4. There is no sign of a cohesive team spirit.
   Frequently ___ Occasionally ___ Rarely ___

5. There is a conspicuous lack of new ideas, innovations, or opportunities reaching senior-level management, and there is a noticeable absence of a workable two-way communication system.
   Frequently ___ Occasionally ___ Rarely ___

6. No consistent procedure is present to encourage and reward employees for innovative suggestions.
   Frequently ___ Occasionally ___ Rarely ___

7. Employees exhibit erratic behavior; appear discouraged, indifferent, fearful; and resist risk-taking.
   Frequently ___ Occasionally ___ Rarely ___

8. Where new market initiatives and competitive encounters have failed, management routinely lays blame primarily on poor employee performance.
   Frequently ___ Occasionally ___ Rarely ___

Part 3: Remedial Actions Based on Parts 1 and 2

Parts 1 and 2 provide qualitative assessments of your overall ability to *build morale*. Based on a self- or team diagnosis of your company's situation, use the following remedies to implement corrective action:

- Communicate a long-term positive vision for the organization with clearly-stated objectives that employees can internalize and get excited about.
- Develop a learning environment that demonstrates to employees management's interest in and support of their development.
- Remove personal and physical barriers that would prevent employees from feeling pride in their work and the organization.
- Create collaborative cross-functional teams with specific duties and responsibilities.
- Encourage constructive communication up and down the organization where self-expression and innovation are encouraged.
- Nurture a corporate culture that positively impacts morale, especially when it is reinforced by an ethical climate and secured by the company's positive history and core values.
- Utilize media tools such as social networking to identify and capitalize on this rapidly growing venue for marketing, messaging, and competitive edge.
- Require teams to submit strategy action plans. It serves as a unifying activity to allow collaboration and encourages the flourishing of team dynamics through creative expression.

Remedial action points: _____

_____

Strategy Guideline 9: Strengthen Your Decision-Making Capabilities to Think Like a Strategist

Leaders use history, market events, and their intuition as guides to sharpening decision-making and strategy skills. In the end, it is mastering the concepts and principles of strategy that can direct marketplace events in your favor.

Part 1: Indications That Strategy Guideline 9 Functions Effectively

1. You actively strengthen your decision-making capability by systematically examining the best practices of other companies and using them to build additional layers of knowledge.

     Frequently ___ Occasionally ___ Rarely ___

2. Where reliable competitive intelligence is lacking, you tend to rely with confidence on your innate intuition, experience, training, and knowledge to arrive at valid decisions.

     Frequently ___ Occasionally ___ Rarely ___

3. To enhance the decision-making skills of front-line employees, you give them ample opportunity and free reign to develop their imaginations and intuitions.

Frequently ___ Occasionally ___ Rarely ___

4. You understand that by valuing your organization's business history and by managing knowledge, you add precision to your decision-making skills.

Frequently ___ Occasionally ___ Rarely ___

Part 2: Symptoms of Strategy Guideline 9 Functioning Ineffectively

1. You lack an organized effort to capture and record the lessons and key strategies of past events. This inhibits the ability to pass them on to the next generation of decision makers.

Frequently ___ Occasionally ___ Rarely ___

2. You do not have a systematic procedure or venue for individuals to share experiences, insights, knowledge, and observations.

Frequently ___ Occasionally ___ Rarely ___

3. Intense competitive situations cause staff to flounder and become dispirited.

Frequently ___ Occasionally ___ Rarely ___

Part 3: Remedial Actions Based on Parts 1 and 2

Parts 1 and 2 provide qualitative assessments of your overall ability to improve the knowledge and the *decision-making capabilities* of individuals to think like strategists. Based on a self- or team diagnosis of your company's situation, use the following remedies to implement corrective action:

- Provide training sessions where key individuals are invited to provide their insights and experiences.
- Set up databases that capture case histories and details of significant business events, as well as noteworthy competitive encounters—both failed and successful.
- Permit individuals to access the assembled information for their personal use, to coach others, and for formal training to think like strategists.

Remedial action points: _____

_____

SUMMARY

This strategy diagnostic system provides a multidimensional view consisting of (1) the human element that elevates the natural worth of people; (2) the company's culture that determines if plans can succeed; (3) strategies that decide the success of a company, business unit, or product line; and (4) guidelines to assist you in determining the culminating point of a campaign.

If you merge them into a solid platform that characterizes you and your leadership, there will be ample opportunities for growth.

APPRAISING INTERNAL AND EXTERNAL CONDITIONS

Used as an audit, the appraisal consists of 100 questions to provide an accurate assessment of your company's operating condition and level of competitiveness.

Taking the time to conduct the evaluation reduces some of the risks of planning, strategizing, and implementing your strategy plan. For instance, you can anticipate the weaknesses and strengths from both your side and that of your competitor and make informed decisions based on analysis and fact— not speculation.

The aim of the audit, therefore, is to highlight a set of symptoms for further evaluation. Then, with the detailed output, you can take corrective actions or modify plans to meet those circumstances. Thus, the appraisal permits you to conduct a structured analysis of internal and external considerations divided into three areas:

1. Your firm's market environment
2. Management procedures and policies
3. Strategy factors

Where possible, use a team approach in conducting the audit to gain varied perspectives on key issues. Also, if feasible, you will find it beneficial to add objective outside opinions from individuals when evaluating your organization's competencies. Should you come across some questions that do not apply to your business, unless they can be modified to fit your purpose, move on to the next section.

APPRAISING INTERNAL AND EXTERNAL CONDITIONS

Part I: Reviewing the Firm's Market Environment

Consumers (End Users)

1. Who are our ultimate buyers?
2. What are the primary physical features and psychological influences in their buying decisions?

3. What are the key factors that make up the demographic and psychographic (behavioral) profiles of our buyers?
4. When and where do they shop for and consume our product? With what frequency are purchases made?
5. What needs do our products or services satisfy?
6. How well do they satisfy compared with similar offerings from competitors?
7. How can we segment our target markets with greater precision?
8. How do prospective buyers perceive our product in their minds? Is there valid research to support the opinions?
9. What are the economic conditions and expectations of our target market over the near and far term?
10. Are our consumers' attitudes, values, or habits changing? Is there a reliable gauge to track changes?

Customers (Intermediaries)

11. Who are our intermediate buyers, such as distributors or retailers? How influential are they?
12. How well do those intermediaries serve our target market?
13. How well do we serve their needs? What are the special areas that would help solidify relationships?
14. What are the central issues that drive their buying decisions? Have there been any changes over the past 12 months? What are the projections for the next 12 months?
15. Has there been any significant movement in their locations relative to the end users?
16. What types of noncompeting products do they carry? What competing product lines do they handle?
17. What percentage of total revenue does each competing product line represent compared with ours?
18. How much support do they give our product? What can be improved?
19. What factors made us select them and they select us?
20. How can we motivate them to work harder for us?
21. Do we need them?
22. Do they need us?
23. Do we use multiple channels, including e-commerce?
24. Would we be better off setting up our own distribution system?
25. Should we go direct? What are the advantages/disadvantages?

Competitors

26. Who are our competitors? What are their strengths and weaknesses?
27. Where are they located relative to our key customers?
28. How big are they overall and, specifically, in our product areas? Where are they vulnerable?

29. What is their product mix? Are there any gaps in their mix that would create an opportunity for us?
30. Is their participation in the market growing or declining? What are the reasons in either situation?
31. Which competitors may be leaving the field? Why? What are the implications for us?
32. What new domestic competitors may be entering the market? What market niches are they filling? Or what comparative advantage are they using?
33. What new foreign competitors may be on the horizon? How threatening are they?
34. Which competitive strategies and tactics appear particularly successful or unsuccessful when used by competitors—and by us?
35. What new directions, if any, are competitors pursuing? Give details of new strategies as they relate to such areas as markets, products, pricing, marketing, supply chain, technologies, leadership, or others.

Other Relevant Environmental Components

36. What legal and environmental constraints affect our marketing efforts? What are the immediate and long-term concerns?
37. To what extent do government regulations restrict our flexibility in making market-related decisions?
38. What do we have to do to comply with regulations?
39. What political or legal developments are looming that will improve or worsen our situation?
40. What threats or opportunities do advances in technology hold for our company?
41. How well do we keep up with technology in day-to-day operations? How do we rank in the industry and against key competitors?
42. What broad cultural shifts are occurring in segments of our market that may impact our business?
43. What consequences will demographic and geographic shifts have for our business?
44. Are any changes in resource availability foreseeable (e.g., finances, equipment, personnel, raw materials, or suppliers)?
45. How do we propose to cope with environmental, social, or "green" issues that can impact our business?

Part II: Reviewing Management Procedures and Policies

Analysis

46. Do we have an internal market research function or do we rely primarily on outside resources? To what extent do staff and outside agents participate in obtaining competitive intelligence?

47. Do we systematically use competitor intelligence for developing plans and strategies? Is it applicable in determining an indirect approach, pinpointing strengths and weaknesses of competitors, and focusing on a decisive point at which to commit resources?
48. Do we subscribe to any regular market data services?
49. Before we introduce a new product or service, do we test its acceptance among customers, as well as consider how it is positioned against competitors?
50. Are all our major market-related decisions based on market research and competitor intelligence?

Planning

51. Do we have a formalized procedure to develop a strategic business plan or strategy action plan?
52. To what extent do we seek collaboration in planning by opening the process to additional levels of the organization and thereby obtaining qualified feedback that leads to higher levels of morale and results in employee buy-in to implement the plan?
53. Do our long- and short-term objectives complement our company's mission or overall strategic direction?
54. What market-driven procedures do we use to locate gaps in customers' needs?
55. Do we develop clearly stated short-term and long-term objectives? How are they prioritized so as to avoid internal conflicts among other business units?
56. Are our objectives realistic, achievable, and measurable?
57. Do we utilize appropriate metrics to assess performance and make essential midcourse corrections?
58. How effective are we in integrating what-if scenarios into our plan and thereby being prepared to react rapidly to competitive challenges and threats?
59. Are our core strategies and tactics for achieving our objectives aligned with our corporate culture?
60. Is there a systematic screening process in place to identify opportunities and threats, such as a SWOT analysis or similar approach?
61. How aggressively are we considering diversification or joint ventures as they relate to planning for growth?
62. How effectively are we segmenting our target market to determine decisive points?
63. Are we committing sufficient resources to accomplish our objectives?
64. Are our resources optimally allocated to the major elements of our marketing mix?
65. How well do we tie in our plans with the other functional plans of our organization?
66. Is our plan realistically followed or just filed away?

67. Do we continuously monitor environmental movements to determine the adequacy of our plan?
68. Do we have a centralized activity to collect and disseminate market and competitor intelligence?
69. Do we have an individual who oversees the sharing of technology and marketing data among business groups?

Organization

70. Does our firm have a high-level function to analyze, plan, and oversee the implementation of our strategic efforts?
71. How capable and dedicated are our personnel?
72. Is there a need for more internal skills and leadership training?
73. Are our managerial responsibilities structured to best support the needs of different products, target markets, and sales territories?
74. Does our organization's culture embrace and practice the market-driven, customer-first concept?

Part III: Reviewing Strategy Factors

Product Policy

75. What is the makeup of our product mix?
76. How effective are our new product development plans?
77. Do they have optimal breadth and depth to maintain customer loyalty and prevent unwelcome entry by aggressive competitors?
78. Should any of our products be phased out?
79. Do we carefully evaluate any negative ripple effects on the remaining product mix before we make a decision to phase out a product?
80. Have we considered modification, repositioning, and/or extension of sagging products?
81. What immediate additions, if any, should be made to our product mix to maintain a competitive edge?
82. Which products are we best equipped to make ourselves and which items should we outsource and resell under our own name?
83. Do we routinely check product safety and product liability?
84. Do we have a formalized and tested product recall procedure? Is it effective?
85. Is any recall imminent?

Pricing

86. How effective are our pricing strategies? To what extent are our prices based on cost, demand, market, and/or competitive considerations?

87. How would our customers likely react to higher prices? What losses can we expect, if any?
88. Do we use temporary price promotions and, if so, how effective are they?
89. Do we suggest resale prices?
90. How do our wholesale or retail margins and discounts compare with those of the competition?

Communications/Promotion

91. Do we state our communication objectives clearly?
92. Do we spend enough, too much, or too little on promotion?
93. Are our communication themes effective?
94. Is our media mix adjusted to the optimal use of the Internet and social media?
95. Do we make aggressive use of sales promotion techniques to stimulate sales and to disrupt competitive actions?

Personal Selling and Distribution

96. Is our sales force (if any) at the right strength to accomplish our objectives, and to what extent will the Internet affect sales force activities?
97. Is it optimally organized to provide market coverage and to meet customers' logistical, technical, and service needs?
98. Is it adequately trained and motivated? Can it be characterized by high morale, ability, and effectiveness?
99. Have we enhanced our supply chain, or are there opportunities for further streamlining?
100. How does our overall marketing mix, including field personnel and senior management, rank against that of our major competitors?

As a final note: Conditions within your company are likely to change. That is unquestionably true of today's volatile markets. Therefore, to make clear-cut decisions (or recommend changes to the next level of management), it is indispensable to skillful management to give your operation a once-a-year (or sooner) checkup.

You will find the preceding appraisal and the strategy diagnostic system highly useful in broadening your perspective to think like a strategist. These tools can assist in clarifying your thinking and permitting you to grasp the core meaning of your firm in its operating environment.

Once again, you can customize the items and questions in the checklists to conform to your company's and market's needs.

Index